TURNING CONTROVERSY INTO CHURCH MINISTRY

TURNING CONTROVERSY INTO CHURCH MINISTRY

A Christlike Response to HOMOSEXUALITY

W. P. CAMPBELL

ZONDERVAN®

ZONDERVAN.com/
AUTHORTRACKER
follow your favorite authors

ZONDERVAN

Turning Controversy into Church Ministry
Copyright © 2010 by William Campbell

This title is also available as a Zondervan ebook. Visit www.zondervan.com/ebooks.

This title is also available in a Zondervan audio edition. Visit www.zondervan.fm.

Requests for information should be addressed to:

Zondervan, Grand Rapids, Michigan 49530

Library of Congress Cataloging-in-Publication Data

Campbell, William P., 1957-
    Turning controversy into church ministry : a Christlike response to homosexuality / William
P. Campbell.
        p. cm.
    Includes bibliographical references.
    ISBN 978-0-310-32132-3 (softcover)
    1. Homosexuality — Religious aspects — Christianity. 2. Church work with gays. I. Title.
BR115.H6C36 2010
259.086'64 — dc22   2010004711

All Scripture quotations, unless otherwise indicated, are taken from the Holy Bible, *New Interna-tional Version®*, NIV®. Copyright © 1973, 1978, 1984 by Biblica, Inc.™ Used by permission of Zonder-van. All rights reserved worldwide.

Scripture quotations marked NASB are taken from the *New American Standard Bible*. Copyright © 1960, 1962, 1963, 1968, 1971, 1972, 1973, 1975, 1977, 1995 by The Lockman Foundation. Used by permission.

Scripture quotations marked TNIV are taken from *The Holy Bible, Today's New International Ver-sion*™. TNIV®. Copyright © 2001, 2005 by International Bible Society. Used by permission of Zonder-van. All rights reserved.

Scripture quotations marked KJV are taken from the *King James Version* of the Bible.

Any Internet addresses (websites, blogs, etc.) and telephone numbers printed in this book are offered as a resource. They are not intended in any way to be or imply an endorsement by Zonder-van, nor does Zondervan vouch for the content of these sites and numbers for the life of this book.

Cover design: Rob Monacelli
Interior design: Ben Fetterley

Printed in the United States of America

10 11 12 13 14 15 /DCI/ 23 22 21 20 19 18 17 16 15 14 13 12 11 10 9 8 7 6 5 4 3 2 1

Contents

PART 1:
ANALYSIS: YOUR CHURCH, CHRIST'S BODY

PART 2:
APPROACH: OVERCOMING CONTROVERSY

Creation and Science: Did God Create Homosexuality?

Standards and Psychology: Which Norms Are Still Relevant?

Compassion and the Church: Does God Really Care?

122298

PART 3:
ACTION: BUILDING MINISTRY

Preface

Two extreme reactions to same-sex attraction and all types of sexual brokenness tend to dominate the church—complete avoidance or unquestioned acceptance. The resultant divide among denominations, within congregations, and even between family members has been devastating to the life and witness of the Christian church.

As a pastor for more than twenty years, I have empathized with the angst and pain of people who wrestle with unwanted homosexual attraction and who believe they will be rejected by the church if they are open about their struggles. Sadly, they are mostly right. Our churches and our society are both suffering from the consequences of sexual experimentation, abuse, and confusion, and it is time to work for solutions. Those who follow Jesus, the healer, should be leading the way.

This book is written to equip Christians and their churches to provide a Christlike response to homosexuality and to people who struggle with unwanted same-sex attractions. Such people are in almost every congregation, often suffering quietly. Some drift as visitors from church to church. They are jostled and torn between the conflicting values of society and of the church. What they need is a safe Christian environment where they can safely be honest about their struggles, feel welcome and loved, and receive grace and guidance to follow Jesus.

Very few pastors or church members understand how their congregations can foster such an environment. Yet the resources needed to make it happen are already within our grasp. It is time to recognize the gospel's relevance and to cease overlooking and shunning this part of our society before our churches become irrelevant to the world. Churches that wisely develop ministry in this one area of need will become healthier and more vibrant overall.

What follows is not a call for compromise but a call to deeper Christian commitment. We do not need a middle way, but a higher ground, which is Christ's way. In the following pages, you will be asked not to abandon your convictions but to embrace truths that will deepen your resolve, strengthen your church, and allow the world to see that Jesus is alive and that he does have the answers. He is waiting to manifest his healing power and grace through Christians and congregations that choose to follow in his steps.

Acknowledgments

A special thanks to my wife, Lin, for her loving support through the process of writing this book—and to my children, Gabriel, Lia, and Michaela, for their patience and understanding. Thank you also to my church family for their encouragement and to Tom Pickens, Ardie Steven, Sonja Martin, and many other warriors for their constant intercession on my behalf. To my brother, Chris Campbell, thank you for your inspiration.

I am grateful for those who put their editing pens to the paper: Lin Campbell, Carolyn Poteet, Pat Garland, and Meleah Allard; and for those who did a final read on the manuscript: Jeff Winter, Kristin Johnson-Tremba, Dan and Betty Rawls, and Peggy Parker.

To David Frees and the team at Zondervan, thank you for your ongoing support and counsel for this project; it was invaluable.

Thank you to those who gave their time for interviews, some through multiple calls or contacts: Tim Wilkins, Alan Chambers, Bob Stith, Jeff Buchanan, Karen Booth, Scott Davis, Andy Comiskey, Frank Worthen, Michael Riley, Ron Smith, Clark Whitten, Patrick Payton, Mike Goeke, Mike Haley, Terrence Toon, Sam Andreades, Doug McIntyre, John Yates, McKrea Game, David Swanson, Jim Thomas, Dale Evrist, Heather Zempel, Rollie delos Reyes II, Roy Blankenship, Joseph Nicolosi, Arthur Goldberg, Bill Henson, Kathleen Christopher, Mark Yarhouse, Ann Cohrs, Eddie Hammett, Chad Thomas, Bryan Kliewer, Bill Berry, and to those of you who have chosen to remain anonymous.

Above all, I give my thanks to God for guiding me to write this book and for providing the inspiration and strength necessary to complete it. May it be used for his glory.

Introduction:
Putting Christ Back
into "Christian"

Instead, speaking the truth in love, we will in all things grow up into him
who is the Head, that is, Christ.

—*Ephesians 4:15*

HE WAS NOT the typical visitor to a pastor's office. His story, however,
was all too typical.

"I'm ready to give up on the church," he said. He was referring to the
church universal and to every church he had known, starting with the congregation of his youth in which his father pastored. Now married with a
family and a good job, he was still engaged in the lifelong pursuit of healing
and help for his unwanted same-sex attractions.

What amazed me most as I listened to his experiences and felt his pain was
that he had not given up. He was motivated by the belief that somewhere,
somehow, local Christian fellowships can become centers of healing and help
for men and women like him who want God's best and who know that the
church should be the first place in which to find it.

That is, unless Christians have set aside their calling to follow Jesus ...

How Jesus Shocked Them All

People gathered just inside the stone gate, undisturbed by the hustle and
bustle of an early morning market town. A small desert caravan rumbled past,
trailed by wandering beggars, their hands reaching toward merchants who
were arranging produce on carts along the wall. Several men clad in white
robes pushed a young woman through an arched stone portal. She stumbled
and fell into the dirt. They pulled her up and forced her through the crowd
and stationed her in front of Jesus. She slumped forward and adjusted her veil

11

to shelter her face. Towering over her, a teacher of the law combed his wiry beard with bent fingers. His lips tightened.

"Teacher, this woman was caught in the act of adultery. In the Law Moses commanded us to stone such women. Now what do you say?"

The crowd quieted. A woman shook her two squabbling boys into silence and motioned for them to listen. Calmly, Jesus bent over and wrote on the ground with his finger. The cloaked men murmured among themselves and stepped closer to interrogate him. He did not look up. The questions quickly escalated into barbed accusations.

Jesus rose slowly, his eyes steady. "If any one of you is without sin, let him be the first to throw a stone at her." He knelt again.

The men exchanged puzzled glances. An aged Pharisee tapped another on the shoulder, then broke ranks and departed. Another followed. Jesus continued writing on the ground, unmoved. The group dissipated slowly until only Jesus and the woman remained. Tears glistened on her cheeks.

"Woman, where are they? Has no one condemned you?"

"No one, sir," she said.

"Then neither do I condemn you. Go now and leave your life of sin" (John 8:1–11, *paraphrased and embellished*).

Fast-Forward

It's the twenty-first century. A minister has gone public about his gay partner. He is being led into the high court of his denomination, aware that everyone has been talking about him, from church leaders to church sextons. He is an item in the Associated Press and on the blogs. The conservatives and the liberals, the pundits and the pew sitters wait for the large gathering to be called to order. People jostle and elbow to find one of the hard wooden pew spaces in the large historic downtown church. Nonelected attendees, who had been restrained outside the door, hustle for the remaining seats high in the balcony. An elderly gentleman nudges his friend. "If he wants to be a gay minister, why doesn't he just go to a denomination that accepts that sort?"

A denominational executive steps to the pulpit and adjusts the mic. He clears his throat, and the crowd quiets as his deep voice carries through the church: "Wouldn't it be nice if Jesus were here to settle this issue? But he isn't." He sweeps his hand through the air, reaching toward people in all parts of the sanctuary. "He has left this one up to us."

Interesting thought: "He has left this one up to us." If that is so, how have we done? Let's look at the scorecard.

The swirling debate about whether homosexuality is a gift from God, a sin before God, or something in between has churned into a tempest in and around the Christian church. Episcopalians and the Evangelical Lutheran Church of America are being fractured under its force, mainline Presbyterians are giving way to its power, and other denominations are being pulled into the vortex. Nearly every Christian is touched on a personal or theological level by this, one of the most unsettling issues ever to confront the American church. Congregations and entire denominations have done a good job of *condemning, affirming,* or *avoiding* homosexuality, but how many have fully embraced *both* the truth and grace Jesus offered?

Most pastors grapple with homosexuality in their congregations but are not sure how to approach it. Parents and children have become alienated, school systems conflicted, and the media tilted. The church is called to be a beacon of light, insight, and wisdom — a guide to all who wander the shadowed paths of this world — yet it has withdrawn its helping hand from many of its sexually conflicted parishioners.

It need not be so. We have the Lord on our side. He is available, through his indwelling Spirit and his Word, to guide us with the wit and wisdom that has always been his and can also be ours. He who settled the matter of the woman caught in adultery offers insight for our every conflict, promising clarity in place of confusion and confidence over cowardice. But we must be willing to follow his guidance; we must approach this difficult and complex topic as he did. Christ calls us to speak the truth while demonstrating grace.

Truth and Grace

Jesus did not hide the truth; he called the adulteress to repentance. But neither did he insult her, condemn her, or throw her out. His grace embraced her and sent her forth to live a better life. If he had demonstrated grace without truth, he would have let her stagger down the path of personal destruction. If he had spoken truth without grace, he would have clubbed her with the law and sentenced her to stoning by the crowd.

Truth and grace — have you ever tried putting those two together without minimizing either? Without God's help, it is a daunting task. Grace without truth pampers, confuses, and even deceives. Truth without grace cuts, wounds, and destroys. Those who approach thorny matters such as sexual addiction, homosexuality, and adultery with only truth become experts at alienation. Those who bring love into such discussions but avoid the truth are unable to confront patterns of behavior that hurt self and society. Both are important; neither can function properly without the other. Salt is essential for the body, but separated into its two elements, sodium and chloride, it can be deadly.

The battle about homosexuality has been raging in the church for several decades, and it has created a polarization between those who focus on love and "grace" and those who lean toward correctness and "truth." Many Christians have become firmly entrenched in one camp or another. Some refuse to be pulled into either extreme and have avoided the battle for so long that they have become a muddled middle. We who claim to follow Christ are called to embody truth and love without compromise, hesitation, or fear (Ephesians 4:15).

Jesus was put on the cross because he spoke the truth; love and grace kept him there. He never told a lie, never twisted Scripture, never played interpretive gymnastics when he taught from the Law, the Psalms, and the Prophets. We don't find Jesus saying, "The Scriptures can't be understood by the average person — in fact, on issues of sexuality, they mean the opposite of what they appear to say. You need to understand a variety of ancient cultural customs and ..."

Nor do we find Jesus rejecting the wayward sinner, the outcasts, and those on the fringes of the religious establishment. He made them his primary focus for a demonstration of love and mercy of a type rarely seen in the church of our day. He did not look for a middle ground between truth and grace but embraced them both perfectly, and on this foundation built a life-transforming ministry.

How the Church Has Failed

I grew up in a mainline Presbyterian denomination, now called the Presbyterian Church (USA). In the early 1980s, when I was studying for ministry at Princeton Seminary, the moderator of the denomination at that time came to visit. I'll never forget his comment to a group of student questioners: "I look forward to the day when practicing homosexuals can be ordained in our denomination." My first thought was, "That's when I need to step out of the denomination." Little did I know what lay ahead for me and for the PCUSA.

Over the past thirty years, an ever-growing minority of denominational executives, pastors, and elders have promoted gay rights causes and forced issues of sexuality and homosexuality to dominate the business of the church. One would hope that a whole generation of focus on the topic would cause church leaders to become experts in understanding and in healing people's wounds. Just the opposite is true. It has resulted in a polarization between parties, and people on both sides of the fence have become experts at contention but have overlooked opportunities for ministry.

The Christian church often reaches out to those wounded by divorce but alienates or avoids those who struggle with same-sex attraction. Congregations that support recovery ministry for alcoholism are numerous, but when people surface who want help with homosexuality in their lives or families, we either turn a cold shoulder or whisk them away to specialized groups outside the church. We form support groups for fellowship, weight loss, marriage recovery, and financial stress but have little interest in or insight about how to minister to sexual brokenness in all of its forms.

My denomination has only one affiliated ministry, called OneByOne, specifically designed to help homosexuals who desire to experience the transforming grace and love of Christ that they might live according to God's standards for marriage and singleness. Jeff Winter, the chairman of the board of OneByOne, has guided the ministry for thirteen years. I once asked him how many of the 11,000 mainline Presbyterian churches had learned to move beyond the debate about homosexuality and had become good examples of healing ministry, without compromising biblical truth. He answered, "I can't point to one. There may be some out there, but I don't know about them." I have since surveyed leaders and congregations in larger and smaller denominations and have discovered a similarly shocking gap in ministry. A number of congregations do stand as bright exceptions to the norm, however, and they have much to teach us.

While writing this book, I was asked to present the "conservative" side for a debate in my local presbytery regarding whether practicing homosexuals should be ordained. After presenting my points, I stepped down from the pulpit and shook my head in dismay. The whole process of debate was once again a setup for failure, regardless of who might win more votes. In my allotted seven minutes, I had given the expected rebuttal to the speaker before me but had little time to express what I believed everyone desperately needed to hear. I wanted more time and a neutral platform from which to call God's people away from debate and into a more holistic, in-depth understanding. I believe most Christians are yearning for such understanding.

There Is Hope

When the church approaches the homosexual dilemma in a Christlike manner, people on both sides of the issue can become unified around the clear teachings of Scripture and minister with the endless compassion of Christ. People who find themselves attracted to the same sex will no longer be subject to mixed messages but will hear one voice affirming their worth in the sight of God and their need to turn to the Savior who heals, forgives, helps, and enables them, along with every human being, to "sin no more." We will no longer be a people with a formula and a quick fix, but humble followers of Christ who invite others to engage in the lifelong process of growth and change.

I believe that if our local congregations had not neglected ministry to people struggling with homosexual attractions twenty years ago, society would not now be rising up in such force against the values of the church. In the pages that follow, you will find definitive reasons to believe that Christians still can have a significant and positive influence on our culture, even in a day when antidiscrimination legislation is on the rise and traditional marriage is losing ground.

I was recently discussing the battle about homosexuality and the church with a writer of some influence in my denomination. We both shared our woes and struggles. I mentioned that I was writing a book on the topic, and she asked me to describe it, adding, "I want you to know up front that I don't agree with your perspectives." Knowing that I embrace a traditional view of Scripture, her personal history in church politics elicited strong emotions that pushed her mind toward assumptions about me before hearing me out. We sat in a lounge, and during the course of ten minutes, I unraveled some of the salient points that you will find in this book. She narrowed her eyes and said repeatedly, "I didn't know that," then straightened and said, "You need to publish that book."

> Ministry Essential #1:
> The best way to avoid
> extremes is to follow
> Christ's example.

You may be starting this book with the assumption that you have heard it all before, with the belief that you have nothing to learn on the topic, or with the conviction that there is no way to unite the church. If so, I challenge you to read on.

By joining me on this journey, you will:

- realize how Christians tend to oversimplify matters related to homosexuality, creating more confusion than resolution for the church, resulting in crippled congregations that are unable to address the needs of our society.
- uncover misinformation about same-sex attraction that has permeated our society and the church, on both sides of the debate.
- recognize that those who wrestle with homosexuality are, at the core, no different than the rest of us. We all have natural-born or acquired weaknesses, addictions, or temptations.
- understand how the average church, regardless of its size, location, or denominational affiliation, can develop vital ministries for those who come to them asking for help and guidance related to sexual brokenness.
- glean wisdom for building ministry that will improve the health and outreach of your church.

This book will show you how to move out of the fray of conflict with ten ministry essentials. A church ministry paradigm will help you discern where your congregation stands, and you will be inspired with stories of transformed lives. Insights from science and theology will guide you on a path of well-

Ten Ministry Essentials

1. The best way to avoid extremes is to follow Christ's example.
2. Churches that blend uncompromised grace and truth are positioned for dynamic ministry.
3. Ministry begins when we connect brokenness in our hearts with brokenness in others.
4. Church leadership is about godly role models, not rights.
5. We must embrace the whole of Scripture to keep our lives whole.
6. Our genes bear the shadow of the fallen creation. They do not overshadow righteous living, however, for those who are new creations in Christ.
7. The law leads us to Christ, who enables us to fulfill it.
8. The goal is not to move from homosexuality to heterosexuality but from homosexuality to holiness.
9. Where sin abounds, God's grace is greater still.
10. With God, nothing is impossible and no one is unreachable.

reasoned logic. Practical steps for establishing Christlike ministry will be laid out for you in six ministry spheres and supplemented by six ministry tips. You will be challenged by ministry models from churches of all sizes and types. As a pastor for more than twenty years and a long-term consultant for a variety of ministries that shape both Christians' and congregations' lives, I write with the conviction that any average church member can work alongside any average pastor in any average church to establish a team and to implement the principles and suggestions in this book. But we must follow the example of Christ.

Our Framework

This book is an expedition into the world of vital facts and human factors set against the landscape of God's revelation. I unapologetically fasten Scripture as a frame around this portrait. The contrasting colors of the law and the gospel, grace and instruction, truth and love must be blended if we are to understand both God's mind and God's heart. A pastor in Nazi Germany who was willing to die for the truth and who was motivated by God's amazing love, the courageous Dietrich Bonhoeffer, wrote:

We must learn to know the Scriptures again, as the reformers and our fathers knew them. We must not grudge the time and the work it takes.... How, for example, shall we ever attain certainty and confidence in our personal and church activity if we do not stand on solid biblical ground? It is not our hearts that determine our course, but God's Word. But who in this day has any proper understanding of the need for scriptural proof? How often we hear innumerable arguments "from life" and "from experience" put forward as the basis for most crucial decisions, but the argument of Scripture is missing. And this authority would perhaps point in exactly the opposite direction. It is not surprising, of course, that the person who attempts to cast discredit upon their wisdom should be the one who himself does not seriously read, know, and study the Scripture.[1]

Part 1

ANALYSIS: YOUR CHURCH, CHRIST'S BODY

Chapter 1

THE FEET
Where Your Church Stands

Examine yourselves to see whether you are in the faith; test yourselves. Do you not realize that Christ Jesus is in you—unless, of course, you fail the test?
— *2 Corinthians 13:5*

I wasn't paying attention to the white-water rafting guide as I threw an inner tube out of the large raft and jumped into the frothing water—but my brother was. Listening carefully to the guide's warnings about the upcoming section of Oregon's Rogue River called "Coffeepot," my brother stared helplessly as I floated ahead of the raft into the bubbling waters described by the guide as violent undercurrents that have been known to suck people down into the depths, into the river's chest, wedged between its immovable ribs with no way out. My brother pointed in dismay, unable to speak as I disappeared under the agitated surface of the water.

I remember the experience of shock when I was pulled down, inner tube and all, and then flipped upside down. I gripped my float for dear life for what seemed an eternity as the watery currents tugged and tore at me, beckoning me into the black unknown. If my dug-in fingernails had slipped from the tube, I would have been sucked into the vortex of death. Finally, the draw slackened and my tube bobbed to the surface. I gasped, sucked in air, paddled to the side of the now quiet river, and climbed onto the rocks. My chest ached as I told myself that I would never forget to be thankful for the next breath or for the next heartbeat. I stood, rejoicing that my feet were on solid ground.

Now, years later, I find a chilling parallel between this incident and the forces that are pummeling the Western church like mighty currents and threatening to pull pastors, congregations, and entire denominations into swirling darkness. Rapid changes in societal values have swept over the

21

church in a torrent that has many pastors holding on for the ride, or holding their breath and looking for a way of escape. Could this be why 80 percent of pastors would find another job if they were able, and 85 percent of pastors' wives are depressed?[1] It is vital that we identify the currents that are coming against the church if we hope to navigate our congregations to safe ground and settle them as outposts of recovery for the needy, the hurting, the drowning people we are called to reach.

Currents That Overwhelm

When I pastored a church in Maryland, I frequently drove to Harpers Ferry, West Virginia, for leadership retreats. Every time I drove into that historic town, I peered into the rippling waters where the Potomac and Shenandoah Rivers merge. Often a serene setting, the lower part of Harpers Ferry has sometimes felt the wrath of these converging rivers.

Local legend has it that Robert Harper, a Philadelphia businessman who settled in the area in the early eighteenth century, was driven out of his cabin by invading water in 1748. Rather than leave the area, he turned disappointment into opportunity and established a ferry across the Potomac in 1761. Thus Harpers Ferry became a vital crossing point for westward-moving settlers seeking new lands in the Shenandoah Valley and beyond. George Washington was captivated by the potential of a town that sat quietly where the mountains break and where a ferry provided passage. The president arranged to have one of our country's two arsenals located there. From that day forward, history records more than a dozen deluges in Harpers Ferry. By highlighting a few devastating floods at key points in history, we can draw a parallel with the raging political, economic, and theological currents that threaten to submerge the church today.

The Flood of 1870 — Politics

In 1870, floodwaters massed upriver from Harpers Ferry and rushed upon the town like two converging trains, catching the residents unaware and sweeping away homes and businesses. Forty-two people died because they were not prepared for the rapidly rising rivers. This flood came on the heels of the Civil War, which had already left the town nearly destitute. From the Sunday evening of October 16, 1859, when abolitionist John Brown and his twenty-one-man army of liberation had seized the town armory and its one hundred thousand weapons, to the day the Federals returned to Harpers Ferry after the Battle of Antietam, the town was submerged by conflicting political currents. Subject to forces outside its control, the town changed hands eight times between 1861 and 1865. Like two vast rivers, different viewpoints from the North and South regarding slavery converged on Harpers Ferry, and the town barely survived, reaching near ghost-town status.

The church of our day, like Harpers Ferry, sits exposed and vulnerable to the mighty rivers of competing interests that fuel our national politics. With regard to gay rights, for example, we can think of the Stonewall riots in 1969, the removal of homosexuality from the American Psychiatric Association's list of disorders in 1973, the Anita Bryant campaign in 1977, Jerry Falwell's founding of the Moral Majority in 1979, the media's overstated claims about the supposedly gay brain in the early 1990s, California's Proposition 8 in 2008, and the emergence of hate crime legislation and state approvals for same-sex marriage in 2009. These are but a few historic watermarks reminding us of the growing strength of two churning political rivers, for and against gay rights, which now converge on the church.

The Flood of 1942 — Economics

In 1942, the Potomac and Shenandoah rivers overwhelmed residents of Lower Town Harpers Ferry once again, this time with an all-time-high flood level of 33.8 feet. There is never a good time for a flood, but this intrusion by nature was especially difficult for the town economy as the Great Depression was just coming to an end.

Analysts will forever debate how invisible forces surprised and then devastated the economies of the Western world to create a depression that lasted more than ten years. In fact, the debate has taken on fresh interest in our day, as our national economy is experiencing gyrations that cause financial gurus to draw comparisons with the financial woes of the Great Depression. Every sector of our economy has felt the force of the economic downturn that began in late 2008, and rival political parties have been quick to cast blame on each other. Christian ministries and churches cannot avoid being swept into converging forces of public irresponsibility and government policies that have ransacked our nation and have sent anxiety rippling into businesses, churches, and homes.

Economics is a hidden force behind the political currents that hammer the church across our land. Regarding the gay rights agenda, for example, funding sources for and against the November 2008 Proposition 8 ballot in California to ban same-sex marriage contributed more than $83 million from all fifty states and from twenty foreign countries. It was the most substantially funded campaign on a state ballot ever. The financing behind this single ballot surpassed every campaign in the country outside the U.S. presidential contest.

It is said that economics drives politics, and politics guides the masses. Yet there is a current deeper than either economics or politics that Christians must contend with. This mighty force flows undetected, yet it has the power to unite or to divide and devastate God's people. This force is the combined pressure of divergent theologies.

The Flood of 1996 — Theology

Only in 1996 did two floods in the lower part of Harpers Ferry bring the water over the 29.8-feet-high watermark in a single year. One of the floods, in January of that year, owed its existence to the blizzard of 1996, followed by torrential rainfall. The second watery invasion came on the heels of the angry Hurricane Fran. Twice the historic town that draws some two million tourists annually was deluged by two swollen rivers.

In the same year, 1996, my denomination, the Presbyterian Church (USA), was so conflicted by pressures from both sides of the theological debate about homosexuality that its national body felt the need to place a statement confirming the traditional viewpoint on marriage in its constitutional document, the Book of Order. That statement, once a high waterline, has been submerged in controversy ever since. Other mainline denominations were likewise inundated in the 1990s with the progressive push for homosexual unions and ordination on one side, and resistance and reactions from conservatives on the other. These streams of thought have risen with fury since the 1990s and are now threatening nearly every Christian church and denomination.

The Two Theological Rivers

There are two strong currents in the Scriptures that were never meant to be separated: grace and truth. When they have become divided throughout history, the church has always suffered. Older terms such as *fundamentalist-modernist* and newer labels such as *progressive-traditional* reflect these currents but cannot be used to measure or understand them.

The theological flows of the Old Testament, which highlights the law — the *truth* of God — and the New Testament, which features the *grace* shown in Jesus Christ, are two parts of one whole. They create an interconnecting pattern throughout the Bible. The Old Testament is about more than the law of God. The Ten Commandments were given through *grace*, through a God who loved the Israelites as his "treasured possession" among all the peoples, "a kingdom of priests and a holy nation" (Exodus 19:5–6). The tabernacle, accompanied by rules and regulations for worship, was an intricately painted portrait of the grace that invites us, through the sacrifice of Christ, into the very presence of God (Exodus 35–40; Hebrews 10:1–25).

The New Testament is about more than the grace of God. Jesus, in the New Testament, upheld the standards of God's law. He said that "not the smallest letter, not the least stroke of a pen, will by any means disappear from the Law until everything is accomplished" (Matthew 5:18). He who came to save us will return to judge those who refuse to believe.

Law and grace flow together throughout the Bible—but have not always done so within the church. In the 1920s and '30s, the influx of liberal theologies from Germany, spurred on by new literary approaches for understanding Scripture, provoked stark reactions from conservative theologians. Hence the fundamentalist-modernist controversy began, creating splits in seminaries and denominations. The battle was not fully settled theologically but rechanneled into manageable currents through church policies (polity).

The effort to divert theological arguments rather than resolve them is but a temporary solution. Today the same two rivers, grace and truth, have risen to flood stage and are raging with destructive force. Many Christian denominations are attempting once again to hold themselves together through polity and procedures but have been unwilling to find the more difficult and lasting solution, which is to bring the two rivers into one. Grace and truth were never meant to be separated. Biblical standards and relevant cultural witness are partners. Evangelism and social action work best when working together. Great movements of renewal throughout history have brought the streams of truth and grace together to create mighty movements of God. This was the case in American history, for example, during three great awakenings (1730–1755; 1790–1840; 1850–1900). May it happen again today.

Examining Grace

The Greek word for grace, *charis*, means "unmerited favor." It is food offered to the homeless person who has just cursed you. It is forgiveness extended toward the boss who cut your hours in half. It is love shown to the teenager or spouse who berated you, the kindness offered to the fellow church member who soiled your name in gossip, and the hug of welcome to the drug addict who stepped into your church for the first time. God's grace, however, is not weak toward injustice, deception, compromised character, and shortcut spirituality. With tenacity and resilience, biblical grace challenges us to grow, to better ourselves, to climb toward the highest rung of godly living.

Those who strip the truth away from grace create a perversion of God's person and plan for humanity. We live in an age of reckless sexuality. Our truthless grace has handed the car keys to teenagers, along with a map to the interstate of sexual experimentation. Nearly half (46 percent) of all fifteen- to nineteen-year-olds in the United States have had sex at least once, and by the age of nineteen, seven in ten teens have engaged in sexual intercourse.[2] Grace with no anchor of truth ignores the high rate of divorce among Christians in our country and is untroubled that the rate of cohabitation rose by a thousand percent between 1960 and 2000.[3] It may even turn a blind eye to the one in four girls and one in six boys who are sexually abused before the age of eighteen, because it has no basis for setting standards for human sexuality or behavior.[4]

Examining Truth

Truth lived in Christ's way, the kind of truth we are called to embrace and proclaim as Christ-followers, has few gray edges. It is clear and straight about God's commandments and God's priorities. It shamelessly names what is right and wrong and does not hide the consequences for obedience and disobedience. It does not cheat on taxes or accept the benefits of a clerk's error in a grocery store. Truth refuses to cover up the weakness of governmental policies or of a pastor's theology. It confronts ethical violations on the job and verbal abuse at home. It will not be bent by majority opinion or bribed with an offer for a better position. Those who live by truth engage in the ongoing challenge of applying God's unchanging standards to our ever-changing society.

Truth devoid of grace, however, is a poison-tipped dagger. It speaks words that wound and promotes acts that kill spirit and hope. It is loveless, merciless, compassionless, and clueless about how to help others improve. Rather than heal wounds, it opens them; rather than allowing time for change, it stifles growth; rather than offering help, it slams the door in the face of human need. It turns opportunity into despondency, and praise for a person's hard work into a list of failures. Truth without grace creates a formal, pious, self-righteous legalism.

Caught in the Wash

There are very few churches or Christians who actually ride their theological rafts in only one river. The extremes of narrow truth and isolated grace are difficult to maintain in the real world. Fred Phelps of Westboro Baptist Church in Topeka, Kansas, who makes it a practice to carry picket signs to the funerals of homosexuals to announce their certain entrance into hell, does not have a big following.[5] Nor has the World Naked Bike Ride movement enjoyed broad denominational endorsement.[6] Most of us, avoiding the unabated flow of the extremes, attempt to plant ourselves in the middle, only to be victims of the backwaters and unexpected floods. The battle over homosexuality in the church has been raging for several decades, and we have built our rafts and lifeboats as we continue to gather for Sunday worship as though nothing has happened. We avoid teachings about sexual addiction among heterosexuals, or words like *gay* and *lesbian* from the pulpit, while many of our members are slipping off of the rafts and sinking. We lift our chins high and pull our rafts together for comfort, not noticing the sounds of those who are alternately going under and coming up, gasping for air because of their conflicted sexuality. Too ashamed to hold out their hands for help, they sink once again.

Many of us feel it is not proper to discuss such issues in or around the church. Those who have gone under will soon be out of sight and out of mind. Better to keep it that way. It is unsettling, however, to acknowledge the sometimes deafening roar of waters on both sides. The sound of new legislation. The knowledge of another church raft that split, sending members into the rapids on both sides. The upcoming denominational assembly called to discuss how to remain safely in the middle. It is difficult to hold on. Some who have gone under might be your own loved ones.

Beyond the Rapids

My favorite part of rafting the Rogue River, following my near-death incident, was the quiet after the rapids. It reminded me of the calm Jesus' disciples must have felt when he got into their boat and quieted the waves. There is nothing quite as peaceful as the face of a gentle river reflecting the bright colors of autumn trees across its surface. Such a scene describes the potential inner tranquility found in the hearts of Christians and churches that have blended grace and truth into one current. Those who steer their rafts into this gentle flow are positioned for Christlike ministry.

Where Does Your Church Stand?

A recent National Congregations Study survey of over fifteen hundred churches found that approximately 19 percent of churches have an openly gay or lesbian couple attending their worship services and welcome their gifts in leadership.[7] It may be about the same percentage of churches that, rather than being *gay affirming*, are either subtly or overtly *gay bashing*. By the terminology the members use and the expression on their faces, visiting gays or lesbians know they are viewed as outcasts. The broad middle, approximately 60 percent of churches, is often either too afraid or too apathetic to take a stand either way. There are a small minority of congregations, however, who follow in the steps of Christ by bringing grace and truth together without compromise to create dynamic healing ministries for the sexually broken. Those who thus avoid the extremes by following the example of our Lord are the exceptions. The hope behind this book is to make them the norm.

One River

A church is a family, with all of its diversity, and no two churches in the world are exactly the same. What is the culture, the aura, and the climate of your congregation? Is your congregation especially welcoming? Stuffy? Joyful? Somber? Which of the five descriptions below best portrays your church family? In general, when faced with the topic of homosexuality, is your church:

1. *gay affirming*—a church that believes and proclaims that homosexuality cannot be changed and is accepted by God, a church that encourages gays and lesbians to embrace and live according to their same-sex propensities?
2. *fearful*—a congregation that feels stuck in the middle of the battle and is afraid to speak about homosexuality at all, whether for or against, because the topic seems too political, too confusing, and potentially divisive?
3. *gay bashing*—a congregation that condemns the practice of homosexuality in such a way that homosexuals do not feel welcome, even as visitors?
4. *apathetic*—a church whose dominant mood is apathy about homosexuality, no matter whether leaning toward the affirmation or rejection of homosexuality, a church whose people are not only silent about this issue, but generally don't care because they find it to be irrelevant to their lives and ministry?
5. *sold on Christ's way*—a church family that embraces Christ's stance and is strong in both grace and truth, a church whose members love homosexuals as much as they love any other member, and yet who clearly proclaim that the practice of homosexuality is a violation of God's purpose?

Find where your church fits in the diagram below.

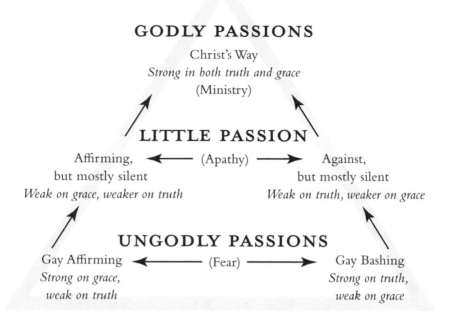

GODLY PASSIONS
Christ's Way
Strong in both truth and grace
(Ministry)

LITTLE PASSION

Affirming,   ⟵   (Apathy)   ⟶   Against,
but mostly silent   but mostly silent
Weak on grace, weaker on truth   *Weak on truth, weaker on grace*

UNGODLY PASSIONS

Gay Affirming   ⟵   (Fear)   ⟶   Gay Bashing
Strong on grace,   *Strong on truth,*
weak on truth   *weak on grace*

Examining our Passions

The passions that drive the lower portion of this triangular preparedness paradigm are not fitting for true Christians. If we are bashing homosexuals, we do not love them as Jesus does. When we affirm the practice of homosexuality, we are not speaking the truth according to God's Word. If we are stuck between the two extremes and are too fearful to discuss and relate to the issue, we are unable to do ministry as Jesus would. None of these three scenarios are options for followers of Christ.

If we find ourselves aligned with the second tier of the paradigm, where apathy lies central, we lack Christlike passions. To the outside world, it may appear that such churches have found a wise middle ground in the midst of the conflict. In the sight of God, however, those who don't side fully with truth while uncompromisingly appropriating God's grace create a distorted view of Christianity.

Jesus told the church of Laodicea, "I know your deeds, that you are neither cold nor hot. I wish you were either one or the other! So, because you are lukewarm—neither hot nor cold—I am about to spit you out of my mouth"

(Revelation 3:15–16). It is believed that both the hot and cold springs that fed the city of Laodicea were quite a distance from the city. The extensive journey to the city through aqueducts cooled the hot springs to lukewarm and warmed the cold water to tepid. Just as the water disgusted Laodicea's residents, a church that lacks Christ's passions is not pleasing to the Lord. In God's eyes, it is better not to call ourselves Christian than to live a distorted Christianity.

The top of the triangle, Christ's way, represents the church motivated by godly passions. In this sector, truth and grace unite, and church ministry flourishes. When we embrace Scripture without compromise and show love without fail, Christ becomes apparent in our midst, and he empowers us to walk in his purposes.

Creating an Environment for Ministry

No church fits perfectly into any one category. The goal of this exercise is to get you thinking about how to move your church forward into the deep and gentle waters where ministry can abound.

For the Gay-Bashing Church

When I recently presented the Church Ministry Preparedness Paradigm at a seminar, a person asked, "What do we do with the people in our church who are just simply against homosexuals, period? If we even mention the subject, the hair rises on the back of their necks."

Even a few such outspoken individuals may push your congregation into this "gay-bashing" realm. If their presence is tangible and if their opinions are audible, they may cast a blanket of darkness and condemnation over persons struggling with same-sex attractions. Those who are so defensive and uptight about this topic usually do not understand the causes of homosexuality, nor do they see that their negativity actually works against the process of recovery that people with unwanted same-sex attractions desperately seek.

Some people who have very strong reactions against homosexuality also have some deep issues of their own that need to be dealt with. Perhaps, for example, they have been abused, and the very topic brings up painful memories. Those who protest the loudest may actually be attempting to cover their own guilt about deviant sexual activities. Don't expect everyone in the gay-bashing category to change overnight. Offer them the truth in love and model the kind of values you wish they would embrace, as you pray for their perspectives to change.

For the Gay-Affirming Church

How should you minister to people who believe that homosexual orientation is sanctioned by God and that the practice of homosexuality is blessed by

God? Again, a few strongly opinionated people in this camp may cast their aura over the whole congregation. Do not attempt to argue people out of their positions or they will resist you. If, however, you carefully reinforce the truths they are lacking about homosexuality, science, Scripture, and many of the factors described in the front half of this book, you may see great inroads into their lives as they change over time.

Many who are strongly entrenched in this camp are either gay themselves or have loved ones who are gay. Having been hurt by church and society, the arguments and opinions that come from the gay-bashing camp only confirm and further establish their opinions. When they are met with Christlike values in church leaders and members who truly care about hurting people, however, they may soften their positions and endorse this Christlike approach.

For the Fearful Church

One of the most common reasons people don't know how to respond to homosexuality is fear. People are afraid of the unknown, and fear can prevent us from searching for understanding. Some of the reasons for this fear include:

- The topic of homosexuality seems so confusing. Through informed teaching and biblical preaching, however, we can turn confusion into clarity in the Christian church.
- Talk about gays and lesbians choosing to be celibate or finding freedom from their past seems politically incorrect. Church members don't want to be labeled as "unloving bigots." It is my experience that when people approach this topic with understanding and love, even those who self-identify as gays and lesbians will appreciate the effort. But the question should be asked: Are we more concerned about our own reputations or that of Christ?
- People are afraid that if they speak about this subject, they might hurt someone's feelings. Actually, the opposite is true. When we nervously cower around the issue and don't converse about it and learn how to approach homosexuals as Jesus would, we create an environment of alienation. When we become transparent and admit to our own weaknesses, however, we often find open doors into the hearts of hurting people and can become their partners in a healing journey.
- Some are afraid that if they are friendly toward a person with same-sex attraction, it will appear they are inviting a sexual relationship. As with any relationship, however, proper discretion can negate this concern.
- Many avoid discussions about homosexuality for fear that such conversation might open up their own issues of sexual brokenness (e.g.,

sexual abuse, addiction, pornography, or marital infidelity). If this is the case, we must deal with our own issues until we are healthy enough to help others.

There are several biblical reasons for not allowing fear to guide our lives and ministries. They include the following:

- Jesus continually reminded his disciples not to fear (Matthew 10:26 – 31; 14:27; 17:17; 28:10). He was with them in bodily form and now is with us in spirit—living within each of us (John 14:17, 26; 15:26; 16:13). He has given his angels to protect us, and his Father is watching over every detail of our lives (Matthew 10:28 – 33; 18:10).
- An unhealthy fear of others reveals a lack of trust in God (Luke 12:4 – 7).
- When we allow our fears to prevent us from doing what is right, we are sinning against God (James 4:17).

Many of our church members are afraid of gays and lesbians because of ignorance and misconceptions. One of the best things you can do for your church is to find a gracious leader of posthomosexual ministry to visit your church.* Most of these individuals were once deeply entrenched in a gay or lesbian lifestyle but have found grace, forgiveness, and strength in Christ to live in holiness. Many are married, have children, and have testimonies and teachings that can alleviate the fears people carry about the unknown.

We must learn to call fear what it is—a barrier to accomplishing God's will for our lives and for our churches. Paul reminded Timothy that he was not given a spirit of fear; neither are we (2 Timothy 1:7).

For Churches with Little Passion

Phrases often heard in the apathetic church and those with little passion related to ministry for homosexuals are, "We don't do that here," or, "We don't have that problem." But if we don't recognize problems, we will not seek solutions. If our pastors and church members don't know anyone struggling with same-sex attractions, perhaps it is because those who have such struggles have not been given reason to believe they will be listened to with understanding and love. Surveys suggest that between 60 and 70 percent of

---

    * The terms *posthomosexual* and *postgay* are being used instead of *ex-gay* in many Christian circles to place emphasis on new life in Christ and an adjoining lifestyle of holiness rather than on a completely changed sexual orientation. While many who struggle with same-sex attractions may find them diminishing significantly or completely over time, others may always wrestle with their inner drives, even while following Christ wholeheartedly.

churchgoers know a loved one who has homosexual attractions.[8] If those who experience same-sex attractions don't sense compassion within us, why would they choose to risk themselves by opening up to us?

Another indication of spiritual apathy is the attempt to please everyone by traveling down the "middle of the road." Through the years, I have known many Christians who label themselves as moderates in their determined effort to stay out of the fray of theological conflict. Some moderates may have deep passions, but many of them are unwilling to take a stand on much of anything. We must examine our hearts on these matters. If we pride

> Ministry Essential #2:
> Churches that blend
> uncompromised grace
> and truth are positioned
> for dynamic ministry.

ourselves in not being fearful, not being antigay, and not being gay rights promoters, but rather middle-of-the-roaders, we must ask ourselves whether we have a passion for ministry based on a burning love for Jesus. If we or our churches are apathetic, we need to ask for a fresh dose of God's Spirit of conviction until our passion is reignited.

The Church of Godly Passions

How do you know if your congregation is drifting in the calm waters that blend grace and truth? Look for these signs:

- Everyone who visits your church will feel welcomed and loved.
- The truth of Scripture and the gospel of salvation will be proclaimed humbly and boldly from the pulpit and in the classrooms.
- Prayer will be a vital part of the church's ministries.
- Worship will be uplifting (regardless of the music style), heartfelt, Christ focused.
- The church will be a safe place for everyone to confess their sins and turn to God.
- Members will be excited about their own spiritual growth.
- The ministries of the church will have an impact on the community and world.

Of course, no church can perfectly bring truth and grace together all of the time. Still, it is God's will that each congregation strive for this ideal and that the leaders in every church lift up both grace and truth in their teaching and through their lives.

Experiencing All Kinds of Churches

Each of the following chapters contains stories and testimonies that demonstrate the power of local congregations, for good or for ill, to influence those who struggle with unwanted same-sex attractions. Few people have had the opportunity to observe as many types of congregations as has Alan Chambers, president of Exodus International, the largest network of postgay ministries.* The following quotes, drawn from our conversations and from his writing, show how different types of churches influence the lives of people around the world—and have influenced his life.

The Gay-Bashing Church

Alan grew up in a church that believed and preached Scripture but lacked compassion and grace. He told me, "I am thankful that the church I grew up in taught me the Scriptures. From my early years I learned the truth. I learned that there is no wiggle room with God's commandments. But at the same time my church didn't offer grace and compassion. It set up a negative image of God in my mind."[9]

In *God's Grace and the Homosexual Next Door*, Alan writes,

> As a teenager, I struggled in silence with unwanted and, to a larger degree, unacted-upon feelings. I felt condemned to hell by a pastor and church that never once shared that there was any hope for someone like me. The guilt, shame, and condemnation became so unbearable that I well remember the day I deliberately ignored the stop sign at a busy intersection and sped through it with my eyes closed, hoping that another car would crash into mine and end it all.
>
> Later, as a college freshman, I vowed never to return to the church because it did not have a life-giving answer or alternative for me. All it promised was deeper guilt and no hope for a way out. It was very easy for me—and it's very easy for many gay men and women today—to run bloodied and bruised into the open arms of a gay community that was more than happy to have me, love me, and save me.[10]

The Gay-Affirming Church

Having experienced gay life and culture, Alan does not appreciate the pandering and soft-pedaling of truth that often occurs in theologically liberal congregations. Alan likes to term congregations that are all about love, but

---

* Exodus International is a nonprofit, interdenominational Christian organization that promotes the message of freedom from homosexuality through the power of Jesus Christ. Exodus is an umbrella for more than 230 local ministries in the United States and Canada.

soft on truth, churches of "sloppy agape." He recognizes that such congregations "may be trying to correct errors of the past, when truth triumphed over
grace, but they have now gone too far the other way. Failing to offer God's
standards, they forget that God not only loves us as we are, but he loves us
too much to leave us that way. God wants us to experience the freedom that
comes when grace and truth are brought together."[11]

The Church of Godly Passions

Alan explained to me that "what we need are churches that are 100 percent committed to grace and 100 percent committed to truth." He added,
"Thankfully there are such churches out there, and churches like these can
reach a lost and dying world. They don't sidestep either truth or grace but
speak clear truth about every issue and are graceful toward every person. This
is what the church is called to be, and it is what people are looking for. It was
a church like this that saved my life."[12]

In 1992 Alan's life was indeed turned around when he began visiting a
church in Orlando, Florida, called Discovery Church. He writes,

> No stranger to those struggling with homosexuality, the people of Discovery
> immediately clued in that I was fighting for my life in regard to homosexual-
> ity. And that made them love me all the more.
>
> Having only attended Discovery Church a few weeks, I remember two
> bold and loving church members walking into a gay bar on Easter Sunday
> 1992 to tell me that God had sent them to remind me that he loved me, they
> love me, and they were committed to walking with me on the journey out
> of homosexuality. Recommitted to obedience, I was restored by that church.
> They taught me that change takes more than just pointing the way; change
> requires grabbing a person's hand and walking with him or her.[13]

In his book *Leaving Homosexuality*, he continues the story:

> Thus began my season at Discovery Church, a place where "community"
> became a reality. I quickly came out to everyone there. It wasn't a secret
> anyway, and no one seemed to really care. My story was common there.
> There was every kind of "former" you could imagine. My sin wasn't a big
> deal because the people at the church categorized all sin the same way. It was
> a little hard to adjust to. I was used to fearing what people thought, but here
> my homosexuality was just another item on the list of what Jesus could heal.
>
> Discovery was a hospital for me — but a hospital that quickly became a
> medical school. They facilitated a process that helped me heal in ways I never
> dreamed possible. In time, that hospital became a university that trained me
> to be a doctor, to do what they had done for me with others. They trained
> me to share and point people to the truth. Church is where healing and
> wholeness occurs.[14]

It was the bringing together of truth and grace that made all the difference:

I was a member of Discovery for just under four years.... I would not be where I am today without them. I speak and write of them often, and even today, more than a dozen years later, the mere thought of how they loved me reduces me to a crying mess.

They weren't wishy-washy about sin either. Sin was called sin, and no one pretended they didn't struggle with it. My sin wasn't overlooked but rather talked about openly in conjunction with every other sin. I learned that I could walk into church with everything out in the open and hold my head up high. I learned that I wouldn't be rebuffed, but embraced. No one ever pointed a finger at me, but hundreds of times I had people take my hand and choose to walk with me on my journey toward wholeness.

That taught me never to be ashamed of myself. For the first time in my life, I began to be who God created me to be and to love even the broken parts just as he does. I found out that God had always loved me as I was, but that he loved me too much to leave me that way.[15]

Chapter 2

THE HEART
How Your Church Cares

> As he went along, he saw a man blind from birth. His disciples asked him, "Rabbi, who sinned, this man or his parents, that he was born blind?"
>
> "Neither this man nor his parents sinned," said Jesus, "but this happened so that the work of God might be displayed in his life."
>
> —*John 9:1–3*

The Consequences of Sin

Lin and I did not suspect there was anything unusual about our firstborn child until he was almost nine months old. Gabe babbled, like any other baby, and he seemed to respond to our voices. But still, something seemed not quite normal. One morning, just to be sure, we snuck up to his crib with kitchen pan lids in hand. Keeping out of sight, we banged the lids with a clamor that could drive rats out of an attic. He didn't blink.

Before we were able to see the doctor, we both recognized a strange sense of promise in our hearts. We somehow knew that if our son was deaf, God had a purpose for it. Within days, medical testing confirmed that Gabe was severely to profoundly deaf. The hope that had brightened our hearts was nearly extinguished by shock and grief. I began a period of fasting and prayer, asking God to show me if there was any sin in my life that caused my son's deafness.

My wife and I brought Gabe to an internationally known faith healer, who declared our baby's full healing in front of a crowd. We had no doubt that God could heal him, and I had seen and experienced miraculous healings in the past. But in this case, it didn't happen. A short time later, an evangelist from India visited our house. Sitting across from him at our dining room table, I asked, "Have you seen the deaf healed?"

"Oh, yes," he replied. "Often."

"Are they always healed?"

His eyes flattened. "At our crusades, there are sometimes those who are not healed."

"Why not? A lack of faith? Sin?"

"That is a mystery," he said, "that we must leave to God."

As we surrendered our son to the Lord, again and again we discovered a renewed sense in our hearts that Gabe's deafness was for the glory of God. There is no doubt that sin and the resultant curse that has come on our world is the source of all hardship, sickness, darkness, and death. But Christ uses everything for good for those who love him (Romans 8:28–30). The man who was blind in John 9 would not have been born blind in a perfect world. But the disciples' natural inclination to attach personal sin and responsibility to the man or his parents for his blindness did not receive a head nod from our Lord. Rather, Jesus recognized this as an opportunity for God to manifest his glory.

I would like to draw a cautious parallel between deafness or blindness and the experience many people have of growing up with unwanted same-sex attraction. This is not a clean analogy, and it has its limitations. Acting out on one's same-sex attractions is sinful; being deaf or blind is not. The homosexual attractions themselves, however, are the result of growing up in a fallen world. Those who experience same-sex attractions generally do not choose their leanings, but they can make daily choices about what to do with them and about whether to seek healing and transformation through Christ.

If you were standing with Jesus when his disciples asked whose sin had caused the blind man's loss of sight, would you have gone along with the crowd's condemnation of the man, or would you have had compassion and yearned for the man's healing? This question is important, because such compassion is foundational to any and all ministry, whether to homosexuals, to the poor, to youth, to alcoholics, or to people of other countries.

When a pastor, a church leadership team, and eventually an entire congregation develop the heart of Christ for the sexually broken, ministry can begin. The initial barriers of fear, defensiveness, and even disgust often experienced by church members when they think of ministering to people with unwanted same-sex attractions is rooted out of hearts as understanding about the causes of homosexuality grows. The compassion of Christ begins to bloom when members begin to understand that homosexual attractions are usually not chosen by those who experience them but are the fallout of a multiplicity of factors such as prenatal dispositions, sexual abuse, parental detachment, and same-sex peer rejection. This helps us to move beyond the unknown and to connect with people's pain, which should be familiar territory for everyone.

Connecting with People's Pain

Once our son's hearing loss was confirmed, my wife and I began a journey of growth and learning. Over the next several months, we focused on learning sign language through videos and classes and began attending Deaf social functions. Because of our son, we were immediately embraced by the Deaf community. Lin and I rejoiced in this new venue for ministry. Already passionate about missions, we were often looking for opportunities to bring the gospel across cultural barriers. For years, I had directed a student ministry, traveling the country and world promoting missions in seminaries. Now an opportunity to be involved with a largely unreached sector of our society had arrived at our doorstep. Little did I realize that our son's deafness would bring ministry even closer—to the doorstep of my heart.

As our family continued to grow, I continued to travel. The strain on our young family became visible, and I thought about settling into a pastorate. There was one barrier, however—funerals. I was allergic to them. One day I received a request from a Deaf friend on our TTY (telecommunication device), who wrote, "We need you to do a funeral." I told her I wasn't available. She didn't budge, saying, "But you are the only one we can find who is an ordained minister and who knows sign language." Still, I refused. Within hours, she called again.

Days later, I conducted my first funeral—in sign language. The parlor was packed with Deaf families and their friends. They overwhelmed me with love, acceptance, and appreciation. As I stumbled through the service, I was welcomed into the Deaf community and into their lives to an extent I never dreamed possible. More than a year's prior effort to become part of this new community did not yield the results achieved in one hour of sharing with them in their grief and sorrow.

A few weeks later, I was invited to do another funeral for another Deaf family. I refused. They insisted. I gave in. Once again, during the service my fears were buried in joy. The walls that had long isolated my heart from the pain of others were falling down around me, brick by brick. Each brick represented the pain I had been avoiding in others because of the grief I had buried within myself. With a stiff upper lip, I had been living lies for years, such as, "A real man doesn't show tears," "A true leader shows no weaknesses," and "A solid faith overcomes rather than experiences sorrow." Hidden in my facade of strength, I was not a whole person and didn't have the capacity to help others who needed healing.

Ironically, I am now serving in a church with a high percentage of retirees and an abundance of funerals—sometimes more than one a week. Still, God is constantly chiseling the rough edges off of my heart and helping me develop his compassion for all kinds of people.

Connecting with Sexual Brokenness

Through years of reading books and researching issues related to homosexuality, it never occurred to me how little of the truth in my head was filling my heart, and how much less was touching the churches I served. Over a twenty-year period, I keenly argued theology and articulated what was right and wrong on this subject, but my own heart was not broken, and the compassion of Christ took a backseat to my passion for correctness. I counseled individuals who struggled with homosexuality and felt the love of God for them but had little vision for helping my church to do the same.

Slowly, God got through to me by means of a variety of experiences, including a visit by a Deaf friend and her counselor. The two showed up for dinner and provided a five-course meal for the soul through their testimonies. Our friend, who had been close and precious to us for many years, shared that several years earlier she had been involved in a lesbian relationship before turning to the Lord in repentance. Her counselor, having once been a lesbian herself, was now helping many with unwanted same-sex attractions find freedom in Christ.

After our friend related her testimony of change, which closes out this chapter, she then discussed the higher incidence of homosexuality among the Deaf compared with the rest of the American population. The reasons, she believed, are several: a disconnect that often happens between parents and their deaf children (90 percent of deaf children are born to hearing parents, and 90 percent of those hearing parents never learn sign language); a feeling of inferiority that develops in most deaf children; the physical, emotional, and even sexual abuse that often becomes a part of the deaf child's world; and the increased pressure that can be placed on students in residential schools for the Deaf to engage in same-sex activity. She then reminded us of the isolation that is often experienced by Deaf people and grieved over the fact that they lack resources to help them with homosexuality.

I began connecting the dots. I had heard through two decades of fellowship and involvement in the Deaf world about the relatively high rate of homosexuality there.[1] Some of our best teachers of sign language were gay, even those in Christian circles. I had noticed pain associated with the Deaf community and had subconsciously recalled similar pain in the lives of homosexuals I had counseled through the years. My heart softened as I gained new insight.

When Your Ministry Begins

When you hear the word *gay* or *lesbian*, do you cringe and recoil inside? Somewhere deep down, do you consider homosexuality to be more of a taboo than adultery or fornication? The first half of this book will provide more than enough information for you to realize that it should be otherwise. But sometimes the short distance between the head and the heart seems impenetrable.

Change for me came through a process that I believe is at work in every Christian. Simply stated, your ministry for the Lord and to others begins at the place where your heart is already broken. For example, think of Bob Pierce, who in 1947 served with Youth for Christ doing evangelistic crusades in China. The evangelist's heart was touched and broken by human need and poverty in that nation. He wrote in the flyleaf of his Bible, "Let my heart be broken with the things that break the heart of God." Dragging a camera across Asia, Pierce captured the heartrending realities of poverty and injustice across Asia, highlighting the tragedy of children orphaned by the Korean War. He showed his pictures and shared his burden with churches in America, and World Vision International was born. It was through the same burden from God that Pierce later founded Samaritan's Purse, another organization that responds to poverty and human need.

I have studied the lives of many people who are engaged in ministry to the sexually conflicted and broken, and I have found a common thread: those who initiate such ministry are first broken by the things that break the heart of God. Many of them have themselves experienced brokenness through unwanted same-sex attractions. Many others are heterosexuals who have experienced sexual brokenness through experiences of abuse, sexual addiction, and the like. These experiences are so common among the average person and in the average church that one would think ministry to homosexuals would be understood and embraced by Christians everywhere, and yet it is one of the most neglected ministry areas in Christendom. Why? Might it be that we have not made the connection? Our hearts are fully capable of being touched with the compassion of Jesus, but we have allowed all of the political noise and resultant confusion to block our minds and hearts from a Christlike response.

Many who have initiated ministry to the sexually conflicted have made the connection in other ways. Some have linked in through the worldwide tragedy of AIDS. Others have connected because of a family member or personal friend who is struggling with issues of sexual brokenness. It is estimated that up to 10 percent of Christians in the average church are sexual addicts, for example.[2] Still others understand the rejection and isolation a person with same-sex attraction may experience because they too have experienced the dark tunnel of loneliness and isolation.

Pain Works Two Ways

When I first challenged my congregation to open their hearts to the sexually broken, I was surprised by some of their responses. Some of the most understanding and compassionate were those who had gay family members, friends, coworkers, or neighbors. Likewise, some of those most opposed to this call to ministry also had gay family members, friends, coworkers, or neighbors. Depending on a person's experience, closeness to gay or lesbian people can either soften or harden that person toward ministry.

If you have been hurt, offended, or wounded by a gay or lesbian person, your challenge is to forgive and move on. If you can't help that person, there are others you *can* help. Better, there are people who struggle with same-sex attractions who can help *you*. Read books or watch DVD testimonies offered by ministries listed in the resources section of this book. Ask God to bring people into your life who can help you understand the human struggle related to same-sex attractions. Hear their stories. Feel their pain. Recognize their need.

How Your Church Can Make the Connection

Each denomination and each local congregation is being shaped by God to meet needs according to its own unique area of gifting, calling, and spiritual burden. Wisdom guides churches to draw the connection between already established ministry and new ministry venues. A rule of thumb for beginning a new type of worship service, for example, is to plan some overlap in the style of music for the new service with the type of worship that the congregation already knows and loves. Such overlap makes it easier to enlist congregational support, involvement, and understanding. In the same way, ministry to homosexuals should begin at your church's most natural point of connection.

Does your church provide counseling through your pastor (or other staff or volunteers) to people in need? Consider beginning there. Offer counseling services for the sexually conflicted. Are your people strong in fellowship—from potlucks to Sunday school programs to retreats? This may be your natural avenue for outreach. Those who struggle with same-sex attractions need to be loved, to be embraced in fellowship, to become known for who they really are, not based on sexuality as much as on interests and personality. Perhaps your congregation is big on social action and on overcoming societal injustice. You are poised to demonstrate deeds of kindness, differentiating in word and deed between the politics of the world and the politics of Christ.

Theologically conservative congregations can make the connection through evangelism and missions. We have learned to target the unreached peoples of the world, and we have come to identify the great opportunity afforded us through unreached peoples in our own country. What about the unreached homosexual population? We recognize the need to bring the gospel to every tribe, tongue, language, and nation—to touch every culture. What about gay culture?

This point has been subtly coming home for me, one who promoted missions to unreached peoples for years. Directing a student-mobilization effort for nearly a decade, I traveled the world, stirring up students and churches for the cause of missions and evangelism. I often spoke about unreached groups around the world, defined not only by geography and language but by cultural distinctives. Gay culture, too, is a reality to contend with.

In the book *God's Grace and the Homosexual Next Door*, Alan Chambers writes:

> But why is it that churches seldom help support a "missionary" to the gay culture? Why is there seldom a ministry reaching gays represented on missionary Sundays? And why are so few churches doing anything proactively to reach the homosexuals around them or help support those who *are* trying to have an impact?
>
> I suppose it's because they don't see the gay-identified community as a true subculture like those based on race, economic status, location, ethnicity, or religion.
>
> This is a notion I'd like to see changed....
>
> Some readers may have a problem with me claiming that the gay-identified community is a valid, recognizable subculture. But I'm here to tell you as an expatriate, there *is* a gay-defined world in the hearts of millions of people who are attracted to their own sex. As a man or woman thinks, so he or she is. As millions of people think, so a "community" is born. This community—or subculture—*exists* as surely as the Waodani tribe portrayed in the missionary movie *The End of the Spear* exists.[3]

I have been involved in ministries to the Deaf. The word *Deaf* with a capital *D* refers to those involved in Deaf culture. Many Deaf adults find a common affinity in their own language and through their shared experiences in residential schools, Deaf clubs, and the challenges faced as minorities in our large hearing world. Our family has been involved in churches for the Deaf, lead by Deaf pastors who sign their services. Their music is loud, led by drumbeats that can be felt by the worshipers. Many churches around the country have sought to make inroads into Deaf culture by providing

> **Ministry Essential #3: Ministry begins when we connect brokenness in our hearts with brokenness in others.**

interpreters in their services, offering classes on sign language and Deaf culture, and supporting missionaries to the Deaf.

Interestingly, most Christians are comfortable supporting ministry to the Deaf but won't even discuss homosexuality, a major concern in Deaf culture. It is also a major concern in hearing culture. We have a lot to learn about bringing Jesus to the gays and lesbians who knock at the doors of our churches.

As you read the following testimony, take note of the pressures faced by my Deaf friend. When she finally got help, it wasn't from someone who stood back and pointed, as the disciples pointed at the man born blind, asking, "Who sinned?" It was rather from someone who took the time to listen, to learn, to reach out in love.

A Testimony of Truth and Grace

I grew up deaf in a hearing family.* I was born deaf, with a little bit of hearing with hearing aids. I received a lot of speech training and was very good at lipreading, so my family did not learn signs. I attended public schools. I initially had contact with a few other deaf kids, then lost contact completely. When I was in college, I started learning American Sign Language (ASL). I was interested in the Deaf world but didn't know where to find it. My family was close-knit. I had a sister who was two years younger than me. We played together a lot.

I got a degree in deaf education. Afterward, I got a job teaching Deaf students in a mainstreamed program. I finally started finding the Deaf world, where I felt I belonged, but in a small community it was still not enough. I taught sign classes in the evenings. I met a hearing woman, Julie, who was very enthusiastic about learning signs. My close hearing friend from church had just moved away, and I had a big void in my heart. Julie came by to visit me at home. Later she invited me to her home. I visited her church, which had a small Deaf ministry. I decided to move to her home. Her town was halfway between my work and the church with a Deaf ministry. I became very involved in the Deaf ministry there. Julie and I became very close emotionally.

---

* The author wishes to remain anonymous.

Looking back, I realize that Julie was very emotionally dependent, and she latched on to me. At that time I was still unaware of her abusive past. I was lonely, and she helped fill the void in my life. Julie struggled with depression and used the threat of suicide to make our relationship become a physical one. I was not comfortable. I felt so close to her, but at the same time I was torn. I didn't understand what was going on. Being deaf, I didn't grow up hearing about sex or gays and lesbians. At first I didn't recognize that our physical relationship was considered sexual. I didn't have anyone to turn to to talk about it.

It was strange that in spite of my religious upbringing, I had minimal struggles about my relationship with Julie and was not eaten up with guilt feelings. At some point, I remember the verses in Romans 1 about homosexuality hitting me like a brick. I had grown up knowing about the passage in Romans 1 but never thought of it applying to me in my relationship. It was as if I had been blind and then all of a sudden able to see what had been going on. God showed me clearly that I had to terminate the physical nature of our relationship. I knew I didn't have an alternative if I wanted to maintain my walk with God. Having God's peace in my heart was the most important thing to me, and I knew that if I went against something God had clearly shown me, I'd be living in misery.

I remember sitting with Julie and explaining to her what the verses in Romans meant. She had never heard that before, even though she had grown up in church too. Julie cried, but I consoled her by saying that we could continue to be friends. God had not shown me yet that I would have to terminate the friendship as well. He took care of that himself when I made a career move a year later.

I moved to Gallaudet and made friends with another hearing student who knew signs. We both liked to discuss intellectual topics. Later the friend confided to me that she wanted a relationship with me. This started a time of turmoil for me. I didn't know if this meant I was gay. I moved to another town and started teaching Deaf students again. A Deaf female staff member struck up a friendship with me. We had a lot in common. We liked to have a good time and were both very active. It wasn't too long before she was telling me she wanted a relationship with me. I was really good friends with this woman, but I was honest with her and told her why I couldn't have a relationship with her. Again, I lost another good friend. This was frustrating for me. I realized I was new in this town, so people were probably testing me to see if I was straight or gay. Again, I struggled with the same question as to why gay women approached me.

Years later, God brought me into contact with Exodus ministry. This ministry helped me a lot by counseling me and providing me with Christian resources dealing with my homosexuality. I wish I would have had this help when I first struggled with this issue. My counselor was a godly role model for me, having come out of a homosexual lifestyle herself years earlier. It meant a lot to me to have someone who had been there, so I knew I didn't have to explain myself or feel ashamed with her. I was able to be more open with her than I had been with anyone. I learned that the root causes of homosexuality are isolation and rejection. I also understand now why I was drawn to other women and was afraid of men. I know that God is my companion, and he is there for me all the time, unlike any human companion. I learned that it's important to keep my times alone with God paramount, since he alone will fulfill the deepest needs of my heart.

As a Deaf person, I feel fortunate to have found a counselor who was willing to work with a Deaf client. Many resources on homosexuality are not available in captions for Deaf people, so that's a critical need for helping Deaf clients. One struggle I did have as a Deaf individual who had struggled with same-sex attraction was wishing I could meet other Deaf Christians who had walked out of homosexuality so I could see how their stories compared to mine.

Another problem in the Deaf community is that it is very small. Once word gets out about something, everyone knows. I have struggled with sharing my testimony with other Deaf people. God has given me the grace to share with more and more of my friends in the hopes that they, too, will stand up for God's design for one-man-one-woman relationships.

Chapter 3

THE HEAD
Who Your Church Follows

Train yourself to be godly. For physical training is of some value, but godliness has value for all things, holding promise for both the present life and the life to come.

— 1 Timothy 4:7–8

Leadership is critical to the life of God's church. Positions of church authority are the long-sought-after prize for the Christian gay rights movement. For many traditional Christians, leadership posts are the last bastion, the final defense, which, if breached, will signal the demise of orthodox Christianity. Leadership standards are the dividing line where currents from the culture wars collide with riptide fury.

A few months ago I was in a presbytery debate that swirled around the topic of church leadership. An elder in favor of the ordination of gays and lesbians concluded her appeal, saying, "I have homosexual friends who say, 'We will not be part of your church. Why should we get involved in a church that will baptize us but won't allow us to become church officers?'"

Even as I type these words, the Presbyterian Church (USA) has just finished its fourth vote in twelve years about whether to allow practicing homosexuals to become elders and pastors. The vote was close, but once again the historic standards prevailed. Soon, though, it may go the other way. Already appeals are being made by gay-affirming congregations for a fifth vote on the same issue. Other denominations are in the thick of battle about ordination standards too.

Why Leadership Matters

Early in my marriage, before I began pastoral ministry, I had the wonderful opportunity of attending churches just to learn, worship, and participate as a regular member. My wife and I settled into a large interdenominational church and enjoyed the worship and the preaching. We came to love and trust the pastor and delighted in his sermons.

Then came the announcement—in the mail. My pastor had left his wife for his secretary. The church had set up a council to work with him in an attempt to restore his marriage, but he refused to leave the new woman. The letter announced the pastor's dismissal and the creation of a support team for the pastor's family.

I was devastated. How could this seemingly godly man veer from the commandments of God to fulfill his own personal desires? If his problems were deep and interpersonal, why did he not seek counseling and recommit to his marriage and family? Similar disappointment and pain must have filled the hearts of nearly every other church member. Like me, they each probably understood the need for him to step down. To allow him to continue in his unrepentant state would be to affirm his misdeeds and to suggest that promiscuity and adultery are acceptable and inconsequential in the lives of Christians.

A leader's life casts a large shadow over the people he or she serves. J. Oswald Sanders, in his book *Spiritual Leadership*, puts it simply: "Leadership is influence."[1] When church members fall into immorality, immediate friends and family grieve. When a leader of the church fails morally, the whole congregation suffers.

Influencing Our Youth

The awesome responsibility of parents and the church related to their youth is summarized in the book of Proverbs: "Train a child in the way he should go, and when he is old he will not turn from it" (Proverbs 22:6). The Hebrew word for *train* carries with it the sense of creating an environment for growth. In home life and in the church, we must do all in our power to create an environment for the healthy growth of our youth. Parents and church leaders carry the responsibility of creating such an environment, and their examples shape that environment.

Steven DeVore grew up with polio. He learned to overcome his disability by watching others walk and then mentally replaying the image in his mind. When he was nineteen, he used the same modeling concept to learn the Finnish language. Later, in college, he watched professional bowlers on television until their movements and styles were imprinted in his mind. He then attempted to copy their techniques and bowled nine strikes in a row, claiming a score of 278 (his highest previous score had been 163). Sharing his bowling experience with a professor of psychology, DeVore was told that observation and learning through role models are the primary ways in which humans learn behavior. DeVore engaged a neuropsychologist at Stanford University to help him with research and applied the concept of learning behavior through role models to develop a multimillion-dollar company that markets instructional videos on everything from golf to weight control. He made a mint on a simple concept: we develop our behavior based on the behavior of others.

Leaders are role models for our youth. Think of the people who have most influenced your life. What influence did leaders have on your ambitions and actions as a youth? It is no wonder that whole denominations are splitting over decisions about whether unrepentant gays or lesbians should be allowed to be pastors and church leaders. For those who believe homosexual behavior is immoral, such a step is tantamount to sanctioning nonrepentant adulterers into positions of power. Those who believe same-sex attraction is an inborn gift of God, however, find it offensive and discriminatory not to allow gays and lesbians into leadership posts.

The Modern Dilemma

In 2003, when the American Anglican Church voted to appoint openly gay Rev. Canon Gene Robinson as a bishop, an ecclesiastical earthquake erupted, causing church splits, court battles, and significant membership flight. No doubt, there were already many homosexuals within the ranks of the Episcopal Church, but most were quietly worshiping or serving. For the denomination to appoint a bishop who publicly endorsed homosexuality by his words and his lifestyle, however, was to proclaim to all people that homosexuality is acceptable in the eyes of God.

The leaders we need are not those who give in to their weaknesses, but those who humbly trust God for the strength to be obedient. Jesus told us we would need to deny ourselves and take up our crosses if we are to be his disciples (Matthew 16:24). In the realm of sexuality, leaders in the church must model faithfulness to God's creative norm, despite struggles they may face as singles who never find mates or as persons locked into marriages that for physiological or psychological reasons preclude sexual expression. Jesus Christ, who was never sexually active, enables us to find deep intimacy and fulfillment in relationships even when sexual expression must be curtailed. The Bible showcases singleness, along with marriage, as a holy calling from God (Matthew 19:10–12, 27–30; 1 Corinthians 7).

Our Manual

Leroy Eims, in his book *Be the Leader You Were Meant to Be*, writes, "We need to look at leadership from the standpoint of the Bible. Both the Old and New

Testaments are alive with eternal truths that bear on this subject."[2] But there are differing perspectives on how to interpret the Bible. Bishop Robinson found his way into a respected leadership post because there were many who believed his self-proclaimed gay lifestyle was acceptable in the eyes of God, and they believed they could support their position scripturally.

The two primary New Testament writings about leadership are found in 1 and 2 Timothy. Each chapter in these two letters describes the qualifications for pastors, and a whole section is devoted to the high standards for church officers (see 1 Timothy 3:1–13, which has a parallel passage in Titus 1:5–9). The clarion call in Paul's letters to Timothy, his frontline pastor and church planter, is for *godliness*. Not giftedness, not prominence, not persuasiveness, and not majority vote, but godliness. Every chapter in these two books upholds godliness as a standard for leadership, as does the whole tenor of the Bible.

The Greek word for *godliness* is a compound of two words, *eu*, meaning "well," and *sebomai*, meaning "devotion" or "worship." Put together, godliness is "well worship," or "true devotion." A godly person lives in a way that honors God, based on a true knowledge of God's Word and will for our lives. The Bible cautions us about religious leaders who cloak themselves in an outward form of godliness but who deny the life-changing power of our Lord. There is a vast difference between *godlikeness* and *godliness*. Godliness encompasses not only appearances but the reality of an inner life that is touched by God's truth and grace right down to the thoughts and attitudes of the heart (2 Timothy 3:5).

The Two Rival Factions

In Christ's day, two major perspectives on godliness were peddled by the two types of religious power brokers — the Sadducees and the Pharisees. The Sadducees were the well-to-do priesthood, the religious aristocracy, the leaders of the mainline church. They were experts at finding caveats and compromises related to the plain teaching of Scripture to make life for the God-follower easier and to make Scripture more accessible for people who struggled with their faith. When they found it necessary or convenient, they denied the existence of angels, the afterlife, and the judgment of God. Looking good in their external show of religious finery, they subtly denied major scriptural truths in exchange for political gain (Mark 12:24). The images of godliness and religious power were nearly synonymous for them.

The Pharisees, on the other hand, held to a strict and literal interpretation of Scripture. Tenaciously, they embraced their faith in God, in the supernatural, in the afterlife, in angels, and in all things sacred. In fact, so great was their devotion to Scripture that they created thousands of their own rules to ensure that even the finest points and interpretations of God's Word were kept with exacting detail. To the Pharisee, godliness was measured not by one's power but by perfection. Their lists of regulations became so laborious that the common person had no hope of keeping them, and even the Pharisees themselves couldn't keep up with them all. Dwelling on the minutiae of God's will, they missed the main point. "You strain out a gnat but swallow a camel" (Matthew 23:24). They tithed their kitchen spices but neglected justice and mercy for the poor and needy.

The Sadducees failed to honor God's truth, and the Pharisees neglected God's grace. Neither lived in a manner that pleased the Lord. Jesus cut to the heart of the issue when he showed love to the outcasts, the poor, the sinners, and the downtrodden. Speaking the truth in love, he taught people everywhere that the life he offered could change their lives. Challenging the Pharisees for their rigid standards (Matthew 23:13–36) and rebuking the Sadducees for their lack of faith (Mark 12:18–27), Jesus' teaching and life confronted ungodliness with all of its religious trappings.

How are we doing today? Do we really embrace Scripture without compromise? If so, are we following the Bible by embracing the priorities given to us by God by caring for the needy, the poor, and the outcasts of society? Throughout history, the coming together of truth and love and the avoidance of the extremes of the Sadducees and Pharisees have always been an indication of life, health, and renewal in the church. When conflicting extremes create a polarized church, however, the need for spiritual renewal becomes glaring.

What Drives the Extremes?

It is typically not wrong values that create heresy and hypocrisy in the church but right values that are out of balance. Heresy is biblical grace twisted on one end, and hypocrisy is biblical truth twisted on the other. Justice, for example, is a value that fuels the progressive theological movement. The call for justice is found throughout the Bible. It is a godly aim, an indisputable passion in the heart of God. With a slight twist, however, it can bend love into immorality and truth into error. On the other extreme, the value of biblical accuracy powers the theologically conservative sectors of the church. When the Bible is taught but not lived out, the church becomes an empty shell, devoid of life and purpose as it motivates church members more by guilt than by the grace of God. Let's briefly consider how both extremes have manifested themselves in the church.

Justice with a Twist

The issue of justice permeates the Scriptures. In the Old Testament, God's people are commanded to reach out to and care for the poor, the alien, and the downtrodden (Zechariah 7:8–10). Jesus set the standard for the church when he did just that (Matthew 9:35–36). His followers are commanded to follow in his steps. Latching on to this mandate, the progressive movement within the church works vigorously to open the gate for practicing homosexuals to serve as ordained pastors. Jack Rogers, in his book *Jesus, the Bible, and Homosexuality*, says that those who hinder such ordinations need only to look back at the history of other injustices to see how wrong it would be to prevent gays and lesbians from serving as church leaders. Likening the issue to slavery and women's rights, Rogers writes:

> How could most Christians for more than two hundred years accept slavery and the subordination of women with not a hint that there was any other view in the Bible? Why did good, intelligent, devout Christian people not see what we now recognize as mitigating factors in the biblical record? Why did we change our minds? How does a church change its course? Potentially, at least, we can learn something relevant to our discussion of homosexuality by discovering the answers to these questions.[3]

Later in the book, Rogers uses similar logic about the church's gradual acceptance of women and then divorced people into leadership. This is a classic example of truth with a twist. The logic of Rogers's argument seems to work on the surface, but with a more careful look, one can find the turning of facts and logic, causing his argument to come apart at the seams. The comparison with slavery is *illogical*, the comparison with the subordination of women is *debatable*, and the comparison with divorce is *irrelevant*. Consider first the slavery issue.

Why Slavery Does Not Fit

Equating race with sexual preference is incongruous. Genes determine skin color and may influence our *preferences*, but they do not dictate our *behavior*. The argument behind this logic goes like this: But homosexuals did not choose to be attracted to the same sex. That statement is true. We do not choose our temptations. But we can choose how to act on them. Overweight people do not choose to be drawn to the dessert menu, but they do make choices about whether to overeat. Joe Smith does not choose to be aroused by his neighbor's wife as he unintentionally sees her undressing through his window. But he can decide to look away and not dwell on his thoughts and feelings or convert them into action.

The very thought of equating slavery with homosexual rights is offensive to many African Americans. In Jack Rogers's defense, one might say his main point of symmetry between slavery and homosexuality is on how leaders have changed their viewpoints around the interpretation of Scripture. But even that comparison is illogical. While slavery is allowed in the Bible, it is nowhere supported. It is tolerated under a general rubric of respect and love for one's fellow humans (Leviticus 19:17–18; 25:39). Homosexual acts, however, are nowhere tolerated in the Bible. Despite the modern gay rights movement's effort to reinterpret Scripture, mainstream scholarship has for two thousand years understood the Bible to stand against homosexual behavior.

Paul stood against inequities in a society that incorporated slavery into its very fabric. It is believed that as many as 40 percent of the populace in Rome was under the bondage of slavery. Many indentured servants, however, were treated fairly and justly, somewhat like employees today. Sadly, many others were abused and mistreated. If Paul had started a campaign to end all slavery, he would have been mocked, imprisoned, and rendered ineffective. Instead, he did something much more powerful. He promoted the godly values of love and justice (Colossians 4:1). With a heart made radical by the love of Christ, Paul called Christian slaves his brothers and sisters (see the book of Philemon). He set the stage for the abolition movement centuries later.

William Wilberforce, one of the best known of the British abolitionists, was a member of the Clapham Sect, an evangelical segment of the Anglican Church. His challenge to the upper class to regain true Christian values, largely based on Paul's writings, was critical to his political success. If the New Testament values that Paul sought to apply to slavery were applied to employee-employer relationships today, the outcome might actually improve relationships in most corporations. It would not be slavery.

What about Women in Leadership?

Questions about women in leadership, biblically, go back to the creation and yet are influenced by culture. Some "conservative" Christians believe that the acceptance of women in leadership posts in the church has opened the door for the ordination of practicing homosexuals. Likewise, some "liberal" Christians argue that just as the church finally came around to accepting women in leadership posts, it is time they do the same for practicing homosexuals. This is Jack Rogers's stance. Both perspectives are flawed.

The issue of whether women should hold leadership posts in the church has been debated from the earliest days of the church, even in some of the most conservative branches of Christendom. Likewise today, some of the more conservative evangelical Christians support women in leadership, and some do not. When we find an issue like this that has been debated by Bible-believing Christians through the ages, we should approach those who differ with us with grace and respect.

The question of whether practicing homosexuals should be allowed into positions of church leadership has not been debated or even considered an option through two thousand years of church history. The first significant challenge to the clear teaching of the Bible on this topic came through Anglican theologian Dr. Derrick S. Bailey in the 1950s in his *Homosexuality and the Western Christian Tradition*.[4]

Not one verse in the Bible affirms homosexual leadership. Dozens of texts, however, describe women in leadership.[5] Questions of gender in leadership and questions about morality are not on the same plane.

The Divorce Question

A third correlation, upheld by the theological left, between the church's historic stance on practicing homosexuals' leadership options and injustice is divorce and remarriage. After describing the changing standards about divorce in the mainline Presbyterian Church, Jack Rogers writes:

> How is this relevant to granting equality to gay and lesbian members of our churches? Jesus' words that divorce is equivalent to adultery are among the clearest statements on a moral issue in Scripture.... If we were to take Jesus' teaching on divorce literally, we would still not be accepting divorced and remarried people as office bearers in the church. Yet church law now asks that we take literally less clear statements regarding homosexual behavior. It is a double standard: current church law permits a pastoral approach concerning marriage and divorce for people who are heterosexual and mandates a legalistic approach toward people who are homosexual.[6]

On the surface, this argument seems to make sense. Recently I had lunch with a man who said, "I've been divorced and remarried three times, and I am in church leadership. I can't see why we don't allow homosexuals to lead in the church if we allow for divorce and remarriage." It took from the time the food was ordered to just before the bill was paid to answer my friend. There is not a simple one-sentence response to this complex issue, and whole books have been written to bring clarity on biblical guidelines for remarriage and divorce. And that is just the point. On matters that are not made clear in the Bible, denominations need to set clear policy guidelines so that their membership is treated fairly and consistently. Same-sex activity is clearly prohibited in the Bible. The conditions on which one is free to remarry, however, can be complex.

The Bible shows clearly that God hates divorce but that he allows for it where the marital bond has been broken by sexual infidelity (Matthew 19:9). Paul offers his personal convictions about other potential exceptions (1 Corinthians 7). Less clarity is found with regard to remarriage, and each pastor and church must develop their own perspectives on this matter and practice them consistently to avoid hurt and confusion among church members. I remember one time when I told a couple that I could not marry them on biblical grounds, based on the particulars of a previous marriage and the situation of a previous spouse. They walked down the street and found a pastor in another denomination who agreed to marry them.

Fortunately, many denominations have written clear position statements about divorce and remarriage. Nearly every statement I have seen emphasizes the importance of repentance for the person getting remarried if the divorce occurred for nonbiblical reasons. The Scriptures tell us to repent for our past sins so that we don't set a bad example for others. Christians can debate whether a divorced person can take a leadership post in a church, but none should debate the importance of purity and permanency in marriage and of repentance for those who divorced for the wrong reasons.

The proper question about homosexuality, when making a comparison with divorced persons being remarried, ought to be, "Should we allow *repentant* homosexuals to be in a position of leadership in the church?" The logical answer ought to be, "Of course," especially for churches that allow *repentant* divorcees to be in leadership. Throughout this book I seek to differentiate between a person who may struggle with same-sex inclinations but who is committed to living in a way that honors God in contrast to the person who promotes same-sex activity by his or her words and life. Other requirements for church leadership should include a life of godliness, spiritual maturity, and God's calling and gifting for the job.

The Other Extreme: Empty Truth

If grace devoid of standards leads to spiritual harm, then a pharisaic approach to Christianity is equally detrimental. Some believers add line upon line of tradition and requirement around God's truth until the original intent of the Scripture is entangled by human-made regulations. The Pharisees drew 613 laws from the Old Testament and loaded them on the backs of their followers. Jesus said, "They tie up heavy loads and put them on men's shoulders, but they themselves are not willing to lift a finger to move them" (Matthew 23:4). Jesus called them "hypocrites" seven times in Matthew 23 alone. The biblical Greek word for *hypocrite* means "actor"; one commentator has "actor on the stage of life."[7] These were religious leaders who put on a good show but inside were uncaring and unloving. They were no godlier than the prostitutes and tax gatherers they rejected. Extremely careful about how they dressed, how they tithed, and how they kept the traditions of their congregations, they overlooked the more important matters of "justice, mercy and faithfulness" (v. 23).

In searching for modern-day examples of hypocrites, I need not look far. I preach weekly to a large congregation just a block from housing projects and a shelter for the homeless. I live on a decent American income, while poverty ravages most of the world. I pray for people to come to Christ and don't share my faith as often as I should. Thus, I often struggle and pray daily that the Lord will help me not to be just another actor on the Christian stage, devoid of heart, passion, and Christian action.

Karen Booth is a woman who has devoted her life to helping Methodist churches develop ministries for those conflicted sexually. I once asked her what she has found to be the biggest barrier to developing ministry for homosexuals in local congregations. Expecting to hear that it was gay rights protestors, or perhaps denominational politics, her answer caught me off guard. She didn't think twice before answering, "The church itself is the barrier." She went on to detail example after example of how reluctant and resistant the average church is to help the sexually conflicted. Prejudice, fear, and legalism abound. There is so little understanding, so little love and compassion. Evangelicals and fundamentalists shake their fingers as they denounce the liberal congregations that affirm homosexuality. But what will it take for those who carry the torch of the truth to themselves be ignited with a love for the people Jesus wants them to reach?

The Heart of the Matter

Debate among Christians about homosexuality is but the fruit of differing perspectives. The way we view Scripture is the *root* problem. We must avoid the extremes of both the Pharisees and the Sadducees. Those who handle key biblical texts about homosexuality properly will find that controversy over this topic diminishes, as we will see in part 2. Based on this understanding, one can successfully build ministry, as described in part 3.

There are more than a dozen biblical texts that either directly or indirectly deal with homosexuality, half of them carrying the greatest significance.[8] These texts can be linked into natural pairs that demonstrate how the Old Testament stories, images, and laws are the alphabet with which the language of the New Testament is written. Each pairing reflects a central aspect of God's person.

Who God is	Old Testament reference	New Testament reference
God as Creator	Genesis 2:21–25	Romans 1:18–32
God as King	Leviticus 18:22; 20:13	1 Timothy 1:8–11
God as Redeemer	Genesis 19	1 Corinthians 6:9–11

Based on the three central roles of the Almighty, we find three practical questions that relate not only to those who struggle with issues of sexuality but also to the challenges every one of us faces on the journey of spiritual transformation:

• • •

1. God as Creator
Question addressed: Did God create me this way?
2. God as King
Question addressed: Is the Old Testament law relevant for today?

3. God as Redeemer
Question addressed: Can God change me?

Creating a Biblical Reality

In his book *Leadership Is an Art,* Max De Pree writes, "The first responsibility of a leader is to define reality."[9] The desperate need of our day is for leaders who will define biblical reality. Avoiding the extremes of the Pharisees and the Sadducees, we need leaders who will proclaim truth with such love and acceptance that they become like Christ to the hurting world. We cannot endorse leaders who embrace a lifestyle of adultery, greed, sensuality, or gossip, however. Nor should we immediately reject leaders who have once fallen but show evidence of transformed lives. It is often those who are overcome by the grace of God who can best help others to overcome.

Regarding ministry to homosexuals, some of the most effective leaders, counselors, and advisers to churches are those who were once trapped in the grip of sexual sin. In fact, I have found that one of the most significant factors held in common by churches that have developed ministry to the sexually conflicted is that they have partnered with one or more persons who have been sexually broken, who have found healing and strength in Christ, and who have dedicated their lives to helping others.

Paul commended posthomosexuals in the church at Corinth for overcoming their sinful ways, saying, "Such were some of you" (1 Corinthians 6:11 NASB). He acknowledged their faith and faithfulness (1:4–9), confirming that their past need not hold them back from living for God's glory today (6:9). Many modern Christians do not share Paul's confidence that lives can be changed and thus are indifferent and even hostile toward posthomosexuals, as though they are a category of untouchables, an especially bad class of sinners.

I have the highest respect for those who are leaders in the posthomosexual movement. Many of them are model Christians by biblical standards. They face great challenges as they seek to help others while being rebuffed, not only by the world, but by Christians on both sides of the theological fence. Those who have come out of homosexuality and now take a stand for Jesus and for holiness may be considered a persecuted silent minority in our country. Many of them labor tirelessly, snatching others from the pit of despair and darkness and

> **Ministry Essential #4:**
> **Church leadership is about godly role models, not rights.**

offering the brightness of hope. They are to be commended and supported for their work. They become a lifeline for gay and lesbian persons who are crying out to God and looking for a church to call home. These heroes of the faith are also some of the best instructors to help equip the church to develop relevant ministries to homosexuals.

Why do some heterosexuals feel awkward or even defensive toward post-homosexuals? Perhaps we have forgotten that God can use our failings to make us stronger, and our sins to teach us grace. Think about it:

- Paul was a persecutor of Christians before he repented and became the great apostle and the author of most of the New Testament.
- Moses committed murder and ran as a fugitive before he repented and led a million Jews to the Land of Promise.
- Rahab was a prostitute who protected God's people and had her name etched in the genealogical line that leads to the Messiah (Matthew 1:5; Hebrews 11:31).
- Abraham and Isaac each had a problem with lying (Genesis 20:9–13; 26:6–9), Jacob could be downright deceptive (Genesis 27:33–36), David fell into sexual sin (2 Samuel 11), and Solomon supported idolatry (1 Kings 11:4–10). James and John were once judgmental (Luke 9:51–56), and Peter outright disowned his Lord (John 18:25–27).

There is not a leader in the world who has never sinned or who will not face temptation in the process of leading others. The desperate need of our day is for godly leaders who will allow their past failures to become channels of grace through which others experience the touch of God's love and redeeming grace. When church leaders are transparent about their weaknesses, those they lead are more likely to come out of their protective shells and ask for help.

The Making of a Leader

Patrick Payton was recently out of seminary.[*] His new church in Midland, Texas—Stonegate Fellowship—was thriving. His success in part came through teaching his members to be open to all kinds of people because the grace of God can change anyone. Then came the challenge—through Mike and Stephanie Goeke, a couple whose troubled marriage had been wonderfully

[*] Patrick Payton is the senior pastor of Stonegate Fellowship in Midland, Texas.

restored. They confessed in the quiet of the pastor's office that their marital problems had been related to Mike's lifelong struggle with same-sex attractions. Patrick listened as Mike described his struggles through childhood, high school, and college, along with the loneliness and the fear of alienation he felt even at Stonegate Church. Patrick left work that day with the realization that Mike and Stephanie's testimony needed to be shared openly with the congregation. In his words:

"Following several weeks of very intense and sometimes personal attack and struggle about the importance of sharing this real-life story in the body of Christ, I had this precious couple speak in front of our entire church family. It was a day I will never forget.

"The auditorium was packed with Stonegate members and with Mike and Stephanie's friends from the community. Our church was filled with people who thought they were there to hear a normal story about how Jesus had saved a marriage. No one knew they were about to experience a *marker day* for Stonegate Fellowship. From that Sunday morning on, everyone would know we were serious when we said, 'We believe Jesus changes lives, and we want you, and all your baggage, so we can journey with you in the new life in Christ.' But not only was Stonegate Fellowship changed; a pastor was changed as well.

"To say the least, I was amazed at what happened that Sunday morning. After the service, people would not leave. So many people stayed to talk with Mike and Stephanie about family members struggling with homosexuality and asked what they could do. Men whom I knew to be very upset about what the Goekes were going to share were in tears, asking for forgiveness from Mike and Stephanie. And the hope I saw on the faces of so many was astounding. I saw in the eyes of people something of a new hope that said, 'If Jesus could do this in Mike and Stephanie's life, then surely he can change my life.' But things were changing in my heart as well.

"I knew from the beginning that my characterization of homosexuality had been wrong. My ideas about homosexuality were formed from the harsh rhetoric of evangelical speakers and the images of mainstream media. I never once thought about white-collar professionals like Mike Goeke who had been suffering with this issue for decades and were drowning in a sea of anonymity right under the nose of the church. Men—and women—living two lives, desperate for help but finding none anywhere they looked. After all, homosexuality was the *worst* sin and surely of a different sort than *normal* sins, such as taking one too many drinks, cheating on taxes, lusting after women, breaking the speed limit, or failing to tithe! I had bought into a way of thinking that set homosexuality apart as the leprosy of the twenty-first century rather than another destructive sin used by Satan to steal away full and meaningful life from those who would follow Jesus. From this moment on, at least for this pastor, homosexuality would not be the serious sin of the worst sinners but rather another sin destroying the lives of everyday people of all social classes.

"I also learned that my words were killing those who most needed the healing touch of the Savior. On another Sunday, not long after the Goekes shared, I was waxing eloquent about an especially popular couple at the time who were openly proud lesbians. I boldly referred to them as perverts and continued on without skipping a beat. Within days, Mike stopped by my office to let me know that when I used words like *pervert* and *queer*, I further alienated those so desperately desiring help from the local church. As much as I wanted to defend myself, I could not. I was damning the very ones Jesus died for by my churchy, harsh words. The more I thought about it, the more I realized Jesus never called anyone names either, except the religious elite of his day. He certainly never called the woman we read about in Luke 7 a whore! He just let her wash his holy feet and taught a humiliating lesson to Simon the Pharisee. As much as I hated to do it, I stood in the pulpit the very next Sunday and issued an apology to our congregation for labeling sinners rather than just labeling sin. I vowed to never make that mistake again.

"I was learning some new things about confession and community as well. Jesus changes a life in an instant, but it takes a lifetime of walking in the new, crucified life in a community of Christ-followers called the local church to truly experience the transformed life Jesus came to offer. But for so many like me, we have grown accustomed to acting like transformed people should act, while deep down inside we are dying a slow death because we are afraid to talk about our struggles. We fear we will be perceived as spiritual losers. After Mike and Stephanie shared the rest of their story, the gauntlet was thrown down in my life and in the life of our church. That gauntlet simply represented the fact that Stonegate would be no place for fakers. We would lean heavily on each other with our deepest struggles so that, as a community of Christ-followers, we could share the life of Christ with each other."

Part 2

APPROACH: OVERCOMING CONTROVERSY

Creation and Science:
Did God Create Homosexuality?

Standards and Psychology:
Which Norms Are Still Relevant?

Compassion and the Church:
Does God Really Care?

THE LANDSCAPE
The Grand Sweep of the Bible

The Controversy

Grace with Compromised Truth: "There are only a few passages in the grand sweep of the Bible that focus on homosexuality. The rest of the Scriptures strongly affirm God's love and acceptance for all people. It is obvious that homosexuality is acceptable to God and that it should be to us."

Truth with Compromised Grace: "There are several biblical passages that specifically focus on homosexuality and proclaim it as deserving damnation, and the rest of the Bible supports them. No question about it: homosexuals need to turn or burn."

Uniting Truth and Grace as a Basis for Ministry

"Do you know how much Jesus said about homosexuality? Do you know?" asked the woman with angst. Her small group of friends who had come to provide their alternative viewpoint at our church seminar nodded as this visiting pastor pursed her lips and wrinkled her brow, pushing her words forth with deep, quiet emotion: "Absolutely nothing." She inhaled with authority and confidence.

I gazed at her, amazed that these words were still being used. My mind unconsciously slipped back to a time in the mid-1970s, during my college years, when a blond student in a San Francisco–based program I was attending cornered me in the hall and inundated me with what was then considered cutting-edge gay Christian theology. Back then, more than three decades earlier, I was hearing all of the arguments for the first time. He asked me the very same question, in a similar tone of voice. From the mid-1970s until the present day, I would watch this and most of the other pro-gay arguments become packaged and repackaged, answered and reanswered, debunked and set aside, only to be picked up year after year and spoken by people who embraced them as though they were new and astounding revelations and were convincing others of the same.

But one thing was different. In the 1970s San Francisco classroom, a hulking black-haired student stood and denounced the blond, presumably gay man, with a public rebuke that included derogatory labels, including "devilish snake." In this most recent seminar, however, our leadership team embraced the "opposition" with hugs and invitations to come back and dialogue further. The way we cared for our guests added validity to the truths presented in our seminar and probably spoke more than our words to many who listened and watched.

To overcome the decades-old controversies on this topic, we must first start with the Bible. We will examine two specific texts about homosexuality, and we will also consider the broad perspective of the Bible to put those texts in the context of God's redemptive story. As we do so, let us remember that it is not enough to find the truth; we must learn to present it to others in love, as did Jesus.

What did Jesus actually say about homosexuality anyway?

What Jesus Said about Homosexuality

Troy Perry, founder of the largest gay denomination, said, "As for the question 'What did Jesus say about homosexuality?' the answer is simple. Jesus said nothing. Not one thing. Nothing! Jesus was more interested in love."[1] On the surface, Troy was right. But an argument from silence is deceptive. Consider the following:

First, we do not know everything that Jesus actually said. Only a small portion of the eighty-nine chapters in the Gospels are actually quotations from his mouth—no more than a person might speak in a few hours of casual conversation. To claim that he never spoke against homosexual behavior or any other sin is pure conjecture.

Second, Jesus was Jewish, his disciples were Jewish, and his ministry was first and foremost among the Jewish people (Matthew 15:24; Romans 1:16; 2:9–10). The people who surrounded him already considered homosexual acts to be a sinful violation of God's purpose, and they stood against it, leaving Jesus little reason to address the topic.[2] Jesus also said nothing about incest or the other forms of improper sexuality that were already condemned in the

Old Testament. He did not address the problems of pedophilia, bestiality, voyeurism, fetishism, sadism, masochism, or necrophilia.

He did speak clearly against adultery, however, because this was an arena in which even some rabbis compromised the teaching of Scripture, and it was a sin trap into which some Jews had fallen.[3] We know Jesus' approach to adultery. He was tough, direct, and uncompromising (Matthew 5:27, 32; 19:3–9; Mark 10:11–12). As seen in the last chapter, his approach to *adulterers*, however, was loving, compassionate, and helpful. We can assume that if Jesus had been asked to speak about homosexuality, his approach would have been the same, and his love toward homosexuals would have been powerfully demonstrated.

Most important, Jesus did something much more forceful than speak against the practice of homosexuality. He affirmed God's original and ongoing plan, as expressed from the beginning, for sexuality to be contained between one man and one woman for life (Matthew 19:3–6; Mark 10:1–12). For all the other deviations from God's intended norm, affirmation of God's standard from the beginning was sufficient. It is the creation account that forms the backdrop for the biblical drama on which our study of homosexuality should be staged.

Back to the Beginning

The word *genesis* means "beginnings." Those who suggest that the Scriptures allow for homosexuality as an alternative Christian lifestyle often begin their study with the Sodom and Gomorrah account and may bypass Genesis 1 and 2 altogether. If we do not reflect on the nature of God's creative act, we miss a vital truth about the nature of humans. We are made in God's image.

In Genesis 2 we read:

> So the LORD God caused the man to fall into a deep sleep; and while he was sleeping, he took one of the man's ribs and closed up the place with flesh. Then the LORD God made a woman from the rib he had taken out of the man, and he brought her to the man.
> The man said,
>
> > "This is now bone of my bones
> > and flesh of my flesh;
> > she shall be called 'woman,'
> > for she was taken out of man."
>
> For this reason a man will leave his father and mother and be united to his wife, and they will become one flesh.
> The man and his wife were both naked, and they felt no shame.
> — *Genesis 2:21–25*

The strength and beauty of this imagery is clear. One man and one woman. In human understanding, one plus one equals two. But in God's wisdom, one plus one becomes one — a team of mutual love and support. The woman was made from a part of the man's side so that he might bring her back to himself, near to his heart, to love and cherish her. The two would become bonded for life by God himself. This unity reflects the very image of God:

> So God created man in his own image,
>   in the image of God he created him;
>   male and female he created them.
>
> — *Genesis 1:27*

The God who said, "Let *us* make man in *our* image" (Genesis 1:26, emphasis added), created people to be a reflection of himself. God is a unity of plurality, three persons with one essence. So, too, humans were not made to be loners. This is not to say that God doesn't bless celibacy, because he does. Jesus was single. Paul commended the single lifestyle as being more effective for God's work than the married counterpart (1 Corinthians 7). But the message is clear: humans were created like God, and marriage is a reflection of his person.

The church is often called "the bride of Christ" (Ephesians 5:32; Revelation 19:7), because there are similarities between the marriage relationship and the kind of union God desires with his people. No institution on earth surpasses marriage for intimacy and longevity. Thus, from the beginning God made them male and female and designed them to remain single or to unite in marriage. From this point forward, Scripture proclaims heterosexual union as the norm, the standard to be followed. By positive affirmation, then, the creation account rules out every form of sexual deviation from God's norm that would later be contrived by the human race. This is why Jesus and his disciples referred to the creation account when addressing issues of sexuality. In the words of C. S. Lewis:

> The Christian idea of marriage is based on Christ's words that a man and wife are to be regarded as a single organism — for that is what the words "one flesh" would be in modern English. And the Christians believe that when he said this he was not expressing a sentiment but stating a fact — just as one is stating a fact when one says that a lock and its key are one mechanism, or that a violin and a bow are one musical instrument. The inventor of the human machine was telling us that its two halves, the male and the female, were made to be combined together in pairs, not simply on a sexual level, but totally combined.[4]

The Bigger Picture

Supporters of the gay Christian movement make the point that if only six to eight primary texts speak directly about homosexuality, it must not have been a significant concern in the mind of God. Let us pause here and ask how many Scripture verses we can find that verbally slap the hand that engages in computer hacking. Where is the chapter and verse that prohibits speeding? How many references can you pull down that specifically prohibit the enjoyment of pornography?

"Wait," some will say, "there are enough warnings to avoid stealing, recklessness, and sexual immorality that it should be assumed that computer hacking, careless driving, and viewing pornography are violations of God's plan for our lives." True, very true. From beginning to end, the Bible calls us to holiness before God around the standards he has set before us. It is a given that if we create new ways to sin that breach God's clearly stated purposes, we have violated Scripture. In other words, the whole of the Bible, from the creation account forward, speaks clearly against computer hacking, dangerous driving, and viewing pornography, though we cannot find a specific verse addressing these topics.

Let's apply this logic to a specific area of sexual sin — incest. There are actually people who seek to justify the practice of incest based on the notion that those who so engage are made that way by God.[5] Such behavior, it is argued, is innate, and genetically induced. But do we listen to these arguments and support the practice? No. Not yet, anyway. But the very arguments that have been used to support the practice of homosexuality in the church could be used with greater force by those who wish to justify their incestuous lifestyles. Proponents would simply call to mind places in the Old Testament where marriage within the family was still allowed, and then point out that whereas there are several clear texts that prohibit homosexual activity in the New Testament, there is only one New Testament reference that comes close to condemning incest (1 Corinthians 5:1–5).

What about pedophilia? Not a single New Testament reference directly prohibits such activity. How about relationships with multiple partners at the same time (polyamory)? A 2009 article in *Newsweek* tells us there are half a million households in the United States today comprised of "ethical non-monogamous" adults, who are each engaged in intimate relationships with more than one person — based on the knowledge and consent of everyone involved.[6] These numbers reflect a growing movement. In 2006, a statement titled "Beyond Same-Sex Marriage" was crafted and then endorsed by over fifteen hundred gay, lesbian, transgendered, and bisexual activists, authors, attorneys, actors, filmmakers, educators, and community leaders calling for legal recognition of multiple-sex-partner relationships.[7] Again, the scriptural arguments based on a supposedly antiquated Old Testament and on the silence of Jesus on these subjects can be used with greater force to offer God's blessing on pedophilia and polyamorous households than it can be used in support of same-sex unions. We can thank God for the clear and unambiguous affirmations made by Jesus and supported by the whole of the Bible for the original and permanent design of marriage given by God through the created order.

Christians who seek to invalidate the creation account in Genesis 1–2 based on its age must ask themselves what right they have to invalidate the Scriptures that Jesus and his disciples affirmed. In the gospel of Mark, Jesus quotes both Genesis 1:27 and 2:24 to emphasize the sanctity of marriage between a man and a woman for all time (Mark 10:5–9). The Old and New Testaments are two inseparable parts of a whole. In the words of Augustine, "The New is in the Old contained; the Old is in the New explained."[8] One of the great principles of biblical interpretations to which church leaders have held throughout the centuries is that the Bible should interpret itself.

Romans 1

One of the longest and strongest New Testament passages about the creation account is Romans 1. It describes those who turned aside from the created order. Notice that people are generally made by God to have an innate knowledge of God's character as revealed in creation:

> The wrath of God is being revealed from heaven against all the godlessness and wickedness of men who suppress the truth by their wickedness, since what may be known about God is plain to them, because God has made it plain to them. For since the creation of the world God's invisible qualities—his eternal power and divine nature—have been clearly seen, being understood from what has been made, so that men are without excuse.
>
> —*Romans 1:18–20*

Choices can be made, however, that cause the truth to be hidden in a veil of darkness and self-deception:

> For although they knew God, they neither glorified him as God nor gave thanks to him, but their thinking became futile and their foolish hearts were darkened. Although they claimed to be wise, they became fools and exchanged the glory of the immortal God for images made to look like mortal man and birds and animals and reptiles.
>
> Therefore God gave them over in the sinful desires of their hearts to sexual impurity for the degrading of their bodies with one another. They

exchanged the truth of God for a lie, and worshiped and served created things
rather than the Creator—who is forever praised. Amen.

—*Romans 1:21–25*

As humans, we were designed to worship God. How easy it is to find
substitutes! The way we think influences the way we worship, and the way
we worship radically affects our lifestyles:

Because of this, God gave them over to shameful lusts. Even their women
exchanged natural relations for unnatural ones. In the same way the men also
abandoned natural relations with women and were inflamed with lust for
one another. Men committed indecent acts with other men, and received in
themselves the due penalty for their perversion.

—*Romans 1:26–27*

We are not here claiming the Bible states that all homosexual (or bisexual) *attractions* are the result of misplaced worship or sinful choices on the part
of the homosexual. What we are affirming, however, is that the Scriptures
state unequivocally that heterosexuality is given to us by the Creator as the
norm, and that to express homosexual *behavior* is a distortion of the created
order.

Interpretation Gymnastics

It is both fascinating and saddening to read the lengthy and in-depth accounts
of those who lift this scriptural passage out of its natural link to the creation
and place it alone in the context of Greek culture. Then, after isolating this
text from God's protective covering, they strike it with culturally based arguments until it is deflated of nearly all relevance for today. Numerous authors,
for example, describe at length the Greek practice of *pederasty*, the use of boys
for sexual pleasure by adult males.[9] This immoral practice becomes the basis
for the argument that Paul must have been condemning a particular type
of especially degrading homosexuality found in his day but *not* consensual
homosexual relationships between adults, which are found more commonly
in our day.

However, Paul's reference is not to his culture but to God's creative
norms. It is significant that Paul did not choose the specific terms used for
pederasty in his day, but rather the terms used to designate adult-to-adult
same-sex relationships.[10] In addition, Paul refers to adult female-to-female
sexual relationships in Romans 1 as perversions of God's standards, which
cannot possibly refer to pederasty.

Furthermore, it seems illogical that Paul would be limiting his comments
to pederasty when we lift the curtain of culture just a bit further and see

what is really there. In Paul's day and context, pederasty was an acceptable norm for homosexuality. Same-sex relationships between consenting adults, however, were considered shameful.[11] If, then, Paul made a special effort to condemn the most common and acceptable form of homosexuality in his day (pederasty) and did not mention consenting adult homosexual relationships, which were then considered distasteful and vulgar, would not his readers have assumed that Paul, who was always so careful with the use of his words, was against all forms of homosexual behavior?

Another perspective held by those supporting homosexual behavior is that Paul spoke against those who act outside the normal bounds of their innate heterosexual nature (perverts) but not against those who are made by God to be homosexual in nature (inverts). This argument does not take seriously the foundational teaching of God as Creator combined with the first established and ongoing pattern given by God for his creation. Paul clearly bases his argument on just these patterns: "since the creation of the world" (v. 20). He selected specific Greek words to make the point that he was referring to biology and what is physiologically natural for a man and woman.[12] He was referring to function and not feelings, plumbing and not proclivity.

Another suggested interpretation is that Paul, in Romans 1, was speaking about homosexual prostitution as part of pagan temple rituals.[13] But if such idolatry was Paul's real concern, what about the other twenty forms of sinful thought and behavior that Paul lists in the same Romans 1 passage, ranging from greed to murder? Are we to assume these sins, too, are acceptable to God when practiced outside the context of temple worship? Certainly not.

Homosexuality was commonly practiced in Paul's day without any connection to idolatry. If the practice of idolatry was his only concern, surely he would have said so. It would be inconsistent for such a careful scholar as Paul, who in all of his letters confronts sin and clouded thinking with precision and clarity, suddenly to make a blanket statement with little concern for its consequences. Consider just a few examples related to other topics. Paul made a clear distinction between the right and wrong grounds for divorce (1 Corinthians 7). Paul describes the right and wrong uses of meat offered to idols (1 Corinthians 8). He distinguishes between a loving rebuke and a judgmental spirit (Romans 2:1–6; 2 Timothy 2:14–26), as well as good and bad uses of the law (1 Timothy 1:1–11). If Paul was so much in the habit of drawing ethical lines for human behavior in other areas of human life and sexuality, why would he suddenly break his pattern when addressing the topic of homosexuality? This point will be reinforced as we note other writings of Paul on this subject in the pages ahead.

This is just a sample of the inventive arguments that have been crafted to minimize the impact of the Romans 1 passage.[14] The barrage of assaults against this text demonstrates the strength and clarity of Paul's writing. His words confront our human propensity for sexual compromise. The sheer number of attacks on this passage also implies a failure of each former effort to denigrate its original meaning as new tactics are brought to the fore. When so many efforts are made to undermine the plain and simple meaning of a portion of the Bible, the arguments themselves, with their countering and sometimes conflicting attempts, begin to appear weak and contrived.

A Vital Principle of Interpretation

Even the scholars who promote the above-mentioned prohomosexual slants on the Romans 1 text will admit they are in the minority. We do well, when studying what Scripture says about a controversial topic such as this, first to ask ourselves what the plain reading of disputed texts seems to say. Having done so, we should rely on the plain meaning, unless the majority opinion from sound scholarship tells us we are overlooking critical factors in our interpretation of these texts. This is a basic, historic principle of biblical interpretation that has been handed down to the church from its earliest days and upheld by the Reformers. Martin Luther urges us to embrace the "literal, ordinary, natural sense of Scripture." He wrote, "No violence is to be done to the words of God, whether by man or angel; but [the Scriptures] are to be retained in their simplest meaning whenever possible, and to be understood in their grammatical and literal sense unless the context plainly forbids."[15]

What if we ignored the plain meaning in other significant portions of the Bible? I speak not of occasional copyist variations or isolated verses but of broad teachings found repeatedly in the Scriptures, like those about the deity of Christ or his second coming, especially when such teachings are supported by the plain reading of the whole? To take such an approach to biblical interpretation would unhinge the most foundational teachings of the faith and threaten the faith altogether. It is this loose and unscrupulous treatment of the Bible that has caused many Christians to raise their hackles much more than the challenge of welcoming homosexuals into their congregations.

Why, then, are well-meaning Christians who support the gay rights movement continuing to push for such reinterpretations of the Bible? They do so out of love and compassion and a concern for justice. Those who fight for justice and compassion can just as easily find themselves bending the clear teachings of the Bible to promote their causes as those who are strong about the truth of Scripture may fail to demonstrate the love of Christ. We must avoid both extremes.

We All Fall Short

At this juncture, it is important to remind ourselves that we all fall short of God's best intentions for our lives. With every other human alive today, I have my faults and sins to confess. C. S. Lewis wrote:

> For there are two things inside me, competing with the human self which I must try to become. They are the Animal self and the Diabolical self. The Diabolical self is the worse of the two. That is why a cold, self-righteous prig who goes regularly to church may be far nearer to hell than a prostitute. But, of course, it is better to be neither.[16]

Christians are called to discern right from wrong but are also cautioned not to hurl condemnation and judgment on others (Matthew 7:3–5; James 4:11–12). If we do not show love and compassion toward our fellow humans, how can we expect God to show compassion toward us? Each of us can identify our own sinful tendencies or practices somewhere in the list given in Paul's Romans 1 passage. Here Paul confronts even the sins of our hearts: "every kind of wickedness, evil, greed and depravity ... full of envy, murder, strife, deceit and malice" (v. 29). Furthermore, Paul includes in the list people who "are gossips, slanderers, God-haters, insolent, arrogant and boastful ... senseless, faithless, heartless, ruthless" (vv. 29–31).

> Ministry Essential #5:
> We must embrace the whole of Scripture to keep our lives whole.

We are all sinners, each falling short of the Creator's original intention. As the letter to the Romans unfolds, Paul urges us each to draw near to God in faith that we might become new creations in Christ. God's desire is to forgive us (Romans 3:21–4:25) and then to empower us to live uprightly (chapters 5–8). None of the vices listed in 1:24–32 need to exert control over our lives. If we call ourselves Christians, we should live like Christ.

The End of the Matter

Our success as Christians depends greatly on our understanding of Scripture. As we have seen in this chapter (and as will be reiterated throughout this book), we must not separate the Old Testament from the New, nor the whole of the Bible from its parts. The content of individual verses should be discerned by their context. Our points of view about sexuality should be enlightened by the grand view of Scripture.

When Truth and Grace Unite

"What do you say about the Romans 1 passage? Doesn't it condemn homosexuals outright?" The questioner sat back in his pew as our guest speaker, Tim Wilkins, stood in front of the packed sanctuary.* He strained to search for the right response. Finally — deliberately, slowly — he spoke.

"The Romans 1 passage is probably used more than any other as a witnessing tool. But it is pushed relentlessly and ground into the listener again and again." He moved his fist through the air, and I could feel the pain that he shared with so many gays and lesbians who had been driven far from the church. "Rather than using it to help them find salvation, many Christians use it to push them away."

As he continued to share from his heart, I thought about how much I had come to appreciate Tim as a man who knows how to bring grace and truth together in a Christlike manner. His story is evidence that Romans 1 is not the end of the story but the first chapter of the most systematic and clear exposition of the gospel in all the Bible. Those who feel the weight of Romans 1 are welcomed to receive the mercy, forgiveness, and life-transforming grace offered by God in the rest of Paul's great letter.

Tim had spent years studying every chapter of the Bible, searching for God's perspectives on homosexuality — searching for his own freedom from it. His study changed his life. God has called him to help churches around the country become what the church had not been for him — a place of healing and wholeness for all kinds of people, including the sexually broken. His testimony follows:

---

* Tim Wilkins is the director of Cross Ministry in Wake Forest, North Carolina, where he lives with his wife, Lisa, and three daughters. To read his full testimony and to learn about his ministry, go to *www.CrossMinistry.org*.

How Scripture Changed My Life, by Tim Wilkins

"Up on your feet so I can knock you down again!" I stood horrified in the middle of our circular hallway as my father shouted those words at my mother, who lay at his feet. He had just knocked her to the living room floor. My parents' altercation had awakened me in the middle of the night.

This was one of my earliest memories as a five- or six-year-old child. I believe I unconsciously made a promise that moment: *I will not be like that man!* Thus began my rejection of masculinity and embracing of homosexuality.

Chaos characterized the place we called "home." Tables were overturned, and traumatizing profanity echoed throughout the house. It was not uncommon to find shards of glass covering the floors many mornings, a domestic battlefield from the night before.

On reaching puberty, I recognized an attraction for guys at school. Listen up! I did not choose to be attracted to members of the same sex; one of life's mysteries is that we don't get to choose what we are tempted by, but I *did* consciously choose to eventually give in to those temptations.

My emotional pain was so severe I wore a tiny piece of paper under my watchband for years on which I had scribbled, almost microscopically, "Lord, I am trusting you for healing." Although at age nine I had given my heart to Jesus, knowing he died for my sin, my emotional turmoil continued.

Abandoned!

When my parents' ballistic tirades reached an intolerable level, Dad left us and went to his parents' house for several months. Mama invited me into her bed for emotional support. Eventually our utilities were turned off. On one occasion, Dad stopped by for a brief visit. As he left our rented house to return to his parents, Mama hit him in the back with a flowerpot.

On an occasion in my early teens, Dad became so angry with me that I fled to the bathroom and locked the door. He pounded the door, demanding that I come out. "Please stop!" I screamed. When I refused to come out for fear of being beaten, he began to kick down the door, while Mama stood alongside him, pleading for me to come out. "Everything will be all right," she said. But I knew everything would *not* be all right! As the door shattered under his strength, I jumped out of the second-floor window and ran to safety, hiding in a nearby vacant house.

It was about this time that I gave in to my same-sex attractions. I had been friends with a guy from school for years. His pleasant and approving smile fascinated me, and he liked me. For the first time in my life, another male liked me. Thus began my sporadic involvement in homosexual activity. I quickly found that homosexuality provided excitement, but not fulfillment. It gratified, but never satisfied.

Life at home remained hell. Mama manipulated me to get at Dad. When I did not cooperate with her wishes, she would accuse me. "You love him more than me, don't you?" I didn't want to choose between them; I simply wanted them to love each other and stop fighting.

On another occasion, she and I argued over an incidental matter. When Dad came home from work, she demanded that he punish me. The resulting purple welts on my legs were conspicuous, so much so that the following morning I woke my mother before going to school and asked her to write an excuse so I wouldn't have to dress out for PE. I was ashamed to dress out for track, knowing the belt marks would draw attention.

Obedience

My homosexual activity continued until my early twenties, when I decided that although I honestly did not know how not to be homosexual, I *did* know how to be obedient.

Although the Bible gives no explicit steps for coming out of homosexuality, the Bible is replete with principles I could apply to my life. The psalmist wrote about turning his eyes away from temptation. I refused to look at pornography and averted my gaze from anything that might cause me to stumble. I had to make major adjustments in my life. To focus on God's best for me rather than my psychological pain, I meditated on Paul's admonition: "Finally, brothers, whatever is true, whatever is noble, whatever is right, whatever is pure, whatever is lovely, whatever is admirable—if anything is excellent or praiseworthy—think about such things" (Philippians 4:8). I asked the Holy Spirit to become my personal mentor and to guide me into all truth. More important, I asked the Holy Spirit to teach me the right way to relate to other men.

I attended college, and then seminary. I was like a dry sponge thrown into a huge lake; I soaked up everything. The Bible became increasingly alive to me. Not only was I receiving a great theological education for a future ministry I knew nothing about; I was applying biblical truth to my sexual brokenness.

Same-sex attractions continued throughout college and seminary, but to a lesser degree. I remained steadfast in refusing to give in. In fact, by this time I had told God, "It doesn't matter if I'm ever attracted to a woman as long as I get you!" That prayer was a milestone. It really didn't matter if I was ever attracted to the opposite sex; what mattered was becoming a follower of Jesus Christ.

After graduation I was called to a pastorate in my hometown—a single man living in a four-bedroom house. During this time, my father went through a foreclosure on his home, a separation from his second wife, struggles with alcoholism, and near suicide. With all the responsibilities of a young single pastor weighing on my shoulders, I took my father into the parsonage and tended to him until I could get him into an alcohol abuse facility—none of this known to my congregation.

I eventually resigned from that pastorate, disillusioned and depressed. I cried out to God, "What do you want from me? I've lived a life of celibacy for more than ten years now. I've followed you as closely as I know how. What do you want from me?"

God's Dramatic Intervention

I was about to find out! A lady friend from seminary visited my city. I remember liking her in seminary but had never pursued her. I experienced, for the first time in my thirty-three years, a dramatic, ecstatic, and romantic attraction for the opposite sex. What had God wanted from me? The faith to trust him unreservedly! This lovely lady and I did not marry; today she is married to a wonderful Christian man, and they know the story and are very supportive. (You know who you are.)

Five years later, on a Thursday, September 17, 1992, at 7:19 p.m., Lisa came into my life. We met at a singles event, and sparks flew, in the best meaning of the phrase. Lisa was everything I longed for, a beautiful godly lady with a smile from heaven. The Bible is right! "Delight yourself in the LORD and he will give you the desires of your heart" (Psalm 37:4).

Lisa and I were married on August 21, 1993. I was thirty-eight. I rejoice to say, "Although I'm no longer gay, I'm the happiest I've ever been, and I owe that to Jesus Christ."

More than a year later, when Lisa and I were convinced I should go public with my testimony, several prominent Christian friends advised against it. One told me, "It will ruin your testimony," to which I replied, "But this *is* my testimony." I was reminded that after Jesus healed a man from the region of the Gerasenes, he told him, "Go ... and tell them how much the Lord has done for you, and how he has had mercy on you" (Mark 5:19). I have been doing that very thing ever since!

God has blessed us with more miracles—three daughters, Clare, Grace, and Ellie. As the song states, "God is good all the time"—indeed, all the time God *is* good!

A final note: God has graciously provided healing within my family. Mama, now with the Lord, is sadly missed. *O God, I long to hear her voice again*. And I will! And prior to Dad's death, we finally became what God had intended from the very start—father and son.

Chapter 5

THE SOURCE
The Genetics Question

The Controversy

Grace with Compromised Truth: "Homosexuals and lesbians are born with their same-sex inclinations. It is in their genes. Not to allow them to act on their God-given proclivities is oppressive and inhuman."

Truth with Compromised Grace: "People choose to be gay, and they can choose not to be gay. They just need to repent and pray, and God will take it away."

Uniting Truth and Grace as a Basis for Ministry

My brother Chris was only thirty-four when dozens of small blood clots began forming throughout his lungs. The standard therapy with blood thinners had no effect on them. Doctors were stymied as more and more of his lung function was destroyed over the course of a few short months, to the point that these clots threatened to take his life. His heart, in the battle to keep blood flowing, swelled to several times the normal size. Specialists around the country could not determine the source of the clotting but acknowledged that it might have a genetic link.

Finally, Chris underwent a double lung transplant in an effort to extend his life. He could hope for about five additional years, doctors said, if all went well. By God's grace, Chris is now forty years old and has beaten the odds—but he's in trouble. The immunosuppressive drugs that have shielded his transplanted lungs from rejection by his body have opened the door to cancer, which has covered and permeated his brain. As I write, I am flying to Washington, D.C., to be with him and to offer support. I know what will happen, however. It has been this way every time I visit. He will encourage and challenge me and send me home staggering under the realization that I should more fully appreciate and use my time and my health for God's glory.

Chris's whole life has been radically altered by a condition that may be genetic in origin. But not his attitude. He has been cheerful, confident in God's grace, and encouraging to everyone he meets. He refuses to allow weakness of body to tarnish his spirit. Genes may influence our bodies, but *we* control our thoughts and behavior.

Genes and Homosexuality

The possibility of a genetic link to homosexuality has been an issue of popular interest and debate in our society. After all, if gayness is caused by genes, it falls into a category with the nearly limitless list of syndromes and abnormalities caused by single or complex genetic disorders linked to everything from autism to asthma. For some ethicists, if gayness is genetically caused, then the expression of homosexuality is natural and certainly not immoral. And for some Christians, a related question arises about God the Creator. If it really is true that God made them that way, how can we say God's creation is wrong?

Is homosexuality genetic in origin? Our answer must be a gently qualified, "Perhaps to a small extent," as you will see as we look at the discoveries of science mentioned in this chapter. This information is widely available to anyone willing to do a bit of research. What is so often lacking, however, is a filter through which to process the information. In other words, we must also consider *why* this information is important, which we will cover here, and *what* we are to do with it, which will be covered in the next chapter. Our goal is not merely to set the record straight but to move beyond controversy and into ministry.

Keeping Perspective

Does scientific evidence show that homosexuality is caused by prebirth influences, or that it is developed as one grows? The nature-versus-nurture question has become a big issue in our day. I believe the importance of genetic factors related to homosexuality has been blown out of proportion. Every one of us has inherited weaknesses and strengths. We also carry scars and stars from the negative and positive experiences that have shaped our lives from our earliest years. The day we surrender our behavior to our genetics is the day we turn what should be a victorious human race into a massive societal defeat. Imagine if Franklin Roosevelt had given in to the weaknesses that plagued him in his childhood, or to the polio he contracted at the age of thirty-nine. As the field of genetics continues to grow, we also need to grow as a people, not becoming defeatist about who we are but becoming yet more confident and determined to be our best, for God's glory.

Still, the genetics issue has become so politicized around agendas on both sides of the controversy that it must be tackled. On the one hand, many Christians make light of the challenges facing a person with same-sex inclinations who wants to change. They do not understand how deep the struggle is. This cavalier attitude creates more problems than it solves. On the other hand, our society has been so thickly blanketed with the message that homosexuals cannot change that it has become almost taboo, even in Christian circles, to discuss it anymore as a possibility. Many think, "The Bible seems to say gays can change, but if science says otherwise ..."

John McNeill, an ordained priest and psychotherapist who was expelled from the Society of Jesus in 1987 for his unorthodox view on homosexuality, writes, "Only a sadistic God would create hundreds of thousands of humans to be inherently homosexual and then deny them the right to sexual intimacy."[1]

Did God really "create hundreds of thousands of humans to be inherently homosexual," as McNeill states? It is true that most gays and many lesbians claim they did not choose their orientations. We will explore the reasons throughout the next several chapters. But how much their actions are spurred on by genetics should be determined not by what people think about themselves or by the conclusions of friends or family members of a homosexual person, but by evidence from the field of science.

The Drive for Biological Proof

Much of the most-publicized research related to biological causes for same-sex orientation has been conducted by individuals and groups who wish to promote societal acceptance for homosexuality. Denny Lee of the Lambda Legal Defense and Education Fund, a gay advocacy group in New York City, said, "On a political level, genetic research does seem to move the debate along a certain path. When people understand that being gay or lesbian is an integral characteristic, they are more open-minded about equality for gay Americans."[2] Such understanding is promulgated by a media that has a strong progay bias, as can be seen by simply turning on the television.

We cannot, in fairness, blame all homosexuals for this relentless media spin. It is perhaps but a small percentage of the homosexual population that is actively fueling the prohomosexual political agenda. Many gays and lesbians are not in favor of the search for a gay gene, for example, because of the gnawing possibility that if such a gene were found, it could become a handle through which a new campaign might be launched to use genetic engineering or other means to isolate and eradicate homosexuality from the planet.[3]

Let us be clear: there is no evidence of a gay gene. National Institutes of Health scientist Dean Hamer, well known for his research related to a possible gay gene, said, "We have not found the gene—which we don't think exists—for sexual orientation."[4]

Part of the blame for the broad public acceptance of the notion that homosexuality has a genetic cause falls at the feet of the average person, who easily accepts information from the newspaper, television, or Internet without scrutiny. Yet the barrage of information based on new studies that have been blasted into public view can seem overwhelming. Misinformation has permeated popular magazines and talk shows, has infiltrated government-funded programs and brochures, has become commonplace in the books that line our libraries, and has filtered through our school systems and colleges. The drive behind the gay rights media campaign has been not simply about a possible gay gene but about any possible angle to show that homosexuality is part of nature, not a result of nurture and environment. Research scientist Neil Whitehead writes:

> A constant stream of media articles—several per year—assures us that there is a link between homosexuality and biological features. These articles mention genes, brain structure, hormone levels in the womb, ear characteristics, fingerprint styles, finger lengths, verbal skills ... and by the time you read this, some others may have appeared. The headlines imply that people are born with tendencies which infallibly will make them gay or lesbian, and that change of sexual orientation will be impossible.[5]

Let us briefly consider a few of these biological features, beginning with the theoretical gay gene. If you would like to explore this topic in more depth, please go to *www.ChurchReflections.com*.

The Search for a Gay Gene

In 1993, Dean Hamer published research related to a possible gay gene in *Science* magazine.[6] Searching for chromosomal variants that might demonstrate a linkage between gay family members, Hamer's results were inconclusive and certainly did not confirm the existence of a gay gene. Nevertheless, on July 15, 1993, news that this article was to be published was announced by National Public Radio with the suggestion that a genetic cause for homosexuality had been discovered. Magazines, including *Time* and *Newsweek*, ran feature articles. The *Wall Street Journal* announced, "Research Points toward a Gay Gene ... Normal Variation."

What the average reader did not understand is that a genetic linkage, even if demonstrated, does not show that homosexuality is caused by genetics any more than is depression, gambling, or a propensity toward obesity. There is a vast difference between a *linkage* and a *trait*. Researchers making public statements to the press don't always explain these differences, leaving those who don't understand the terms under the illusion that there has been a new scientific breakthrough.

When pressed by the scientific community, however, researchers who have enjoyed the attention of the public may find themselves backpedaling and speaking more cautiously. When asked by *Scientific American* if homosexuality is rooted solely in biology, for example, Dr. Hamer replied, "Absolutely not. From twin studies, we already know that half or more of the variability in sexual orientation is not inherited. Our studies try to pinpoint the genetic factors ... not negate the psychosocial factors."[7] Hamer claimed to find nothing more than a potential genetic linkage, which means very little. In the words of research scientist Neil Whitehead, "We can confidently predict half a dozen linkages will be 'discovered' between genes and behavior each year. But the important lesson is this: any linkages probably affect only a small proportion of people to a very minor extent."[8]

Even today, scientists are far from developing a precise blueprint of the various causes of homosexuality or, for that matter, of any behavioral condition. What they do agree on is this: behavior in humans is at best *influenced* by genes and is the product of a mosaic of prenatal and postnatal factors. In other words, "Genes make proteins, not (sexual) preferences."[9]

Other Genetics Studies

From the time of Dean Hamer's studies in the early 1990s until the present day, there has been no evidence of a genetic cause for homosexuality. Twin studies, brain studies, and all other efforts to demonstrate a strictly genetic origin for homosexuality have failed.

In their book *My Genes Made Me Do It!* researchers Neil and Briar White-head say that if homosexuality were actually caused by our DNA, it would almost certainly have bred itself out of our population through several generations and would not exist today. A gene continues in a gene pool over time only if one or more children are born to every adult having that gene. Among persons claiming to be exclusively homosexual, only one in five has a child, not enough to perpetuate a trait or characteristic. When factoring into the equation the married and the bisexual gays in our country, the average number of children produced is still less than one child per person, about 0.9 percent, which would not be enough to sustain homosexuality if it were a genetic condition.[10]

Extensive data, ranging from Alfred Kinsey's controversial progay surveys in 1948 and 1953 to the most current statistics, show that sexual behavior among homosexuals is not set but fluid, often changing through life from heterosexual to homosexual and back again.[11] Furthermore, ongoing studies have demonstrated that the rate of homosexuality is dramatically influenced by social factors such as age, education level, and rural versus urban demographics.[12]

Geneticists tell us that if homosexuality or any such behavioral trait (as compared to a mere physical trait) were determined by genes, it would appear in every major culture. Yet researchers Clellan Ford and Frank Beach found homosexuality rare or absent in twenty-nine out of seventy-nine cultures surveyed.[13]

David Greenberg, a gay rights advocate, has written extensively about the social construction of homosexuality through history. He discovered four general types of homosexual behavior:

- intergenerational, in which sexual partnerships occur between various generations
- class structured, in which partners belong to different social classes, such as slave and freeman
- transgenderal, in which one partner adopts the identity of the opposite sex
- egalitarian, involving two partners of a socially equal status

Historically, various models would occur at the same time. In fact, three of them can be observed in the world today. Greenberg found that some cultures had no traces of homosexuality and that the four types of behavior occurred sometimes concurrently and overall with great discontinuity. Because of these results, Greenberg concluded that homosexual behavior is strongly shaped by cultures and that homosexuality cannot be an immutable genetic condition.[14] The practice of same-sex behavior between two consenting adults, the Western model, is relatively new on the world scene and is highly politicized.

A Variety of Factors

A more reasonable viewpoint, based on science and experience, accepts that sexual orientation forms in the average person through a blend of innate tendencies, environmental influences, and life experiences. Sociologist Steven Goldberg writes,

> Virtually all of the evidence argues against there being a determinative physiological causal factor, and I know of no researcher who believes that such a determinative factor exists ... such factors play a predisposing, not a determinative role....
>
> I know of no one in the field who argues that homosexuality can be explained without reference to environmental factors.[15]

Brain researcher Dr. Simon LeVay states, "At this point, the most widely held opinion [on causation of homosexuality] is that multiple factors play a role." He refers to a survey conducted in 1998 by Tinkle Hake, a member of Parents, Families and Friends of Lesbians and Gays (PFLAG), a support network that deemphasizes the notion that gays or lesbians can change their sexual orientation. The survey posed this statement and question: "Many observers believe that a person's sexual orientation is determined by one or more of the following factors: genetic, hormonal, psychological, or social. Based on today's state-of-the-art science, what is your opinion?"

The answers given by influential PFLAG leaders clearly pointed to a variety of causal factors for homosexuality: "all of the above in concert" (Alan Bell), "all of these variables" (Richard Green), "multiple factors" (Gilbert Herdt), "a combination of all the factors named" (Evelyn Hooker), "all of these factors" (Judd Marmor), "a combination of causes" (Richard Pillard), "possibly genetic and hormonal, but juvenile sexual rehearsal play is particularly important" (John Money), and "genetic and hormonal factors, and perhaps also some early childhood experiences" (James Weinrich).[16]

The American Psychological Association concurs:

> There is no consensus among scientists about the exact reasons that an individual develops a heterosexual, bisexual, gay, or lesbian orientation. Although much research has examined the possible genetic, hormonal, developmental, social, and cultural influences on sexual orientation, no findings have emerged that permit scientists to conclude that sexual orientation is determined by any particular factor or factors. Many think that nature and nurture both play complex roles.[17]

Genetic Disposition

A good descriptive word for the greatest impact genetics may have on a person's sexual behavior is *disposition*. An example of a person's predisposition can be seen for example in the field of academics. According to the U.S. Census Bureau, approximately 27.4 percent of Americans over age twenty-five have graduated from college with a bachelor's degree or greater.[18] Some people seem to be genetically inclined toward intellectual pursuits more than others. But whether those same individuals chose to attend college will also depend on the expectations of their parents, the resources at their disposal, their exposure to intellectually stimulating environments, and various other mitigating circumstances in their lives. If one is born with a predisposition toward intellectual pursuits, those leanings do not box a person into any one academic track, nor do they require that person to pursue a graduate degree. Many intelligent people — Thomas Edison, for example — did not earn a college degree.

We can also think about genetic disposition through examples that society labels as negative behavior. Alcoholism is considered to be heritable at a rate as high as 50 to 60 percent.[19] Homosexuality is considered 50 percent or less heritable, even by gay rights advocates. This higher heritability factor for alcoholism does not cause us to dismiss alcoholic behavior. Similarly, genetic linkage has been demonstrated as influential for the misdeeds of certain classes of criminals. We don't allow orientation in such cases to excuse behavior. The fact is that we all have natural inclinations toward patterns of behavior that we need not, and should not, act on. This is the human condition.

A Fair Look at the Other Side

The conservative Christian movement has been so focused on fighting the notion that homosexuality might be caused by chromosomes that we have forgotten compassion. Perhaps we have failed to recognize that the same scientists who cannot substantiate the degree to which combined prenatal factors influence same-sex attraction in a person also tell us that such influences cannot be completely ruled out. Some of us are so set on arguing the point that gayness isn't completely caused by genes that we haven't considered the difficulty homosexuals may have in overcoming their predispositions. If a person is biologically inclined toward weight gain, outbursts of anger, or alcohol addiction, we allow them time and space to deal with their weaknesses and to grow. But what about the homosexual?

Gays and lesbians who turn to Jesus don't find their inclinations simply disappearing like a bad toothache treated by the dentist. Most find that their struggles diminish significantly over time—but don't disappear completely. Like the rest of us human beings, their wounds may heal, but they may be left with residual tenderness that needs to be guarded. Some who come to salvation in the Lord may find a smooth road to recovery, and others may encounter a long, hard climb. No two people are the same.

"One Fits All" Has Failed for Homosexuality

When faced with complicated, messy, and hurtful situations, we humans look for oversimplified explanations and quick-fix solutions. Discussions about whether loved ones with homosexual attractions can and should change are loaded with moral implications, emotional angst, political pressures, and suppositions about prebirth and developmental causes. Is it any wonder that extreme camps have formed around the topic? Mounting societal pressure has forced advocates on both sides to the rigid edges. Posthomosexual leaders through the years have sometimes found it difficult to talk publicly about some who are living faithfully for the Lord but whose same-sex inclinations do not seem to go away. Progay leaders continue to support overstated claims that no homosexual ever can or will change, for fear that their movement will lose its moorings. They also claim that efforts to change can be harmful to the homosexual seeking it. Warriors for change highlight their success stories. Advocates for the difficulty of change highlight the "ex-gay" failures and the stories of those who found change to be impossible. In response, if both parties would simply acknowledge the great diversity of people in the world and the potential differences, person to person, based on both prenatal and developmental influences, it would be a step away from controversy and toward constructive conversation.

Clarity for the Christian

The Christian church is called to bring light into this complicated and painful situation. Recognition of the complexity of this topic should cause us to speak carefully and thoughtfully. The pain associated with homosexuality that has built up through more than thirty years of debate in church circles, however, makes us want to avoid the topic altogether. But we cannot. We have an obligation to speak truth, goodness, and redemption to all the people in the world. To avoid one biblical theme is to surrender the relevance of the Bible in every area. Martin Luther stated the following:

> If I profess with the loudest voice and clearest exposition every portion of the truth of God except precisely that little point which the world and devil are at that moment attacking, I am not confessing Christ, however boldly I may be professing Christ.
>
> Where the battle rages, there the loyalty of the soldier is proved, and to be steady on all the battlefields besides, is mere flight and disgrace if he flinches at that point.[20]

Spiritual Genetics

Paul explains in Romans 5:12–21 that we inherited our sin condition from Adam. This is spiritual genetics. Because the spiritual world is foundational to things physical, it should not be a surprise to us that once the world fell into sin, our physical gene codes would also be flawed. Fortunately, God came to help us through his Son. Through Christ's sacrifice on the cross, we are given the right to eternal life, to reconciliation with God, to the forgiveness of our sins, and to the power to live rightly through the indwelling Spirit of God. God does not take away the taint of darkness in our genetic coding, but he helps us live with it and, to some extent, overcome it.

It is not easy to live in a fallen world. No human can honestly say that he or she is not tempted by cravings of the body, by pride, by ambition, and by the desire to have more. Even Jesus Christ, the sinless one, was tempted. God the Father used temptation to make Jesus stronger and to prepare him for ministry (Matthew 4:1−17). So, we are promised, our temptations can be sources of challenge and growth in our lives (Romans 5:1−5; James 1:2−5).

We Are in This Together

Those who struggle with same-sex attraction and who hold biblical convictions that cause them to refrain from sexual intimacy are not alone in the challenges they face. The percentage of our population that declares itself to be homosexual, according to the best current research, is between 2 and 3 percent. The unmarried adult heterosexual population, however, is larger than the entire homosexual community by a factor of more than ten to one. Those within this huge demographic who follow Jesus also face the challenge of remaining sexually pure. Add to this the married couples who do not experience sexual fulfillment due to physiological and psychological barriers, and it becomes clear that homosexual and heterosexual persons share in tandem the pain of our fallen world.

Jesus was single and celibate. Our Lord described situations in which a person might likewise remain celibate from birth, whether due to nature or by choice (Matthew 19:10−12). The Roman Catholic Church's philosophy of ministry toward those who struggle with same-sex attraction, not surprisingly, falls along these lines.[21] With the long tradition of priests who take vows of celibacy, it is not a stretch for priests who have built and guided the Catholic outreach to homosexuals to embrace this perspective.

Most Protestant ministries to those who seek freedom from the gay lifestyle consider abstinence an option while emphasizing the possibility of partial or complete change in sexual orientation. We will look at research, testimonies, and common logic about the potential for change in the following chapters. The point to be made here, however, is that none of us will ever find lasting fulfillment through the pursuit of sexual desires. Those who seek to be made complete

> **Ministry Essential #6:**
> **Our genes bear the shadow of the fallen creation. They do not overshadow righteous living, however, for those who are new creations in Christ.**

through sexual activity or unhealthy relationships are taking a shortcut to a dead end.

The Deep Struggle

About homosexuality, the British research psychologist and theologian Elizabeth Moberly writes, "From the present evidence it would seem clear that the homosexual condition does not involve abnormal needs, but normal needs that have, abnormally, been left unmet in the ordinary process of growth. The needs as such are normal; their lack of fulfillment, and the barrier to their fulfillment, is abnormal."[22] In other words, homosexuality is not all about sex. Most who struggle with same-sex attraction will tell you that it is more about identity. It is about being loved and accepted. It is about fulfillment and joy on the deepest level. The church has been given to the world to proclaim that this fulfillment can only ultimately be found in Jesus Christ.

Complete in Christ

Bill Henson, twenty-three years old, had graduated from a university and was launching into his career when he became severely depressed and almost suicidal.[*] The suppression of his homosexual desires for twelve years had taken its toll. He sought therapy. He informed his parents. Still not satisfied, he found a male lover and pursued his dreams to live a gay lifestyle for the next five years. He also began attending church and seeking God. His Christian brothers and sisters didn't know he was living a homosexual lifestyle, and he didn't think to tell them. But God began speaking to Bill's heart through Scripture. In Bill's words:

"The Religious Right was condemning me to hell, while pro-gay theologians were saying that *any* consensual sex was OK. I decided I could not believe either of them, so I journeyed through the Bible to find out what Jesus had to say about my life. I was disturbed and disappointed to find many verses that described homosexual relationships as sin. The more I read, the more I

---

[*] Bill Henson is the founder and director of Fish on the Other Side (FOTOS) ministries and of the *Lead Them Home* radio program.
To learn more, see *www.fishontheotherside.org*.

became convinced that God's Word was true. I was attending church regularly and getting more and more involved in discovering that God had a purpose for my life."

Unaware of Bill's lifestyle, the church was unable to call Bill to repentance. But God would use a mission trip to speak to Bill's heart. In 1995, he went with a team to Siberia and saw the desperate need in the eyes and hearts of the people he encountered. "It was everything antithetical to the American experience. Everything that I saw challenged my worldview," he told me. As he held orphans who were malnourished and yet grotesquely muscular from working in the potato fields, he realized that he had come out of an unreal, Hollywood world. Bill also saw a widow who wept as she touched the gate surrounding a condemned cathedral—"she did not weep because it was closed—it had been closed for seventy-five years," Bill said. "She wept for joy that she finally had the freedom to touch the gate as an expression of her faith." Bill concluded, "God ended up doing a mission trip on me!"

The Siberian experience followed Bill everywhere. When he returned, he accepted a job transfer to New England, leaving his lover, family, and friends behind. Soon he began feeling isolated and lonely, and he drew closer than ever to the Lord. "God gently showed me that we all have needs—we have hunger needs, sleep needs, relational needs, sex needs, success needs. And while all of these are important, God showed me we will never get *all* of our needs met. Jesus taught me that the gospel does *not* mean that God is love and therefore we can have *all* of our own needs met, but that through the gospel Jesus gives us strength, love, peace, and comfort when all our needs are *not* met!

"After many weeks of resisting God's call to surrender my life to him, the day finally came. It was late in the night in 1995, and I was wrestling with God, holding on to my own will. With my spiritual eyes, God showed me Jesus nailed to the cross, and his bleeding head was down against his chest. Jesus lifted his head, and the most loving, compassionate gaze peered from his eyes into mine. And God asked, 'Do you want my Son?'

"I wrestled with God. I said, 'Lord, you can have my whole heart, but I just can't let go of the one person I love so much.

Can't I just keep this small part of my life but give you everything else?' God seemed to say that maybe my lover and my homosexual identity were not such a small part of my heart. He was right. While I had a very integrated life that was not solely defined by my sexuality, how could the one I love and how I experience love not be a huge part of my life? The fact is, my lover and my life meant the world to me.

"Then I thought, 'Lord, OK, I'll give you my lover and my identity and invite you more into how I live out my life in this area.' I mouthed the words, but my heart knew I was not willing to let go and surrender this to him. After much resistance, I finally collapsed to the floor weeping. I felt all my strength go out of me, and I felt a peace come over me as I said, 'OK, Lord, I am yours.'"

Now, ten years later, Bill is happily married, but he did not pursue marriage as a "cure." Bill leads a ministry that calls others who struggle with same-sex attractions to come to Christ for salvation and to live in holiness. Bill doesn't tell people that their homosexual attractions must disappear before they come to Jesus, but rather that they must surrender everything and leave the process of inner healing and change to the Lord. Bill adds, "I can never identify as ex-gay. Who wants to be ex-anything? It is a meaningless cliché compared to the riches of being found in Christ. I am not so different from GLBT people.* None of us are. My identity is in Christ alone—not in what I'm not."

---

* Gay, Lesbian, Bisexual, or Transgendered.

THE LAW

Separating Temporal from Eternal

The Controversy

Grace with Compromised Truth: "If we are to apply the prohibitions in Leviticus about homosexuality to modern society, then consistency requires us also to follow Levitical prohibitions about eating pork and shaving sideburns."

Truth with Compromised Grace: "Based on my reading of Leviticus, homosexuality is an abomination, plain and simple."

Uniting Truth and Grace as a Basis for Ministry

One of the most controversial biblical passages about homosexuality is found in Leviticus 18–20, often called the "holiness code." On the one hand, the statements there about homosexuality are stark and glaring, labeling same-sex activity as "an abomination." On the other hand, prohibitions against trimming the edges of one's beard and reaping the corners of one's field are mixed into this same portion of the Bible. When progay theologians address this text, they consistently highlight this apparently glaring inconsistency in the argument against homosexuality. But are they correct? Is this really an inconsistency? And if not, does God hate gay people? To find the answer to these questions we must consider the meaning and use of God's law.

The Importance of God's Law

For those who live under democratic rule, it can be difficult to imagine what it would be like to live under a monarchy in which a king's word is law. The

Bible, however, was written in the shadow of dictatorships. In the era of the New Testament church, calling on Christ as Lord was an affront to the ruling Caesar of Rome. In the days of the Old Testament exile, refusing to worship a statue of the king of Babylon was tantamount to suicide. And before the days when Israel had their own ruler, God was the absolute sovereign, reigning over his people in a theocracy.

Margaret Landon's book *Anna and the King of Siam* captures the essence of how it feels to be transplanted into a land where a king rules absolutely. Based on the 1860s memoirs of Anna Leonowens, a widow with two young children, this semifictionalized biographical novel describes Anna's experiences in teaching King Mongkut's children and wives the English language and introducing them to British customs. The five-year span of her visit is packed with gripping, enchanting, and even humorous accounts of how she learned to work with an arrogant and demanding man whose word was law for the Siamese people.

Kings rule with laws. When the Persian king Xerxes made a law, it could not be broken—even by himself (Esther 3; Daniel 6:8). How much more binding, then, would be rules and decrees established by the King of kings, Creator of the universe, the only true Judge, the unchanging God?

While there is no true theocracy in the world today, those who call on Jesus Christ as Lord acknowledge him to be their King (Matthew 21:5; John 12:13; Acts 17:7; 1 Timothy 1:17; Revelation 15:3; 17:14; 19:16). Jesus appeared on the human scene, announcing that "the kingdom of heaven is near" (Matthew 4:17). In the Gospels, the terms *kingdom, kingdom of God, kingdom of heaven*, and the like appear more than a hundred times. Wherever Christ reigns, his kingdom is present. His throne is found on the heart of every person who believes in and lives for him.

The Lord's expectation is that we obey the law of God, for it is grounded in the unchanging character of God. Thus, while societies throughout history have more or less followed the decrees from heaven as grounded in the history of the Bible, individuals and groups that claim allegiance to Jesus and his kingdom are expected to abide by them. Jesus said, "Do not think that I have come to abolish the Law or the Prophets; I have not come to abolish them but to fulfill them" (Matthew 5:17).

Paul, writing to his disciple Timothy about those in his day who either ignored or perverted the laws of God, made this statement:

> Some have wandered away ... and turned to meaningless talk. They want to be teachers of the law, but they do not know what they are talking about or what they so confidently affirm.
>
> We know that the law is good if one uses it properly. We also know that law is made not for the righteous but for lawbreakers and rebels, the ungodly

and sinful, the unholy and irreligious; for those who kill their fathers or mothers, for murderers, for adulterers and perverts, for slave traders and liars and perjurers—and for whatever else is contrary to the sound doctrine that conforms to the glorious gospel of the blessed God, which he entrusted to me.

— 1 Timothy 1:6– 11

The Meaning of *Law* in the New Testament

The word *law* in the New Testament carries various shades of meaning, depending on context:

- a *law* established by a government—often the way we use the term today (1 Corinthians 6:6)
- a general principle, relating to a *law*—much as we today discuss the "laws" of physics (Romans 7:21; 8:2)
- a general teaching or body of instruction (James 1:25)
- a portion of the Old Testament (e.g., the Pentateuch, as in Matthew 12:5, or everything but the Psalms and Prophets, as in Luke 24:44), or possibly the whole of the Old Testament (John 10:34; 1 Corinthians 14:21)

Theologians throughout the ages, however, have recognized a further distinction that is important for our current study. The term *law* is used in the Scriptures to describe three classes or types of guidelines given by God:

- The *ceremonial* laws given to the Israelites, tied to their practices of worship. These laws changed as God led his people from the wandering desert tabernacle to an established temple in Jerusalem. Such laws changed again during the exile and again when our Lord rose from the dead and the church was born.
- The *civil* laws given to the Israelites to establish guidelines for a theocracy. These civil laws, for example, stipulated patterns for living in the desert. There were guidelines that ranged from how to care for animals to when to enact capital punishment. Israel's theocracy yielded to a monarchy, which became anarchy as corruption clutched the hearts of their kings. With the disintegration of their great kingdom, Israel's civil laws lost their efficacy.
- The *moral* laws given to the Jewish people. These laws find their summation in the great command to love God with all your heart and to love your neighbor as yourself. Such laws did not change through time and will not be altered until Christ returns, for they reflect the

character of God. They find their roots in the Ten Commandments—the same code of ethics we teach to our children today.

The often confusing challenge as we examine Old Testament law is to rightly discern which restrictions are ceremonial, which are civil, and which are moral. In many sections of the Old Testament, all three types of law blended together. They were all relevant for their time, although they are not all relevant for us today. Our distinctions, as we will see, cannot be based solely on which book, section, or chapter of the Bible they are found in. Rather, we should look to the New Testament writers to see how the Old Testament law is to be applied. This is the only sure, safe, and consistent principle for interpreting Old Testament teachings for the modern church.

The Law for Today

If we look again at 1 Timothy 1, it becomes clear that Paul is describing the moral and ethical law of God, unchanging in time and culture. It is interesting to note the parallels of Paul's lists with the Ten Commandments. Many scholars feel that Paul was actually referring to and applying these commandments to his own culture and audience. Notice that Paul's list of lawless deeds parallels the last six of the Ten Commandments—specifically the commands oriented toward loving our neighbors as ourselves:

Exodus 20:12: "Honor your father and your mother, so that you may live long in the land the LORD your God is giving you."

• "those who kill their fathers or mothers" (1 Timothy 1:9)

Exodus 20:13 "You shall not murder."

• "murderers" (1 Timothy 1:9)

Exodus 20:14 "You shall not commit adultery."

• "the sexually immoral, for those practicing homosexuality" (1 Timothy 1:10 TNIV)

Exodus 20:15 "You shall not steal."

• "slave traders" (1 Timothy 1:10; NASB, "kidnappers")

Exodus 20:16: "You shall not give false testimony against your neighbor."

• "liars and perjurers" (1 Timothy 1:10)

Exodus 20:17: "You shall not covet." (This is the great and final catch-all command, confronting the heart attitude from which so many lawless deeds arise.)

- "whatever else is contrary to the sound doctrine that conforms to the glorious gospel of the blessed God"—the lawless and rebellious, the unholy and sinners (1 Timothy 1:10–11)

Paul makes his case against homosexuality on the same basis that he argues against all the sins described in the above list: They violate the very person and purpose of God as reflected in the moral law of God. Because God is unchanging, his hatred of the sins listed here will not diminish. God our Creator is God our King. He who made us knows what makes us happy and healthy. He who designed us has designed laws to protect us and has given us principles to guide us. If we violate the laws of our King, we will face consequences, for we are violating the very patterns established by God at creation.

In summary, one of the linchpin arguments used by gay Christian theologians is that the laws of God have changed throughout history, and what's more, we no longer live under the law. Their logic crumbles, as we have seen, once we begin to explore the meaning of the word *law* and insist that its meaning be clarified for its particular use in each scriptural context. Regarding the moral law, the unchanging principles given to the human race to help us know and follow God, our Lord says:

> Do not think that I have come to abolish the Law or the Prophets; I have not come to abolish them but to fulfill them. I tell you the truth, until heaven and earth disappear, not the smallest letter, not the least stroke of a pen, will by any means disappear from the Law until everything is accomplished. Anyone who breaks one of the least of these commandments and teaches others to do the same will be called least in the kingdom of heaven, but whoever practices and teaches these commands will be called great in the kingdom of heaven.
>
> —*Matthew 5:17–19*

The Levitical Holiness Code

Now let's look at what is commonly called the "holiness code" in the book of Leviticus, especially focusing on the two verses that speak directly to the issue of homosexuality:

> Do not lie with a man as one lies with a woman; that is detestable.
>
> —*Leviticus 18:22*

> If a man lies with a man as one lies with a woman, both of them have done what is detestable. They must be put to death; their blood will be on their own heads.
>
> —*Leviticus 20:13*

Supporters of homosexuality commonly argue that these particular prohibitions against homosexuality are part of a code that is outdated. These laws, they say, were given to the Israelites at a particular point in their history and are not binding on Christians today. Other decrees and commandments of God in the same section of Leviticus, it is often argued, include rules that we would not consider enforcing on ourselves, such as, "Do not mate different kinds of animals. Do not plant your field with two kinds of seed. Do not wear clothing woven of two kinds of material" (Leviticus 19:19).

Thus, continues the logic, if the Levitical holiness code is still binding on us today, we must immediately prevent breeders from breeding mules, confront farmers who mix their seed, and rebuke people who wear cotton-polyester blend shirts, for they are violating the expressed will of God as expressed in the laws given to Israel. If these prohibitions are not binding on us today, however (and the average church member would agree they are not), then why do we consider other prohibitions found in the same section of Leviticus, such as the verses referring to homosexuality, to have any binding relevance in our lives?

The argument against the relevance of the Levitical holiness code sounds so strong and logical, and the book of Leviticus seems so ancient, that the average person may feel nervous or ill-equipped to study it on his or her own. However, a thoughtful look at the passages in Leviticus makes it clear that not all prohibitions listed in these guidelines from God are equal. The guidelines in Leviticus 19:19 about animals, plants, and clothes have no punishment prescribed for their violation or any statement attached regarding their degree of abhorrence in the eyes of God. The two previously quoted verses, however (Leviticus 18:22; 20:13), label homosexuality as "detestable" (NIV; NASB, "an abomination").

It has been suggested that the Hebrew term *tôʿēbâ*, translated "detestable" or "abomination," may refer only to idolatry or ceremonial uncleanness. That is an old argument that has been refuted through the years, and yet people continue to resurrect it.[1] The term *detestable* is indeed generally used to refer to idolatry but can specifically describe immoral behavior that violates the timeless purposes of God, whether or not idolatry is involved (Deuteronomy 12:31; 2 Chronicles 28:3; Proverbs 6:16). If one takes a few minutes to read through Leviticus 18 and 20, it is clear that the word *detestable* in this context is nearly always linked to the most destructive transgressions, including acts of sexual and moral perversion, such as incest and child sacrifice, that left the perpetrators and the whole nation of Israel under the severe judgment of God.[2] The punishment, too, could not be more severe: "they must be put to death" (Leviticus 20:13). Contrast this to the prohibitions in Leviticus 19:19 (related to sowing two kinds of seeds, etc.) for which no punishment is prescribed.

To accept the standard progay line of thought, claiming that homosexual practice is OK if it isn't tied to idolatry is to suggest that incest, adultery, and bestiality are also acceptable to God whenever they not associated with the worship of false gods.

The Unchanging Character of God

In studying the 1 Timothy passage, we saw that the moral/ethical laws given by God were not bound or shaped by time. They reflect the unchanging purpose of our immutable God. It is interesting to note that the seventh commandment ("You shall not commit adultery") has been traditionally understood by Jewish rabbis and by many early church fathers to include not only the breaking of the marital covenant but sexual violations of all kinds that deviate from God's originally established norms for marriage. Adultery is wrong, but so is fornication. General lasciviousness is condemned, as is homosexuality. Any sexual relations outside a monogamous heterosexual marriage were (and still should be) considered a violation of this seventh commandment. Again, as we saw in 1 Timothy 1, Paul was almost certainly contemplating the Ten Commandments when he drew up his list of violations against the moral laws of God and included the words, "those practicing homosexuality" (1 Timothy 1:10 TNIV), referring back to the seventh commandment.

The point is clear: the same God who condemned homosexual practice through Moses *before* the time of Christ condemned homosexual practice through Paul *after* the time of Christ. The law was given to lead us to Christ, who helps us to obey it (Galatians 3:24). All this is in keeping with the teachings of Christ himself, who proclaimed the unchanging nature of the moral law of God.

A basic principle for the study of Scripture is to allow the Bible to interpret itself. Our opinions about the laws in the Old Testament are not as important as are those of Christ, Paul, and the other apostles. As relating to the issue of homosexuality, assumptions that all of the laws in Leviticus are outdated must be weighed against Paul's statements that show moral laws in the Old Testament to be timeless and relevant for today.

Some argue that the *law* of God has been replaced by the *love* of God. The Ten Commandments, for example, can be summed up by the Great Commandment to love God with all your heart and to love your neighbor as yourself. Why not, then, get beyond the law and focus on loving, monogamous relationships, whether heterosexual or homosexual? The answer is clear: the same Lord who tells us that God's laws are based on love warns us never to compromise the law, which he himself came to fulfill (Matthew 5:17). The laws of God, in fact, are given to us because God loves us. And, John tells us, "This is love for God: to obey his commands" (1 John 5:3).

It is because God loves us that he is not content to leave us as we are. He enables us to change. In like manner, we should approach all kinds of people, even those engaged in various stages of spiritual or moral compromise, with a love that flows from the heart of the one true God.

Application for the Church Today

If we embrace God's truth and teach what is wrong about same-sex practice today, we also must proclaim God's grace and provide alternatives. Law and grace are bound inseparably throughout the Bible, and our congregations should manifest this wonderful balance as well.

The Deeper Meaning of Abomination

In his book *Light in the Closet*, Arthur Goldberg traces the meaning of the Hebrew *tô‘ēbâ* through the Talmud to demonstrate that the translation "abomination" or "abhorrent" does not capture the full essence of the word. In the context of God's relationship with his people, the concept of "alienation" or being "led astray" is at the heart of the meaning, along with the implications that one can find the way back.[3]

If ever we use the word *abomination* in relation to human beings, we must emphasize that it is not people who are abhorrent to God, but their destructive behavior. Like a parent grieving over an alienated child, God is calling each of us back home and is troubled by any behavior that causes us harm—you see, he loves us.

A Baptist pastor in my community, Greg Mathis, preached a sermon on homosexuality in which he challenged people to recognize how much God loves all people, how deeply each of us has fallen into sin, and how wrong it is to throw the word *abomination* around in a condemning manner toward one group of people. That sermon, along with a leadership training seminar, positioned his church to minister to homosexuals who come to his church for help.

The Misuse of Statistics Today

We must be careful when using Scripture or statistics to warn people about the negative consequences of homosexual behavior. Our efforts to warn others can also alienate them. Regarding statistics, for example, there may be legitimate reasons to point out that the percentage of homosexuals in our country is somewhere between 2 and 3 percent, not the 10 percent figure that has been floating around for years, or that national statistical data clearly demonstrates negative health implications for homosexual activity.[4] But in our day of ongoing surveys and public opinion results, statistics sometimes become sharp implements that wound and drive away the very people we should be trying to help.

Chad Thompson leads a ministry that addresses homosexuality on high school and college campuses. Working with the younger generation, he has learned sensitivity in tone and terminology when addressing the topic. In his book *Loving Homosexuals as Jesus Would*, Chad challenges us to get beyond hurtful rhetoric and barbed statistics. Having struggled with same-sex attraction himself and having experienced what it is like to be on the receiving end of statistics, Chad writes:

> Many studies claim to prove that fidelity among homosexual partnership is virtually nonexistent. One study says the average lifespan of a homosexual is forty-two years; another study says 43 percent of male homosexuals reported having more than five hundred partners during their lifetimes....
>
> I won't take time to dissect the research methods used to draw these conclusions. I will only say that while some of the findings in such studies are true, throwing these numbers around while talking to LGBT [lesbian, gay, bisexual, and transgendered] people will only reinforce, in their minds, the fact that you have stereotyped them. Can you imagine telling your son or daughter that heterosexuality is inherently evil because America has a divorce rate estimated at 43 percent or because 30 percent of women killed in the United States die at the hands of a husband or boyfriend?...
>
> As Christians, we can be as well-intentioned as we want to be, but if our approach alienates those who we are trying to love, it may be time to try something else."[5]

Chad reminds us, "Many lesbian and gay people *need* Christians to be hateful and ignorant in order to convince themselves that our message is the result of ignorance, homophobia, or some massive right-wing conspiracy. But if we take the time to understand them, showing genuine concern for the things that trouble them, they might actually consider our message on its merits."[6]

What about Governmental Laws Today?

During the year I have been writing this book, I have watched hate crime legislation and gay marriage rights make major inroads in our country. The trend that swept across England and descended over Canada is now spreading its wings and descending on America. Recently a friend described how an employee in England was not even near to her place of employment when she bumped into a fellow employee who, in the course of their conversation, asked her what she thought about homosexuality. The woman replied that she did not approve of it. Word got back to her boss, and she immediately lost her job. If the trend continues, such stories may soon be commonplace in the United States.

How do we remain true to the law of God when the laws of the land oppose us? The answer can be seen in the pages of the Bible and through the annals of history. Again and again, God's people have been placed in situations where the truths of Scripture conflict directly with rules established by human governments. Christians are called to be obedient first to their Lord and Master, and in every way possible also to show respect to rulers who govern the land. In the words of Peter and John, when they were told to stop preaching the gospel, "Judge for yourselves whether it is right in God's sight to obey you rather than God. For we cannot help speaking about what we have seen and heard" (Acts 4:19–20).

> ## Ministry Essential #7:
> The law leads us to Christ, who enables us to fulfill it.

Your church and mine can and should provide ministry to those who are conflicted sexually and who ask for help. This can be done without violating any laws of the land, even as gay marriage comes on the scene. As a pastor, I sometimes refuse to perform weddings for people I feel are not ready for marriage because their lives do not conform to the teachings of Christ. It would not be discriminatory for me to apply the same standards to a gay couple. I must follow my conscience. The call to be involved politically and to push for change in legislation, however, is a special burden that God will also place on some Christians and perhaps on whole congregations. But that is not the focus of this book. There will always be a need for ministry that meets the needs of people with Christlike compassion, and the more secular our country becomes, the greater will be the need. We must never minimize the teachings of Scripture, however. For in so doing, our ministries will present distorted images of the God we claim to serve.

When Truth and Grace Unite

Mike Goeke attended law school at Baylor Law School and embarked on a career as an attorney.* A married man, he could not shake the homosexual attractions that had plagued him from his youth. His reflections below express how his life was turned around because people loved him enough to confront him with a higher law that is based on unchanging truths in Scripture.

---

* Mike is on the pastoral staff of Stonegate Fellowship Church in Midland, Texas, and is the executive director of Cross Power Ministries. Mike can be contacted at atcpm@stonegatefellowship.com.

Offended: How My Family Offended Me and Brought Me Back to Christ, by Mike Goeke

A recent article in the *San Francisco Chronicle* touted the merger of 1,400 "open and affirming" churches (meaning churches that affirm homosexual identity and behavior) with the National Gay and Lesbian Task Force. The article stated that leaders in the gay rights movement consider their biggest challenge to be that of convincing Christians that homosexual behavior is not a sin. I witnessed something of this movement when I spoke recently at a gathering of pastors and church leaders from a denomination that is heavily divided over the issue of homosexuality. One man spoke of his desire that everyone be welcome at his church and that they be "inclusive" and especially that no one leave their church "offended" by what he or she hears. Of course, this was not the first time I had heard these types of thoughts. Many people I talk to, including pastors and parents and friends, are concerned that they not "offend" gay people.

Let me just say a hearty thank you to my wife and my parents, family, and friends who cared enough about me to offend me! I get a sick feeling in the pit of my stomach when I consider the ramifications in my life had the people in my world bought in to the lie that to love me was to affirm my homosexuality. When I left my wife to pursue homosexuality, she boldly told me that she knew God could work in me and in our marriage and that she would not pursue divorce. She protected her interests but always professed her love for me and her desire to work through this together. My parents (and other family members) told me that what I was doing was wrong. They found out about Exodus International, got materials, and tried to get me to talk to a counselor. They also called frequently to check on me, sent me money when I needed it, came to see me on my birthday, and flew me home for holidays. My friends drove hours to talk to me about what I was doing and told me what they believed. They flew from other towns to take me to dinner and tried to convince me to get help and to turn from what I was doing. They also sent me cards and letters full of love and affirmation of our friendship.

And each of them offended me. Each of them made me angry. I viewed them as bigoted, unenlightened, ignorant, prejudiced, and hateful. If they truly loved me, I told them, they would accept my homosexuality and affirm me in the lifestyle I was living. I ignored their calls, and I viewed these people with skepticism. I did my best to sever my relationships with those who were offending me. But they would not let me go. They did not coddle me, but they refused to give up on me.

When I finally took the book *You Don't Have to Be Gay* from my dad, just to shut him up, I was ready to draw a line in the sand and cut all ties with my wife, my family, and my friends.[7] But the time planned by God for the piercing of my heart had come. As I have said many times, that book showed me more than the sentimental, saccharine love of Jesus that gay theology had sold me. It showed me the powerful love of the risen Savior, and I was compelled back to him by that love. The offending parties in my life were waiting, as loving and gracious as they had ever been — not holding my sin against me, but standing there, ready to walk the journey out of homosexuality alongside me.

Today my marriage is restored and has grown beyond my imagination. I have three beautiful children and am living out the call on my life to vocational ministry. Healing has happened in my family relationships, and I am closer to that cadre of friends than ever before. As I listen to people debate the "gay" issue and talk of affirmation and inclusivity of homosexuality, I wonder where I would be today had my wife, Stephanie, accepted my claim that I had always been gay and would always be gay and had pursued divorce like I wanted her to do. I wonder where I would be if my parents had joined PFLAG (Parents, Families, and Friends of Lesbians and Gays) and supported me in my quest to live homosexually. I wonder where I would be if my friends had encouraged me to divorce Stephanie and had rallied around me in my homosexuality. I wonder where I would be if my pastors and spiritual shepherds had encouraged me to accept the very thing I needed to lay before the cross of Christ. I shudder at the thought. I know it must have killed them to think of losing me, but they loved me enough to take that risk. Thank you, dear friends, for your offense to me. At the time, the truth you shared was the aroma of death to me (2 Corinthians 2:15), but today it is the sweet fragrance of life.

Chapter 7

THE WISDOM
Insights from Psychology

The Controversy

Grace with Compromised Truth: "Most mental health professionals refuse to treat homosexuality anymore because they believe it will harm the person who attempts to change. We must encourage gays, lesbians, bisexuals, and transgender persons to accept their orientations."

Truth with Compromised Grace: "Send the homosexuals to counselors. Once they have changed, they are welcome here in our church. But don't let them near our children."

Uniting Truth and Grace as a Basis for Ministry

On April 14, 1912, the great luxury liner forged through quiet waters, unaware that a formidable giant was waiting quietly at its fore. When the iceberg was finally spotted, the *Titanic*'s crew fought madly to turn the hulking ship. It was too late. The *Titanic*'s hull ground against ragged edges of white ice, came apart at the seams, and began gulping seawater. Within two hours and forty minutes, one of the deadliest peacetime maritime disasters left 1,517 people dead and 46,000 tons of metal wreckage buried in a muddy grave two and a half miles beneath the surface.

It was long assumed that the opulent 900-foot cruise ship went down because of a mighty gash in its armor. But the international team of divers and scientists that used sound waves to probe the wreckage in 1985 was surprised to find minimal damage caused by the ice. Instead of a huge gash, they found six relatively narrow slits across the six watertight holds. Had the ship hit the iceberg head-on, it might not have sunk. By scraping against the sharp edges of the frozen mountain, however, the ship's buckling hull popped its riveted buttons over a length of 299 feet, opening its steel jacket for invading seawater.

History's graveyard is riddled with conspicuous sepulchres where many "greats" have been brought down by subtle, often unseen forces. We will forever remember, for example, the great stock market crash of 1929, the explosion of the *Hindenburg* in 1937, the disintegration of space shuttle *Challenger* in 1986, and the collapse of the Soviet Union in 1991. A lesser-known demise of special relevance to this book is the radical revision of the American Psychiatric Association's long-held understanding that homosexuality is a psychological disorder. This demise of century-old perspectives on people with same-sex attractions created a domino effect in more than a dozen other mental health associations.

The change might not have occurred if there had been a head-on collision of values revealed in a huge national study with clashing perspectives brought to the fore for debate and research. Instead, sharp-edged political pressure was brought to bear along the ideological seams of the association's national conventions and power structures, quietly popping century-old rivets of psychological and scientific research and creating an inrush of new understandings.

How the APA Relates to Homosexuality

It was more than a well-organized and persistent effort of gay rights promoters who brought down long-held perspectives in groups like the American Psychiatric Association (APA), the umbrella for some 38,000 psychiatrists, and the American Psychological Association (which also uses the acronym APA), with its 150,000 psychologists. These individuals were but the tip of the iceberg. The American Psychiatric Association and other umbrella associations that cover mental health professionals collided with unseen forces of iceberglike dimensions. Deep under the surface of the associations' debates were new sexual ethics empowered by discoveries in the scientific community about possible biological linkages to human behavior.

The demise of historic understandings in the American Psychiatric Association helped forge new perspectives in society and church about whether a person with same-sex attractions can actually "change." In a marked shift over a ten-year period, they revised their official position to say that homosexuality is not a disease but an orientation. Their next step in the same direction was to declare it harmful to treat those who wish to overcome their same-sex attractions.

The current position of the American Psychiatric Association on homosexuality is rigid and extreme. It would also be extreme, however, to claim that one approach to therapy works for all homosexuals or that every gay or lesbian can be expected to overcome their same-sex attractions. Oversimplification itself is what will eventually be most harmful for individuals, for homosexuality is caused by a multiplicity of factors, and each person's story is unique. Whether every gay or lesbian seeking help eventually overcomes inner struggles, the rallying point for the Christian community should be the *biblical call to obedience*, not a particular approach to therapy.

I write with a humble recognition of the great help many psychiatrists, psychologists, and trained counselors are providing to countless individuals around the country. It saddens me, however, that some of today's mental health professionals are edging into the arena of religion and ethics, where they do not belong. Psychology does not have the final word on human behavior. God's truth (his "law"), based on his eternal wisdom, is as relevant for our health and happiness today as it was in the day Jesus taught it. Where mental health professionals fail, God still may step in.

How the American Psychiatric Association Shifted

In 1963, the Committee on Public Health for the New York Academy of Medicine reported conclusions that had been held by psychiatrists for decades: "Homosexuality is indeed an illness. The homosexual is an emotionally disturbed individual who has not acquired the normal capacity to develop satisfying heterosexual relations."[1]

It was only ten years later, in 1973, that the American Psychiatric Association voted to strike homosexuality from its approved list of psychiatric illnesses. We might expect such a drastic alteration of historically held positions came about through the normal process of the study of documented research over time, through which reliable conclusions were reached. But this was not the case. The APA reached its conclusions, not based on a scientific consensus, but through political pressure. Ronald Bayer, then a fellow at the Hastings Institute in New York, reported how in 1970 the leadership of a homosexual faction within the American Psychiatric Association (APA) planned a "systematic effort to disrupt the annual meetings of the American Psychiatric Association."[2] Bayer summarizes the process: "The American Psychiatric Association had fallen victim to the disorder of a tumultuous era, when disruptive elements threatened to politicize every aspect of American social life. A furious egalitarianism ... compelled psychiatric experts to negotiate the pathological status of homosexuality with homosexuals themselves."[3]

When the American Psychiatric Association made its radical shift, not all of its representative psychiatrists were in agreement, and only 58 percent of its

30,000 members voted to ratify it.[4] A survey by the *Medical Aspects of Human Sexuality* journal four years later showed that 69 percent of psychiatrists opposed the 1973 action.[5] Yet the decision would gradually stifle professional research and debate about homosexuality as a treatable disorder. In the eight-year span between 1966 and 1974, the Medline database listed over a thousand articles on the treatment of homosexuality. Following the APA's decision that homosexuality was not a disorder, such articles disappeared. In the three years from 1992 to 1994, for example, of the 1,581 Medline database articles referencing homosexuality, only one, from France, suggests homosexuality might be an undesired condition that should be treated.[6] Neil Whitehead writes, "In my decades of experience as a research scientist and biochemist, I have seen no parallel in any other professional society. This politicization of the facts may represent the most extreme example ever, outside of Communist societies. I suggest the APA should be declared of unsound mind."[7]

In 1975, two years after the American Psychiatric Association had removed homosexuality from its list of approved psychological disorders, the American Psychological Association followed suit. This new definition opened the door for new sociopolitical agendas. Research psychologist Merton Strommen writes: "To illustrate, the 1999 American Psychological Association Convention in Boston had twenty-nine presentations on gay, lesbian, bisexual, and transgender issues. Each was in favor of increasing rights for gays and discouraging efforts to change an individual's sexual orientation."[8]

An organization's values are made evident in the way it screens its publications. In 1998, the *Psychological Bulletin* ran an article describing pedophilia as not harmful to children when they are willing participants. The same article referred to sexual abuse as a "value–neutral term" and suggested that adult-adolescent sex may fall within the normal range.[9] In the *American Psychologist*, the one journal sent to every member of the APA, an article titled "Deconstructing the Essential Father" promoted a new family model in which the role of the father is unimportant to the health of children.[10]

One would assume such articles were allowed publication by the American Psychological Association for the sake of freedom of expression and the exchange of ideas to maintain intellectual freedom. But at the same time these articles were being published, the APA refused to publish any articles from the National Association for Research and Therapy of Homosexuality (NARTH), an association of more than a thousand members who believe homosexuality can be overcome with proper therapy. Strommen concludes: "The APA seemingly has closed its doors on information that contradicts its position. It is this politicization of the APA, an organization that makes a PhD a requirement of membership and prides itself in seeking truth through objective research, which many psychologists find disturbing."[11]

Joseph Nicolosi, past president of NARTH, notes that "when we break through the media filter and go back to the academic community and the scientist, we invariably hear that homosexuality is due to a combination of physiological, social, and biological factors working in concert." He then raises an obvious concern:

> But one question remains oddly unaddressed: if the researchers themselves admit no one is "born gay," then why is the American Psychological Association not interested in studying the family and social influences that lead to a homosexual identity? I believe the answer is clear: gay activists in the association do not want them to. In fact, whenever the National Association for Research and Therapy of Homosexuality (of which I am president) addresses a letter to the president of the American Psychological Association, it is routed to the Office of Gay and Lesbian Concerns — a group of gay activists. They are determined not to address that vitally important issue of causation.[12]

Psychologists Rogers Wright and Nicholas Cummings's book, *Destructive Trends in Mental Health*, documents how social activism has squelched scientific inquiry in the American Psychological Association. Eminent leaders in their field and self-proclaimed lifelong liberal activists, Wright and Cummings were themselves deeply entrenched in the social activism that drives the APA. Cummings, for example, supported the development of the first task force that championed the mental health needs of gays, lesbians, and bisexuals. As practical observers of the mental health profession for four decades, Wright and Cummings write:

> In the current climate, it is inevitable that conflict arises among the various subgroups in the marketplace. For example, gay groups within the APA [American Psychological Association] have repeatedly tried to persuade the association to adopt ethical standards that prohibit therapists from offering psychotherapeutic services designed to ameliorate "gayness" on the basis that such efforts are unsuccessful and harmful to the consumer. Psychologists who do not agree are termed homophobic. Such efforts are especially troubling because they abrogate the patient's right to choose the therapist and determine therapeutic goals. They also deny the reality of data demonstrating that psychotherapy can be effective in changing sexual preferences in patients who have a desire to do so.[13]

Lamenting that diversity and open-mindedness has been narrowed into a science-squelching, tunnel-shaped political viewpoint that summarily dismisses or overly punishes alternative worldviews, they explain that things have become so bad that "it has become politically incorrect to question political correctness."[14]

The American Psychological Association's response to Wright and Cummings's book initially was to prohibit its member publications from reviewing the book, and then not to respond to it in hopes that it would be ignored. Dr. Wright later commented, "So much for diversity and open-mindedness."[15]

It is astonishing how radically the paradigm has shifted from one in which homosexuality was treated as a disorder to one in which those who seek to treat homosexuality are discredited. Since the 1970s, these mighty associations have been unable to correct their ideological imbalance, creating distrust and frustration among many of their own members, as well as between mental health professionals and major segments of the church and society. Dr. Robert Spitzer, who chaired the task force that encouraged the APA to remove homosexuality as a disorder from the diagnostic manual, later became convinced that change is indeed possible for homosexuals. When he published findings to support his viewpoint in the *Archives of Sexual Behavior* in October 2003, however, his colleagues were outraged and his voice was effectively silenced. He doesn't believe the APA will ever soften its stance on the treatment of homosexuality due to the strength of vocal gay activists within the APA.[16]

Factors the APA Generally Ignores

While the APA admits that homosexuality is caused by a variety of factors and that it is not simply genetically induced, they give at best a passing nod to the significance of environmental influences for the cause of same-sex attraction.

The Psychoanalytic Theory

One of the predominant theories for causes of homosexuality through time has been the *psychoanalytic* theory. Based in part on research by Sigmund Freud, a trained neurologist who developed psychoanalysis in the early 1900s, the psychoanalytic theory assumes a failure in the normal development of a secure male identity, often because of an absent or detached father and a close and dominant mother. Over time, factors that cause a diminished relationship with the father and an unhealthy attachment to the mother can result in a compromised sense of secure "maleness," eventually giving way to an erotic attraction toward males.[17] In 1989, Seymour Fischer and Roger Greenberg analyzed fifty-eight empirical studies related to parents of homosexuals and found that a large majority showed homosexual sons who perceived their fathers as negative, distant, unfriendly figures. The support of close and controlling mothers, however, was not as strong. Fischer and Greenberg concluded, "There is not a single even moderately well-controlled study that we have been able to locate in which male homosexuals refer to the father positively or affectionately. On the contrary, they consistently regard him as an antagonist. He easily fills the unusually intense, competitive Oedipal role Freud ascribed to him."[18]

Even though psychoanalysts have suggested many variations on this theme and few believe there is any single cause for homosexuality, the influence of the family has over time been arguably one of the most regularly suggested sources for homosexual behavior. Dr. Jeffrey Satinover writes:

> One of the most consistent findings from the studies of homosexuality is that a familial factor—or factors—strongly influences later sexual behavior.... In its decision that homosexuality was not an illness, the APA ignored nearly eighty years worth of psychoanalytic and psychotherapeutic observation. The gist of these practitioners' observations is consistent with what more rigorous scientific data demonstrates (even the biased studies such as Bailey and Pillard), namely, that the family environment plays a critical role in the development of homosexuality.
>
> What did psychoanalysts learn that activists want us to forget? That in the lives of their homosexual patients there was usually often an emotional mismatch between the child and same-sex parent (such as a father who subtly or overtly rejects a son who has many "feminine" traits); or an emotional mismatch between the child and the opposite sex parent; or sexual abuse of a child by either the same sex or opposite sex parent; and most often the rejection of a child by same-sex peers.[19]

Even gay activist and author Andrew Sullivan, in his book *Love Undetectable*, says that any "honest homosexual" who considers his family background from the perspective of the classic "distant father/overclose mother" theory will acknowledge it as a contributing factor to homosexual orientation. Sullivan says it would be self-deception to assume a purely genetic source for homosexuality.[20]

This classical understanding about the origins of homosexuality focused on deficits in a person's gender identity due to missing pieces in the sometimes complex puzzle of growth from infancy to adulthood. Simply put, years of observation show often-repeated patterns. If young boys, for example, do not receive proper affection and love from their fathers, and if their mothers are overly enmeshed in their lives, these youngsters may develop an aversion to males and develop behaviors that cause them to be rejected by other boys. Over time, if a sense of rejection from other males works itself deep within their souls, they may reject their own masculinity and begin to crave in others what they lack in themselves, leading to same-sex attractions and fantasies. Once adolescence hits and hormones rage, the youngster, longing to be made whole, may seek intimacy with another male through a sexual encounter. Finding pleasure and temporary fulfillment through this experience, a young man may assume that he was always homosexual. There are many variations on the theme, and no doubt many other factors are involved in the process of developing a same-sex identity, but the common thread of *detachment from one's own gender* because of issues that impact the normal maturation process is central to the classical model.

Over time, this classical model was eclipsed by the biological model, which makes homosexuality a mere function of genes and inborn factors. In reality, the classical model has never been disproven, and there is a wealth of research to support its relevance for today.[21] A partial eclipse of the two models, which recognizes some genetic influence but not enough to force a person to act out homosexually, is a reasonable approximation of reality. Nevertheless, many leaders in the field of psychology have acquiesced to the pressure of political activists to embrace a totally biological model without sufficient scientific proof.

Sexual Experimentation and Abuse

Another well-documented causative factor for homosexuality is abuse and sexual stimulation by peers or older adults. The baby boomer generation has sown the seeds of sexual experimentation and is reaping the harvest with broken homes, marriages, and lives. Unprecedented numbers of youth are experimenting sexually. Nearly 50 percent of all high school students report that they have had sexual intercourse.[22] Sexual addiction, even among Christians, is estimated by experts to be up to 10 percent, and two-thirds of Christian men admit to struggling with pornography. In one study, 40 percent of pastors surveyed confessed to looking at pornography.[23] Sexual arousal through fantasizing, the viewing of pornography, and experimentation can be habit forming. Escaping from the addictive influence of sex can be as difficult as is withdrawing from hard drugs. Describing the addictive effect of sexual pleasure on the brain, Satinover writes:

> In the case of pleasure, the chemical released from the nerve endings is a special type called an "opioid," meaning "opiumlike." Of all behaviors, none would appear to be accompanied by so intense a burst of internal opioids as sex. Therefore, apart from the repetitive ingestion of such external opiates as heroin—the classic example of addiction—no experience is more intensely pleasurable. This fact sheds light on the ease with which repeated sexual behaviors are especially strongly reinforced....
>
> The experience of pleasure creates powerful, behavior-shaping incentives. For this reason, when biological impulses ... are *not* at least partially resisted ..., the pressure to seek their immediate fulfillment becomes deeply embedded in the neural network of the brain. Furthermore, the particular individualized patterns by which we seek this fulfillment will also become deeply implanted....

In short order, therefore, unregulated sexual tendencies become habits, then compulsions, and finally something barely distinguishable from addictions.[24]

Dr. William Consiglio, founder and director of HOPE ministries, has concluded through his own research and his years of extensive counseling with homosexuals that human sexuality is like a rapidly moving stream. Sexual experimentation, trauma, experiences in a dysfunctional family upbringing, and other environmental factors may cause a break in the protective banks of the normal flow of sexuality. Once water flows in a new direction and cuts a new channel, Consiglio reasons, it is difficult to redirect it back into its channel. He has found that restoration is possible, however, with proper motivation, support, guidance, and therapy as necessary.[25]

Sexual abuse has been demonstrated to be a significant factor in the development of homosexuality. Although most research about the causes for homosexuality has focused on men, it appears that sexual abuse is a greater causative factor for the development of same-sex attractions in women. In her book *Restoring Sexual Identity*, Anne Paulk describes a survey she conducted among 1,912 women who were overcoming or had overcome homosexuality. She found that an astonishing 91 percent of the women had experienced some form of abuse when growing up — 69 percent emotional abuse, 66 percent sexual abuse, and 53 percent verbal abuse. Three-fourths of the women who were victims of sexual abuse were first sexually molested between three and ten years of age. Of those molested, 85 percent were sexually molested by a male.[26]

Similar studies have been done among males. David Finkelhor's research in 1984 showed that boys abused by older men were four times more likely to be currently involved in homosexuality than nonvictims. Both Finkelhor's study and a 1987 study by Robert L. Johnson and Diane Shrier demonstrated that young boys who were developing heterosexually at a young age and then experienced abuse often became homosexual later in life.[27]

Gender Identity Disorder

The glaring inconsistency of the American Psychiatric Association's decision to remove homosexuality from their list of disorders can be seen in the fact that they continue to label children who begin to manifest signs of homosexuality (those with gender identity disorder) as having a psychiatric illness. If sexual identity is not important for adults, why should it matter for youngsters? It doesn't take a trained mental health professional to see the internal conflict in an association that allows a prehomosexual child to be given a diagnosis and treatment, while adult homosexuals are considered normal. Even the gay rights activists see this inconsistency and have been steadily and quietly working to remove gender identity disorder from the list of diagnoses.[28]

Rather than develop clear and consistent guidelines for their definitions of psychiatric illnesses and disorders, the APA has flexed with the mores of the age. Scientific method has been clouded by the political imperatives of homosexual activists. In this instance, human opinion has co-opted science, and the two have risen in mutiny against the King of kings to create a socially driven ethic. How easily the laws established by God have been trampled by ambitious humans. Fortunately, not all mental health professionals accept the party line, and well-documented research can provide a balance to the equation.

The Mental Health Profession and the Healing of Homosexuality

Behind the associations that represent mental health professionals today are the psychiatrists and clinical psychologists who face the daily challenge of helping people live healthy and productive lives. In the crises of life and the quiet of counselors' offices, the reality of the human condition comes to the fore. Not all mental health professionals agree with the definitions found in their official diagnostics manual. Despite political pressure and professional ramifications, many mental health professionals still treat homosexuality and believe that those who come to them desiring change may, in fact, be able to find it.

The Diagnostic and Statistical Manual of Mental Disorders (DSM), published by the American Psychiatric Association, initially evolved from statistical data–collecting systems in psychiatric hospitals and from a manual developed by the U.S. Army. Undergoing its sixth revision since its first publication in 1952, the DSM lists standard diagnostic criteria for mental disorders by clinicians, researchers, pharmaceutical companies, and policy makers, and has both its supporters and critics. There is general awareness in the psychiatric community that the removal of homosexuality from the APA's approved list of illnesses is not the same as endorsing the homosexual lifestyle or orientation as "healthy." Psychiatrists often treat people with conditions or behaviors that are not listed or easily identified in the DSM but for which their clients seek change. Stanton Jones and Mark Yarhouse write:

> Removal of a diagnostic category from the DSM is not the same thing as an endorsement of homosexual orientation or lifestyle as healthy or wholesome.... By analogy, a person can certainly be in a condition where he or she fails to manifest an identifiable physical disease, yet also fails to be an exemplar of health and fitness.

> The removal of homosexuality from the DSM does not conclusively decide the issue of the pathological status of homosexuality. There is no absolute standard for judging normality or abnormality.[29]

Twenty years after the APA decided homosexuality would no longer be labeled a disorder, its Office of International Affairs conducted a survey and found that a majority of psychiatrists around the world recognized same-sex behavior as signaling mental illness.[30] Psychiatrists who treat homosexuality have seen over a period of eighty years, and even now see, significant cure rates. Satinover, for example, highlights a cross section from sixty years of published research dating from 1930 to 1986 and finds an overall success rate of over 50 percent.[31] In the 1970s, sex researchers Masters and Johnson found an unusually high success rate of 71.6 percent for eighty-one gays desiring reorientation. They concluded, "No longer should qualified psychotherapists avoid the responsibility of either accepting the homosexual client in treatment or referring him or her to an acceptable treatment source."[32] After reviewing all published reports on reparative therapy for homosexuality in eighty-three scientific journals in 1998, Dr. Warren Throckmorton concluded that such therapy is effective and can be conducted in an ethical manner.[33] More recently he has partially shifted his position, however, and cautions that no single therapy should be seen as a cure-all, and that even if a client does not find complete freedom from unwanted same-sex attractions through therapy, he or she can learn to live a fulfilled celibate life.[34]

In August 2009, the APA adopted a resolution reaffirming the stance that mental health professionals should avoid telling clients that they can alter their sexual orientation through therapy or other treatments. They also encouraged a creative approach to their clients' religious faith, encouraging mental health care providers to help their clients "explore possible life paths that address the reality of their sexual orientation, reduce the stigma associated with homosexuality, respect the client's religious beliefs, and consider possibilities for a religiously and spiritually meaningful and rewarding life."[35]

This "rewarding life" may be difficult to find, however, for church members with same-sex attractions who find themselves pulled between the values of Christianity and those held by the APA.

Avoiding Irrational Reactions

The swirling controversy in the mental health profession has brought its turbulence into the church. It is important that Christians avoid three overreactions to this confusion as they focus on ministries of healing for homosexuals, for their families, and for the church at large: *silence, blind support,* and *oversimplification.*

Overcoming Silence

The politicized climate surrounding homosexuality that has stifled research and treatment among health care professionals has also muffled conversation in church and society about providing help for those who wish to overcome same-sex desires. The average person may be afraid even to discuss the topic, lest she or he be branded "homophobic." *Phobia* is a term used in psychology for one whose fears cause stress, panic, and inability to function. While we should reject prejudice and unloving bias against any of our fellow human beings, the term *homophobic* has been used, sometimes intentionally, to intimidate those who wish to have honest dialogue on the topic.

When a person finds a new job, becomes engaged, or is diagnosed with cancer, conversation flows naturally among family and friends about the adjustments that need to be made. When a person struggles with issues of sexuality, however, silence often prevails among loved ones, and feelings of anxiety and hopelessness can become deep-seated. When we allow fear, ignorance, or mistrust to stifle communication about important issues that hamper our relationships, such issues do not simply slip through the cracks of broken relationships like small seeds of division, to be forgotten forever. No, they soon arise as weeds, taunting us for our neglect. The lack of meaningful, loving, and factually based conversations about homosexuality in the church and in families has enabled division to grow and wounds to fester.

If you are struggling with same-sex attraction, talk to your pastor, a counselor, or a friend who can keep a confidence. If you have a family member who has come out of the closet and is seeking your support, avail yourself of the resources listed in the appendix of this book. If your church is quietly but deeply divided about issues of sexuality, encourage your pastor and church leaders to engage in a ministry of renewal and understanding as described in the second half of this book. Silence is not a viable solution for the divisions that have been created by squelching conversation about this topic in our families, churches, and society.

Don't Offer Blind Support

If most families and Christian congregations are being negatively affected by their ignorance and silence about issues of sexuality, many who are willing to discuss these issues openly have developed a response that lacks integrity and truth. Some congregations have accepted the label "affirming" in an effort to show the love of Christ to everyone. It is hoped that every church will welcome all who come to their worship services to learn about Jesus. But the gospel does not end there. We are the redeemed community. We believe in the power of God to help us change and grow, to live the truth and proclaim it in love. Christians who unwittingly endorse the gay agenda add to societal confusion and dilute the message of God. The Scriptures admonish us to treat gently those who have veered from God's path, being careful to offer correctives and to protect the values of Christ's kingdom (Galatians 6:1).

Avoiding Oversimplification

A third extreme we must avoid when talking about homosexuality is oversimplification. In combating the notion that same-sex attractions are an innate and unalterable phenomenon that should not be treated, let us not create an opposite and equally unbalanced scenario that insists that complete change will occur 100 percent of the time for everyone who seeks it. Even the most conservative Christian therapist will tell you, without flinching, that not all homosexuals who seek a heterosexual orientation will succeed.[36] There are many complicated reasons for the temptations with which we all struggle, and some of our internal conflicts may not be fully resolved this side of heaven.

One of the most significant studies of religiously mediated reorientation therapy was done in 2007 by Jones and Yarhouse. Their longitudinal study is the most methodologically rigorous research to date on both the possibility of changing sexual orientation and of not being harmed through the attempt. Their study focused on ninety-eight men and women who were at least eighteen years old and who were seeking help to resolve unwanted same-sex attractions and behaviors through various ministries of Exodus International. Their results found 38 percent claiming success, 29 percent reporting only a diminution of homosexual attractions, 27 percent having no significant change but not giving up on the process, and 12 percent who were confused or had given up on counseling.[37] Significantly, nearly all participants in this study acknowledged personal gains from their counseling experiences even if their sexual attractions did not change to the degree they had initially desired.

The report, available in book form, concludes, "Taken together, these findings would appear to contradict the commonly expressed view of the mental health establishment that change of sexual orientation is impossible and that the attempt to change is highly likely to produce harm for those who make such an attempt."[38] Jones and Yarhouse's study is significant to this book, because many church members who seek to diminish their homosexual attractions turn to Exodus-affiliated counselors. Even a cursory analysis of the results of the study should help us avoid illogical extremes about the change process.

Defining Change

Part of the confusion about "change" related to homosexuality in Christian circles is semantic. Are we talking about a change of behavior or a deeper

eaders are not there anymore

change in attractions? If a married man is caught having an ongoing affair and he agrees to break it off, is that not change? The extent to which he longs for the other woman or even for just one more daring adulterous sexual encounter, however, relates to a deeper level of change. In the same way, people who have walked away from a homosexual lifestyle may still struggle, with same-sex attractions. A deeper change, the diminishing of such attractions, will likely occur over time, but such attractions may never completely disappear. This is the reality of the human condition. We are all in process. God's call is for obedience and holiness. We can be faithful to that call, yet still struggle. God promises grace for the journey but not necessarily an easy path.

> **Ministry Essential #8:**
> **The goal is not to move from homosexuality to heterosexuality but from homosexuality to holiness.**

A Balanced Approach

The American Psychiatric Association has embraced an oversimplified and unbalanced position on homosexuality; the church must not overreact by doing the same thing in the opposite direction. If the APA claims that none can change, we must not declare that all are guaranteed the ability to change completely. Christians are not so simplistic and unrealistic about any other human vice, whether sexual, relational, or spiritual. We are given grace for repentance and a change of behavior, but the deeper work that influences our thoughts, longings, and desires is an ongoing process through the grace of God. One thing is clear: those who love Jesus are called to live in sexual fidelity. As is often stated by leaders in Exodus International, "the opposite of homosexuality is not heterosexuality—it's holiness."[39]

Finding Our Way

A few weeks ago, a man approached me, explaining that he grew up with unwanted same-sex attractions. He described his therapy with a secular psychoanalyst who put him into a support group designed to help him accept himself as a homosexual. "But that's not what I wanted," he told me angrily. "The therapist wouldn't listen. I wanted to find someone who would help me overcome these feelings."

The APA encourages its members to respect religious and personal convictions. However, it does not encourage its members to treat homosexuality. A well-trained Christian therapist can bring the best insights the world has to offer, combine them with God's truth, and do her or his best to assure that God's wisdom prevails. Every pastor should know qualified Christian therapists to whom he or she can refer the sexually conflicted. Every church should consider adopting the goal of offering its own counseling services for all kinds of people and needs. Smaller congregations can unite together to offer such services.

For decades, many Christians have taken extreme positions on mental health therapy. Some have avoided professional counselors at all costs. Others have referred everyone with sexual issues to mental health professionals without recognizing the vital contribution to the recovery process that can be provided by their own congregations. Ideally, both worlds can come together. Excellent Christian counseling can be supported by vital church ministries that enable those with same-sex attractions to live in a way that honors God, whether their sexual affinities completely change or not.

When Grace and Truth Meet

What If?

Mel White was once a ghostwriter for prominent evangelical figures, including Billy Graham, Jerry Falwell, and Pat Robertson. Even as he served the evangelical community, Mel struggled quietly with homosexual feelings. Attempting for years to overcome his same-sex attractions, he finally got married. Still, he found no relief. In his book *Stranger at the Gate*, Mel describes his ongoing efforts to gain victory through various forms of therapy and Christian counseling, ranging from focused prayer to shock therapy. Mel believed, based on what he heard from the church, that as long as he had these homosexual desires, he was the worst kind of sinner, deserving God's damnation. What he apparently did not hear from Christians is that we are fellow strugglers on the pathway of sanctification and that many, if not most, of us are likewise limping along as a result of past wounds or secret insecurities. The Christian life is not meant to be lived alone. We should depend on one another and support one another to walk in holiness.

Mel continued to fantasize about other men and fell into an affair. He and his wife concluded that he could not change and that he should be free to live the gay lifestyle. Mel not only lived it; he promoted it through his writings. He became a leader in the influential gay denomination, the Metropolitan Community Church.

In his book, Mel confesses that from his earliest days, he didn't hear a redemptive message from the church:

> I can't recall one sermon on homosexuality in all my early years of church and Sunday school attendance. In fact, I hardly remember anyone, including my loving parents, mentioning sex at all....
>
> Looking back now, I thank God for that silence. Imagine what young gays or lesbians face today in the churches of their childhood with televangelists calling gays "a plague upon the nation"; with pastors and Sunday school teachers calling our love "an abomination" and our feelings "straight from the devil"; with books, films, and videotapes shown in homes and churches viciously caricaturing and defaming gay and lesbian people and even declaring that in the ancient days of Moses "homosexuals were castrated, imprisoned, and executed for their sin," implying, sometimes stating outright, that it should be the same today.
>
> Perhaps silence was a kinder enemy, but I still bear the scars of that terrible silence.[40]

What if Mel had met Christians who understood his plight from the start? What if, while not compromising truth, those around Mel had shown him uncompromised love? What if they told him that he wasn't going to hell because of his inclinations any more than were the rest of us for our sinful tendencies? What if, while proclaiming the power of God to change our lives, believers around Mel had also shown the grace of God as they acknowledged that his struggle might be lifelong, but that obedience is what God demands from each of us in all of our areas of weakness and struggle? We will never know.

What we can be sure of, however, is that we must do a better job of bringing the message of truth and love to those around us today. We must not oversimplify the causes and cures of homosexuality, but we should make the message of salvation through Jesus and the call to holiness as simple and clear as possible. By proclaiming that most who struggle with same-sex attractions can be partially or totally freed from their struggles, we bring a message of hope. And by recognizing that there are some who may never fully overcome their attractions, but that every one of them can live in a God-honoring manner, we speak the truth.

THE GRACE
Sodom Revisited

The Controversy

Grace with Compromised Truth: "The historic Christian viewpoint of the Sodom and Gomorrah account is a perfect example of how homophobia has caused a misinterpretation of the biblical text. Actually, it's not a story about homosexuality at all, but about hospitality customs."

Truth with Compromised Grace: "If you ever had a doubt about God's sure judgment on sodomites today, just read the story of Sodom and Gomorrah—and tremble."

Uniting Truth and Grace as a Basis for Ministry

The inferno that engulfed Sodom and Gomorrah left a charred mark on the line of human history. It is still a glowing memory in the world's mind. Just as the flood of Noah brought a promise that God would not again destroy the world with water, the fire of Sodom was God's guarantee that one day everything will be destroyed by flames.

Judgment is coming.

But grace is already here.

We must look for it.

Undying Grace

I let the sledgehammer crunch into another charred beam, and a whole section of the blackened house frame buckled and crashed into the ground, sending a cloud of charcoal dust into the crisp Colorado mountain air. I leaned on the wooden handle and wiped my brow, unintentionally spreading black soot deeper into my pores.

Looking down at the piles of burnt rubble, something caught my eye. There before me was a small clump of violet flowers sending their charm from between the edge of the forest and the crumbled cinders. During a summer of volunteer service at Young Life's Frontier Ranch, this was one picture that became permanently etched in my mind. As I gazed in wonder at the blossoms, images from the last hour flashed through my mind: a charred family picture, a singed bonnet, broken and melted jewelry, and scorched pieces of furniture—unfortunate remnants from an unknown couple's ruined home, all of which had to be cleared out by our work crew. The contrast was striking, almost impossible, yet so real and true to life. A couple had lost everything they owned. And there on the edge of death's blanket was a beautiful spray of wildflowers, soaking up yesterday's remains for their nourishment and growth.

Grace is like that. The word *grace* means "unmerited favor," "an undeserved gift." No matter how dark life becomes around us and no matter how desperate our lives seem, God steps in to create new life, new hope, new purpose. This is the recurrent story of the Bible and the regular story of every believer in the risen Christ. Pain works for growth, disappointment becomes ministry, brokenness is the path to intimacy with God and each other, and death itself is the gateway to new life.

Noah's flood was the promise of a new start, David's adultery has saved countless a wandering eye, Ananias's and Sapphira's deaths spared early Christians from the notion that God doesn't care about petty sins of the heart, and Peter's disowning of Jesus became an inspiration for every backslidden believer. Adam and Eve's sin was covered with animal hide, signifying that the grace of God is great enough to cover every mistake and shameful deed brought on by the human race. Everyone who comes to God in faith through his Son will avoid the final judgment and be ushered into God's majestic and eternal reign.

In between all of this, we have the story of the fiery destruction of Sodom and Gomorrah. But where is grace in this ancient holocaust of nuclear proportions?

Look.

Right there.

In the midst of the blazing flames and the hellish sulfur.

Looking up at us like a delicate flower.

For all to see.

God's grace.

The judgment on Sodom prefigures the ultimate unleashing of God's fury on our world of sin when every element will be stripped bare so that God might make all things new. We live in a period of grace, between Sodom and the final judgment. Our lives and our churches are meant to demonstrate this grace until God re-creates all things and ushers in an age filled with more joy and goodness than this world can contain.

The Sodom and Gomorrah story was not set up to promote a worldwide condemnation of those who struggle with same-sex attractions, but rather to sound a warning about a whole world of sin concentrated in the lush valley of our human pleasures and raised as a mountainous assault against God. Read the Genesis 19 account again and compare it with other biblical references to the Sodom account, which are referenced below. You will note in these texts that this ancient conflagration of divine wrath against human rebellion is a reminder of the grace we all need because of our

- adultery, lies, and wickedness (Jeremiah 23:14)
- shameless sins of all kinds, which we carry as banners in a parade, inviting our own destruction (Isaiah 3:9)
- arrogance and a lack of compassion, which act as masks for "detestable" acts (Ezekiel 16:48–50)
- indifference and careless living (Luke 17:28–29)
- ungodliness, and "the corrupt desire of the sinful nature" (2 Peter 2:6–7, 10)
- immorality and perversion (Jude 7)

While the above texts allude to homosexuality as one of the sins for which God punished Sodom, the verse in Jude speaks most clearly: "In a similar way, Sodom and Gomorrah and the surrounding towns gave themselves up to sexual immorality and perversion. They serve as an example of those who suffer the punishment of eternal fire."

Sodom was a town filled with a gang-rape mentality and a brutal hatred of God and of all that is decent. It was the sleaziest and most dangerous sections of today's most notorious cities combined into one small town minus everything good. To equate Sodom with every person who struggles with same-sex attraction is unfair; to associate it only with homosexual sin is unbiblical.

People who surrender their unwanted same-sex attractions to the Lord need time and support to fulfill God's plan for their lives. As with each of us, they need love, acceptance, and accountability to grow. As we stand alongside them and support their growth, however, the very factors that fostered same-sex leanings inside of them can blossom and flower into tokens of God's grace.

Sizing Up Judgment

Let us put the story of Sodom and Gomorrah in context. When Abraham and Lot came into Canaan, Lot decided to live in the lush Valley of Siddim, where Sodom and Gomorrah were located. Those who receive their fill of the good things in this world are most apt to ignore God and his exhortations to prepare for the world to come. So it was for many inhabitants in the Valley of Siddim. Evil and sin had grown rampant there, and the residents of Sodom and Gomorrah were in the process of destroying themselves by their own corruptions (Genesis 13:10–13). Lest the cancer in these cities spread over the world, God found it necessary to destroy them (Genesis 19).

Let us make no mistake about it, the Sodom and Gomorrah account is a horrific warning. This story, like the Bible as a whole, is a two-edged sword, with grace and judgment coming together to make a point that will be felt by all. Sodom and Gomorrah is a glaring signal to the rebellious heterosexual and to the unrepentant homosexual. It is a fire of caution to any halfhearted, spiritually lethargic soul, gay or not, who places personal desire and ambition ahead of obedience and surrender to the commands of Christ. Two ancient cities were demolished by a turbulence from heaven as a graphic sign about the judgment of God that will fall not only on a world of wickedness but on a false religion that has taken some portions of the church by stealth and some parts by storm. It is a dreadful thing to fall into the hands of an angry God (Hebrews 10:31).

Jesus warned about those who wear the Christian label but don't live like Jesus: "Why do you call me 'Lord, Lord,' and do not do what I say?" (Luke 6:46). Jesus warned that many self-deceived "Christians" will come before his throne on the day of judgment and wish they had heeded his offer of true salvation, of a personal relationship that leads to a changed life: "Many will say to me on that day, 'Lord, Lord, did we not prophesy in your name, and in your name drive out demons and perform many miracles?' Then I will tell them plainly, 'I never knew you. Away from me, you evildoers!'" (Matthew 7:22–23).

What about Homosexuality?

The many progay writers who contend that the sin for which Sodom was destroyed was not homosexual activity but general sexual lust are both right and wrong. While it is clear that homosexuality is not the *only* sin for which the people of Sodom fell into horrific judgment, there is no reason to doubt that homosexuality is encompassed in the broad biblical category of "sexual immorality and perversion" that Jude 7 describes. A study of comments on the Sodom account by early church fathers and extrabiblical literature accentuates this assertion.[1]

Some authors theorize that the sin for which God judged Sodom was not sexual at all. This line of reasoning is based on the translation of the Hebrew word *yādaᶜ* ("to know").[2] They emphasize that the word is used more than 940 times in the Bible to mean "get acquainted with," and only fifteen times does it specifically refer to sexual intercourse. Thus, they say, the actual reason for God's judgment was that Lot violated ancient Middle Eastern hospitality laws when he entertained guests without the permission of the city's elders. The elders insisted that the guests come out, that they might "know" them. What supporters of this perspective fail to acknowledge, however, is that words in the Bible must be defined by their context. In the very same account, Lot offers the men of Sodom his two daughters, "which have not *known* man" (Genesis 19:8 KJV, italics added). In the parallel passage, the story of the Levite's concubine (Judges 19:22–25), the word *yādaᶜ* is used again in a sense that can only mean sexual intercourse. Considering other instances of the word in Genesis alone, it is only wishful thinking that would change the proper rendering of the word *yādaᶜ* in these contexts to "get acquainted with."[3] As a result, few scholars today, even among progay theologians, support this line of reasoning.[4]

It has been suggested that judgment rained on Sodom because its townspeople attempted violent sex on angelic beings (Genesis 19:5). In support of this notion, some point to Peter's description of "those who follow the corrupt desire of the sinful nature and despise authority. Bold and arrogant, these men are not afraid to slander celestial beings" (2 Peter 2:10). No doubt the attempted homosexual rape of angels was wrong, as would be any forced sex. But there is no indication from the text that this one incident alone elicited God's judgment over two entire cities. It is more likely that gross immorality, selfishness, and sexual perversion joined together to create an environment that, in God's eyes, needed immediate change (Genesis 18:20). It should also be apparent that to seek to justify any one of the sins of Sodom by sheltering it under the rest is to play with fire. We cannot justify our sin with the excuse that another type of sin is worse. God does not want us to justify our wrongdoing but to ask him for the help to change.

Paul tells us:

> Do you not know that the wicked will not inherit the kingdom of God? Do not be deceived: Neither the sexually immoral nor idolaters nor adulterers nor male prostitutes nor homosexual offenders nor thieves nor the greedy nor drunkards nor slanderers nor swindlers will inherit the kingdom of God. And that is what some of you were. But you were washed, you were sanctified, you were justified in the name of the Lord Jesus Christ and by the Spirit of our God.
>
> — *1 Corinthians 6:9–11*

These words from the apostle parallel the account in Genesis 19 with a stark warning of judgment followed by the gracious promise of salvation. It begins with bad news and ends with good news. The bad news is that God's judgment is coming, and we all deserve it. In a sense, we are all living in Sodom. None of us are perfectly righteous; no one is worthy of God's grace and his promised heaven. The good news is that if we turn to him for help, we will find it.

The words Paul uses in this text for "male prostitutes" and "homosexual offenders" describe the passive, more effeminate partner and the aggressive complement. Paul here states that both partners who engage willingly in homoerotic activity are sinning before God. Progay advocate Robin Scroggs argues that the word used here for homosexual offenders, *arsenokoitēs* (found also in 1 Timothy 1:10), refers only to those engaged in homosexual prostitution,[5] implying that homosexual practice in the context of more loving and committed relationships is acceptable.

Dr. David Wright, however, demonstrates that *arsenokoitēs* was most likely derived from the Greek translation of the Levitical holiness code that we already considered (cf. Leviticus 18:22; 20:13) — texts that condemn homosexual practice. This forges a strong and timeless connection between the Old Testament sexual standards and the expectations of God for the church of today.[6] Dr. Robert Gagnon also provides a comprehensive overview of the way *arsenokoitēs* was used in Scripture and extrabiblical literature, leading to the convincing conclusion that Paul coined the term to refer to every kind of homosexual practice.[7]

Our Christian Response

Flip through the Gospels and notice who received the fieriest call to repentance from Jesus. Was it the people caught in the web of sexual sin? Was it those who defrauded others financially? Was it those afflicted with brokenness and disease? No, no, and again, no. The Lord saved his most stinging rebukes for the pride-filled and judgmental Pharisees and teachers of the law.

What right do we, the followers of Jesus, have to hurl condemnation on the sexually, socially, or relationally broken members of our society? There is not one verse in the Bible to support such behavior. Our responsibility is to share the gospel of salvation with everyone. God himself will judge those who refuse to repent and believe.

If We Don't Get It Right

In the book *unChristian*, David Kinnaman and Gabe Lyons reveal the results of an extensive poll by the Barna Group showing that a large segment of our population between ages sixteen and twenty-nine view the Christian church as hypocritical (85 percent), judgmental (87 percent), and antigay (91 percent).[8] Interestingly, 80 percent of Christians agreed with the antigay label. We have a problem here.

Christians need to learn to stand *against* sexual compromise while standing *for* those who are caught in the web of sexual sin. If the best we can do is say that we are "antigay," we will continue to lose our relevance to the world, especially to the younger generations we need to reach. Kinnaman writes, "The antihomosexual perception has now become sort of the Geiger counter of Christians' ability to love and work with people."[9]

My recent series of sermons on homosexuality bothered some people in my congregation. It was too much for them, especially for some of the older generation. I explained to them that the same heart of compassion that allows us to develop ministry for people with unwanted homosexual attractions will strengthen our resolve to help the poor, to overcome racial prejudices, to do innovative youth ministry, and to be more like Christ in responding to a hurting world. I believe that was when many of them began to relax. Or maybe they were simply relieved because my sermon series was finally over!

Some people think that developing ministry to sexually and relationally broken people will cause their congregations to become fractured and fall apart. If done carefully, methodically, and wisely, however, the very process you go through to develop such ministry will make your congregation more dynamic in outreach and growth, and more relevant to the world.

Our Untouchables

Shortly after I took up my first pastorate in Arlington, Virginia, a man wandered into the church kitchen looking for food. His skin was white and peeling; he looked like he had leprosy. He explained that he was suffering with AIDS. Since that time, HIV, the virus that causes AIDS, has continued to spread throughout our country. The disease is treated in our country much like leprosy might be treated in India. As with AIDS sufferers, gays and lesbians are treated by some of us as untouchables in America.

In my travels through much of India, I have climbed over rows of sleeping bodies in train stations and observed masses of humanity taking shelter under bridges. I have recoiled at beggars whose fingers and toes were ravaged by leprosy. Most of these people were part of India's more than 160 million untouchables, or Dalits (*dalit* means "crushed" or "broken to pieces"). They do not have access to the same jobs, temples, or tea stalls that the rest of the nation's society enjoys. Comprising 90 percent of India's poor and 95 percent of their illiterate, the untouchables are in constant fear of being beaten, raped, or paraded naked down public streets to be kept in their place by the Hindu upper caste. Despite India's rapid advances in technology and its constitution's outlawing of discrimination and untouchability, the fifteen-hundred-year-old practice of social stratification is firmly entrenched in Hindu society, especially in rural areas.

Leprosy, also known as Hanson's disease, takes a special toll among India's Dalits due to their difficult and unsanitary living conditions. Despite new advances in medicine, India is home to 60 percent of the new leprosy cases worldwide and to over a thousand leprosy camps. Compassionate ministries, such as the one carried out by Mother Teresa's Sisters of Charity, have fought to eradicate leprosy and to help many in the grip of India's caste system. Nevertheless, even among the Christians in India, remnants of Hindu social stratification remain, and the back of injustice has not been broken.

Many Christians who feel compassion for the untouchables way over there in India have difficulty showing grace and love toward a certain sector of our own society. We remember the poor, the mentally ill, the disabled, the elderly, immigrants, and other neglected and oppressed people in our homeland and feel a tinge of national guilt, or perhaps anger, for the injustices shown to them.

But what about homosexuals? Perhaps part of the reason Hollywood works so hard to portray homosexuality in a positive light is that society marginalized, isolated, and even oppressed gays and lesbians for so many years. The diseases of relationship, soul, and body that may result from homosexuality are often masked by promoters of gay rights as they champion the cry for societal acceptance. Is it possible that some Christians who readily publish facts about the negative consequences of homosexuality actually see gays, lesbians, bisexuals, and transgendered people in much the same light as Hindus see their untouchables? Until followers of Christ learn how to respond to the pain in the gay world with the compassion of the Lord, ministry to homosexuals will remain minimal and inconsequential. Our special concern in this book is not so much focused on the gay activist but on the person who silently suffers with unwanted same-sex attractions and who is looking for help from the church.

When Opportunity Comes Knocking

A gentleman came into my office recently to tell me about his journey. He explained that he had tried for years to find a church that would accept him for who he is—married with children, the holder of a good job, a person who is dedicated and faithful to God, and someone who is seeking freedom from the pull of same-sex attractions. He pinpointed the sense of abandonment he experienced in his younger years to his father giving his attention to the other boys in the family who were into athletics, hunting, and other things his father considered manly. With tears, this gentleman expressed the hunger for a father's love that he has carried in his heart through life, a void he believes can be filled by a church that will simply embrace him. He especially needs Christian men who will understand him and befriend him. Without such support from other men, he said, he will remain overwhelmed by the pull toward quick and easy sexual answers to his pain and continue to teeter on the brink of survival.

With pain in his eyes, he described friends he has in town who are gay, who also are married, and who also suffer silently. Perhaps they, too, thought that marriage would fill the void, the yearning to be a man, the longing for a father's love. These men all need Christian males who will be godly fathers and brothers in Christ to them. Likewise, there are women with unwanted homosexual feelings who need female companions and mentors in the faith.

It doesn't take a professional counselor or a new program to extend kindness to a person with unwanted same-sex attractions. It takes people of the same gender, men for men and women for women, who will become "God with skin on," showing them the same kind of grace God has extended to us.

AIDS: A Burden and Opportunity for All

More than a million people in our country are infected with HIV—somewhere between .3 and .6 percent of our population.[10] The Centers for Disease Control and Infection estimate that approximately 48 percent of those living with HIV were infected through male-to-male sexual contact.[11] With about 1.4 percent of the males in our country identifying themselves as homosexuals, it becomes evident that the incidence of AIDS among American homosexual men is *several hundred* times greater than it is in the heterosexual male population. Based on estimates of epidemiologists, 30 percent of all twenty-year-old homosexual males will be HIV positive or dead of AIDS by the time they are thirty.[12] Rather than hide these truths, we should acknowledge them with broken hearts and join together in acts of kindness through ministries of compassion.

Still, it would be inaccurate and unloving to label AIDS as a gay disease. Because homosexuals comprise a small percentage of the population in the United States, more heterosexuals have AIDS than homosexuals. The disease is sweeping our prisons, and in the southeastern United States, the lower-income African-American population is hardest hit. More than 33 million people are infected with HIV worldwide. In 2007, 68 percent of AIDS-related deaths occurred in sub-Saharan Africa, where promiscuity is rampant and where HIV is spreading like wildfire.

It is unfortunate that some Christians pronounce that AIDS is God's judgment on gays and lesbians. Who are we to speak for God? The more obvious message of God from Scripture is that we reap what we sow and that we all deserve God's judgment. Those who violate God's laws hurt themselves and society, and sexual promiscuity in general has brought a dramatic increase in HIV and many other sexually transmitted diseases into the world's populations. Promiscuous heterosexuals have become the most substantial carriers of HIV worldwide.

Our Windows of Grace

The Sodom and Gomorrah account is about God's judgment. It is also about God's grace. Abraham pleaded with God to spare Sodom. Lot attempted to save some in his family from God's imminent wrath. We must take advantage of opportunities to help people and to tell them about the way of salvation while we can.

Responding to AIDS

In 2002, Kay Warren was seriously disturbed by magazine images of frail African men, women, and orphans who were infected by AIDS. She decided to visit Africa firsthand, and her life was deeply influenced. As described in her book *Dangerous Surrender*, she now travels worldwide and gives special focus to educating and inspiring the American church to get involved in fighting this disease. The wife of Saddleback Church's pastor Rick Warren, she is also mobilizing her own church into action. She encourages churches to

- care for and support the sick.
- encourage people to get tested or actually host or become testing centers.
- recruit volunteers.
- reduce the stigma. When the church says it's not a sin to be sick, it changes the way everybody in the community looks at people who are HIV positive.
- promote God's standards of behavior and ask for behavior change.[13]

We can also help fight AIDS overseas by partnering with African churches and ministry centers. Jim Thomas is the founder and president of Africa Rising. An associate professor of epidemiology and director of the program in public health ethics at the University of North Carolina, Jim stands ready to guide any interested church to partner with leaders in African nations and to help native experts win the battle against the HIV pandemic (learn more at *www.africarising.org*).

Educating Our Youth

We also need to educate our youth about the devastating results of sexual promiscuity. Messages about the consequences of sexual experimentation and of homosexual behavior have been so overshadowed by the political agendas that influence our country that the negative implications are often buried. Government and educational agencies warn our youth about the dangers of smoking and boast about resultant changes in teen behavior because of the warnings. Many youth learn in school and from the media, however, that homosexuality is not only optional but a "cool" alternative.[14] The church has an opportunity and a responsibility to bring a balancing message to today's youth.

A friend of mine who has come out of more than fifteen years in gay culture recently complained, "Even the progay websites and medical experts warn about STDs and the high risk of homosexual behavior. Public health data is no friend to the LGBT movement. They try to blame societal pressure and homophobia for their high suicide and depression rates. But these factors only become worse in environments where acceptance of LGBT identity is the highest." And yet our society acts as though these problems don't exist.

> Ministry Essential #9:
> Where sin abounds,
> God's grace is greater
> still.

Government and school programs today promote "safe sex." But how can any behavior that falls outside of the expressed purpose of God, whether we are talking about same-sex activity or sex between boys and girls, be safe? The potentially damaging effects on body, family, church, and society associated with sexual activity outside of marriage run deeper than perhaps any of us can fully appreciate. Brokenness in marriages, families, and people's lives has left its litter and debris in nearly every home and house of worship. We have gotten into this mess together, and together is the only way we will find a way out—with the help of God.

The Beauty of Grace

The grace God offers us to set us free from the destructive forces of the world is a gift that keeps on giving for those who are willing to receive it. Paul describes it as a package designed to meet every need in our lives—past, present, and future. He writes, "And that is what some of you were. But you were washed, you were sanctified, you were justified in the name of the Lord Jesus Christ and by the Spirit of our God" (1 Corinthians 6:11).

If you have been *washed* (past tense) by embracing Jesus Christ as your Lord and Savior, then you are *justified* (in the present)—your sins are completely forgiven by God. You are also in the process of being *sanctified* (from this point on), being shaped and molded into the very image of God. Step by step, day by day, we become stronger in our walk with God. None of us are perfect (Philippians 3:7–16), but if we humbly lay hold of the promises of God, the process of sanctification will continue in our lives (2 Peter 1:3–11).

Mercy, love, and forgiveness, as revealed in God's plan of redemption, together encompass the overriding theme of Scripture. God's judgment is overcome by his loving mercy. The arrows of his wrath are held back by his hand of grace. As he spared and delivered Lot and his family, he promises to come to the aid of any who call on him for help. God gives to us not what we deserve but what we need.[15] We all need God's redeeming grace!

Back to Colorado

When the charred remains of the burned-out house were finally cleared away, I joined my work crew on the next project—loading a flatbed truck with hay. Once the stacks were piled high, we climbed on top of them, and the truck began rumbling down the highway toward our camp. The largest guy, whom we had nicknamed "Mongo," suddenly yelled. I looked back to see the hay coming apart and Mongo bouncing and then rolling onto the highway. The truck pulled off, and we were grateful that Mongo, tough to the core, stood up, dusted himself off, and limped to the side of the road with bones and head intact, and with a few abrasion wounds to boast about. I realized it could have been me—and that I wasn't so tough. I may not have survived.

Every time I meet a person who suffers from addiction, I realize this could have been me. The person who carries the wounds of past abuse could have been me. By the grace of God I am still "on the wagon," and it is only grace that will keep me there. I want to extend the same grace to everyone I meet, remembering that where sin is abundant, God's grace is more abundant (Romans 5:20).

Where Grace and Truth Unite

Terrence Toon assumed he was born gay.* Firmly committed to
the gay lifestyle for over two decades, he became a gay activist,
organizing conferences that attracted thousands. He was addicted
to drugs and alcohol, and he worked sixteen hours a day to support weekends of binge drinking. When he needed to lay off staff
under his supervision because they were caught drinking at work,
however, he was convicted by his own hypocrisy; he had also
been drinking at work. Just before his fortieth birthday, his soul
was so overwhelmed by sin and shame that he decided to end it
all. His life today is a testimony to the grace of God.

The Power of God's Grace, by Terrence Toon

On a hot summer evening in August 1990, I was ready to die.
It was Sunday, and my weekend had been consumed once again
by alcohol. My regular weekend ritual was to drink until early
Sunday evening and then sober up enough to go to work the next
morning. That particular night I was used up; I was finished. All
I could see were endless years of isolation, loneliness, humiliation,
and despair. That night I was determined to end it once and for
all.

Something intervened. I was prepared to hang myself in my
closet, with the noose already around my neck, when the phone
rang. My mother was calling to "see how I was." It was one thirty
in the morning her time. How could she know to call me; why
would she even think about calling me at such an hour? Perhaps because it's rude to kill yourself right after talking with your
mother, or perhaps because I realized that one person in the world
would miss me if I were dead, or perhaps because I realized that
something supernatural had intervened in that moment, I put the
rope aside and didn't die that night.

Instead, I began a search that spanned a decade—a search for
the supernatural agency that had intervened. I knew it couldn't
be a Christian God. I was a gay man. I had been proudly gay for
twenty years, and I was politically and socially active. I knew how

---

* Terrence Toon serves on the staff of WestGate Church in San Jose, California. You
can contact him at Terrence@westgatechurch.org.

the Christian God felt about queers: "God hates fags"—I'd seen the signs at the parades. So I looked in a lot of different places for this higher power.

Eventually my quest brought me back to the God of the Bible. Christian friends started popping up all over the place. Old friends began professing faith in Christ! I liked what I saw. I was meeting Christians who actually showed me kindness, even though they knew I was gay. They were gracious toward me, yet not apologetic about their faith. I began to check out several churches and started a systematic study of the Bible. Eventually I became convinced of the reliability of the Bible. The central question became: If I believe that the Bible is true, can I accept the claims about Jesus?

On a Saturday night in June 2001, I was alone in my apartment once again. This time I was wrestling with the question of Jesus. Finally, I simply surrendered and asked Jesus to be the Lord of my life. The change was immediate. I was filled with great joy!

My life has been transformed. I ended a thirty-year career in the restaurant industry to work for my church. I returned to school to study theology and Christian leadership. In 2005, I traveled to Vietnam to share the story of Jesus with the people there. As I reviewed the list of people who funded my trip, I realized that 90 percent of my funding came from people I had not known when I became a Christian four years earlier! My life is rich in relationships.

I asked Jesus to be "The Boss," with no expectation that my sexual orientation would change. I believed that I was born gay and that my sexual orientation was unchangeable. I understood from my reading of Scripture that God wanted me to live my life in a different way, and I was prepared to structure my life in a manner pleasing to God.

But as I prayed and read Scripture with new eyes and began fellowshipping with the WestGate Church community, the Holy Spirit began to show me that something else was possible. Involvement in the meetings of a ministry called Transformed Image helped me to see the world through God's eyes. I began to question the inevitability of sexual orientation, and I began to understand that real change was possible. I discovered that healing was available at deeply profound levels of my body, mind, and soul, and over time I was set free from the bondage of a gay sexual orientation. WestGate invited me to serve on the staff of the church, and I became their "designated expert" on same-sex attraction issues for people who desire the freedom I found.

Grateful for the grace God had shown to me through my pastor and Christians who were willing to walk with me on the journey of Christian growth and change, I sought ways to show grace to others. WestGate was involved in ministry to an orphanage in Zimbabwe, Africa. After I attended a local symposium on AIDS, I realized that as nice as it was to love cute AIDS orphans fifteen thousand miles away, I was being called to the more difficult task of loving the neighbor with AIDS next door. I helped our church draft a position statement on sexuality. Without compromising our stance on Scripture, we got involved with the San Francisco AIDS walk—a huge step for a conservative evangelical church to take! This opened the heart of our church members to do something about AIDS in our own community in San Jose. We began involvement with the Living Center, a drop-in facility for people who have AIDS. We helped with food delivery, helped them put in a new heating and air-conditioning system, and brought gifts for Christmas (a group of women manufactured over a hundred scarves). Our fifth grade Sunday school class took up collections of cans to help them purchase a new washer and dryer.

The gay community was perplexed. Why would a conservative church like ours be so gracious and generous toward them? Because of the service and compassion we have shown them, we have earned a voice in their lives and the opportunity to share with them and be Jesus to them.

Looking back at the night when I almost took my life, I am eternally grateful that Jesus gave me more than my life back. I have *eternal life* in him. He also gave me a ministry that is changing lives. I would not be where I am today if Christians had not shown God's grace to me.

Chapter 9

THE POTENTIAL
Life - Changing Power

The Controversy

Grace with Compromised Truth: "Gays and lesbians are born with their sexual orientations and should be given freedom to exercise their gifts in the church through the power of the Holy Spirit."

Truth with Compromised Grace: "Homosexuality is a demonic spirit that needs to be driven out. More churches need deliverance ministries."

Uniting Truth and Grace as a Basis for Ministry

I leaned into the turn and shifted through the gears as my bicycle gained speed. Ducking into the wind, I thought about the Illinois tourist I had just met at the overlook on top of the mountain. A biker himself, he described with a smile of satisfaction how he and his friends skirted the Chicago lakefront when a mighty tailwind placed its hand on their backs and propelled them to speeds of up to—what did he say?—fifty miles per hour. Amazing.

I had grinned right back and explained how, up here in the mountains, we can use the pull of gravity to help us do at least as well. And now I would prove it to myself and to that boastful biker. I had nearly reached fifty miles per hour often at this particular spot, a steep but short-lived downhill straightaway in the mountains of western North Carolina. In fact, I could do better than him. I would *break* the invisible fifty-mile-per-hour barrier.

Releasing the brakes and sliding back on the seat, I pulled my arms and legs tight. The wind tore into my body and pressed into my face. As I dropped into the mountain pass, I was just climbing above fifty miles per hour when my bike began waffling as though both wheels were bent wildly out of shape. I was forced to the left, into the washed-out gravel shoulder. I pummeled through the jagged trough, still going about fifty, with two realizations: (1) I had been forced off the road by a mighty blast of wind; and (2) I was rocketing toward a crossroad that abruptly ended my gravel ditch with a jagged sewer mound that would send me flying.

I had seconds to attempt to pull my bike out of the rut and over the deep asphalt lip that was between my front wheel and safety. But even if I could work against the wind, my tire would likely catch the ridge, with disastrous results. Jerking the front wheel over the berm, I popped back onto the road, pumped the brakes hard, and began to slow. My heart was pounding as the bike coasted smoothly to a stop.

My mind began to work. Never before had I experienced such a mighty blast of wind. If the wind had not stopped as quickly as it had come, I wouldn't have been able to avert a wreck.

Contending with the Wind

Never underestimate the power of the wind. A blast through a mountain pass can propel a biker forward or can push him off of his chosen path. In a funnel, it can lift the roof off of a house. In hurricane fury, it can remove a town from the map. In the Bible, it represents the Spirit of God, who can create the world, reshape the church, and change the course of our lives.

The word for "spirit" is *rûach* in the Hebrew and *pneuma* in the Greek. Both words also mean "wind" or "breath." There are several symbols for the Holy Spirit of God, but *wind* is more than a symbol; it is his defining characteristic, his name. At the creation, the "Spirit of God was hovering over the waters" (Genesis 1:2). God the Father spoke through Christ the Word and moved through his Spirit to make all things (John 1:1–3). This unity of three distinct persons, which we traditionally call the Trinity, is described throughout the Bible. The Father sent the Son, and they together send to us the Spirit, the acting agent who changes our circumstances and our lives. The Holy Spirit is fully God, inseparable in person and purpose from God the Father and the Son.

In Acts 2, the Holy Spirit came with power, "like the blowing of a violent wind" (Acts 2:2). The same Spirit who gave birth to the church is able to renew it and change it today. In the book *Like a Mighty Wind*, Mel Tari describes how the Spirit of God blew through Indonesia in the early 1970s with demonstrations of supernatural power, changing the complexion of the church and sweeping great numbers into the kingdom of God. Stanley Mooneyham, then vice president of international relations for the Billy

Graham Evangelistic Association, is quoted as saying, "What the Holy Spirit is doing in Indonesia today is more like another chapter added to the book of Acts than anything else. The Indonesia Bible Society, which tries to chart the results, has found it impossible to keep up with the statistics. Churches in Central Java, for example, which reported 30,000 members in 1961, now number more than 100,000 — almost doubling annually."[1]

Last week, at a lunch with fellow pastors, one pastor described his experience in 1970 as a student at Asbury Seminary. He saw the wind of the Holy Spirit blast through a typical Christian campus and turn everything upside down, soon affecting campuses around the country. About the Asbury revival, Billy Graham wrote, "The unusual revival which came to Asbury College early in 1970 and spread to scores of campuses across America is evidence that God is still at work in his world, lifting men and women out of self-centeredness, secularism, and boredom."[2]

God continues to move with great reviving power in many parts of the world. Sectors of Asia, Africa, and South America are bursting with the renewing work of God. Even portions of the Western world that seem to have been overtaken by spiritual lethargy are experiencing spiritual awakening.[3]

The Wind and the Word

Great revivals through history were sparked and sustained through conviction about the truth of God's Word.[4] From King Josiah's discovery and proclamation of Scripture to Jonathan Edwards's preaching about the mysteries of God, great awakenings occur when Scripture comes to life. The same Spirit of God who inspired prophets and apostles to write Scripture also inspires people through it. When individuals, churches, and even whole cities become stirred up to obey God through emotionalism alone, the embers of enthusiasm are easily quenched. Revivals based on the solid foundation of God's character as revealed in Scripture, however, run much deeper and longer than mere emotionalism. They are the very breath of God, blasting forth like a crosswind to knock the church back on course with heaven's priorities.

The Need for Personal Revival

We should all hope and pray for a massive sweeping of God's Spirit and truth across the world to awaken the church and to accelerate God's mission. This is, in fact, happening in select portions of nearly every continent. Most of us wish to see a mighty move of God in our own churches, but do we understand that it must begin with us?

Gipsy Smith, a British evangelist in the late 1800s, was asked why God used him so powerfully to stir up people and whole churches for God. He replied, "Go home, lock yourself in your room, kneel down in the middle of your floor. Draw a chalk mark all around yourself, and ask God to start the revival inside that chalk mark. When he has answered your prayer, the revival will be on."[5] How true. When we become awakened to the realities in God's Word through the power of God's Spirit, God can use us to touch a few others, who may influence yet more people, until renewal begins in our churches.

A mission leader who influenced my life greatly when I was in college, Bill Pencille, said, "We can experience personal revival every day." He also showed us how. Daily he guided me and a summer mission team in Columbia, South America, to spend time in God's Word. He taught us how to study the Scriptures prayerfully and devotionally. I took that experience home with me and applied it day after day. It changed my life. A daily study of Scripture can become the source of change and renewal for anyone's life.

D. L. Moody once said, "If prayer is how we speak to God, Scripture is how God speaks to us." The question is: Are we listening? Through daily insights from God's Word, we can purify our thoughts and intentions and confirm that our lives are on track with the Lord (Hebrews 4:12). James described Scripture as a mirror that shows us our spiritual condition (James 1:22–25). We wouldn't think about running out into our busy day without first looking into a mirror to be sure our hair is neat and our faces are clean. How much more important it is to be spiritually fit before launching into each day.

Why Scripture Matters

Years ago, a church member came to my office, upset that our congregation didn't support the ordination of practicing homosexuals. I sent him home with some reading material that demonstrated clearly the biblical perspective. Two weeks later, he returned, unconvinced. When I reminded him that our church was seeking to follow the clear teachings of Scripture on this matter, he responded, "I don't care what the Scriptures say."

We *should* care. Jesus warned the wayward religious leaders in his day that the Scriptures themselves would stand in judgment against them on the day of reckoning and that they were foolish to ignore them (John 12:47–50). Those who claim to be Christians and who teach others to violate clear precepts of Scripture should think about the implications of Jesus' words. If his statement is accurate, our destinies depend on obedience to Scripture. If Jesus' words are not true, neither is Christianity. We have no basis for our faith.

Inspiration and Faith

Paul wrote, "All Scripture is God-breathed and is useful for teaching, rebuking, correcting and training in righteousness, so that the man of God may be thoroughly equipped for every good work" (2 Timothy 3:16–17). The Greek word for *inspiration, theopneustos,* is here translated "God-breathed." The classic understanding is that God worked through the unique personalities and circumstances of the more than forty biblical authors to create his Word. Much like a ghostwriter, God superintended the composition of "all Scripture." The Greek words *pasa graphē* literally mean "everything that was written." Paul is claiming that one can trust the Bible, as a whole and in all of its parts, as given to us by the hand of God. But do we really believe it?

For the centuries preceding the eighteenth-century Enlightenment, people regarded the Bible as the very Word of God. When confidence in human logic and ability tipped the scales, human reason began to dominate God's revelation. Over time, the notion that the Bible could be analyzed and scrutinized, based on its historical context, caused many theologians to accept the perspective that perhaps the Bible had little or no divine authority.

While I was a student at Princeton Seminary, I approached one of my biblical studies professors in the quiet of his office, asking why the textbooks we used and the reading list he provided were so one-sided toward what I considered a low view of inspiration. He explained that he used to take the simplistic approach toward the Bible that I did but that his higher education in Germany had changed his perspective.

After graduation, I began traveling to seminaries across America and in other countries, speaking in chapels and classrooms and forming missionary fellowships. Usually spending several days at a school, I experienced the spiritual climate in each and saw firsthand what the seminaries were teaching future pastors about the inspiration and authority of Scripture, and how it might influence the direction of these schools, of their graduates, and eventually of their respective denominations. In the course of a single decade, as I observed indicators of a downward drift in some of the institutions' positions on biblical authority and inspiration as seen in the classes offered and the teaching approaches taken by key professors.

Charles Ryrie makes this interesting observation:

> Not many years ago all one had to say to affirm his belief in the full inspiration of the Bible was that he believed it was "the Word of God." Then it became necessary to add "the inspired Word of God." Later he had to include "the verbally, inspired Word of God." Then to mean the same thing he had to say "the plenary (fully), verbally, inspired Word of God." Then came the necessity to say "the plenary, verbally, infallible, inspired Word of God." Today one has to say "the plenary, verbally, infallible, inspired, and inerrant-in-the-original-manuscripts Word of God." And even then, he may not communicate clearly![6]

Regardless of the words we use to define our view of the Scriptures, it is clear that an increasing number of Christians are treating the Bible as a book of inspired opinions rather than as the inspired Word of God. The anchor that has held the church from drifting in the sea of relativity has come loose. Not believing the Bible to be a guiding light, many in the baby boomer generation did not teach it to their children. Not knowing the Bible, many of the boomers' children, our upcoming crop of leaders, lack strong convictions about the moral standards that have long guided God's people.

Why You Can Trust the Scripture

We can trust that the Bible is the very word of God. Jesus taught that every truth in Scripture is important (Matthew 5:18) and that the entire Bible bears witness to him (John 5:39, 47). As the one who fulfilled Old Testament prophecies (Mark 8:31; Luke 24:27), Jesus depended on Scripture as the basis for his teachings and logic (Mark 12:24–26). Our Lord taught that "the Scripture cannot be broken" (John 10:35). The word *broken* means a loosening of its binding force of authority. Jesus believed that the whole Bible has the stamp of God's divine authorship on it. This authority is supported by the wealth of evidence in archaeology, the statistical impossibility of fulfilled prophecy, the reliable process of manuscript transmission, the historical evidence supporting Jesus' resurrection, and the miracle of changed lives through history. A plethora of books are available to explore these and related topics in depth so that any searching mind can be satisfied about the trustworthiness of God's Word.[7]

The Common Drift

Throughout the Bible, we are reminded of the importance of knowing Scripture, meditating on it, teaching it, and being careful to follow its truths (Joshua 1:8–9). When we fail to keep it alive in our minds and hearts, we can lose God's blessing and drift from his purpose (Psalm 1). The drift that has occurred in our country is rather dramatic.

For years I have spent time with Christians who support the gay agenda and have questioned and listened to them, seeking to discern how they have come to their conclusions. In general, either they grew up with homosexual inclinations or they have a gay or lesbian family member or friend who believes he or she was born that way. Many of them originally believed the Scriptures clearly teach that same-sex activity is wrong. Still, they struggled. How could a loving God label something as wrong that a person couldn't change? Eventually, they learned about gay "Christian" theology. At that point, everything seemed to click into place. It settled well with them, based on their experience, and hope or compassion moved them to give their homosexual loved one the benefit of the doubt. Furthermore, the alternative of a mean or hateful approach to gays and lesbians adopted by church and society was clearly not acceptable.

But there is a better alternative. A person can embrace Scripture as being trustworthy in its whole and parts, as did Jesus, and can love those who do not so trust God's Word. I am thankful for the great number of Christians who avoid both the extremes of condoning and of condemning homosexuals and who show the compassion of Jesus toward people who feel conflicted about their sexuality. They typically have friends who have come out of a homosexual lifestyle and who are living victoriously in the Lord; they may also have friends or family members who identify themselves as gay or lesbian and are praying for them to come to a place of salvation and freedom through Christ. They hold to the orthodox, plain meaning of Scripture on sexuality.

Bringing Scripture to Life

Peter wrote, "But know this first of all, that no prophecy of Scripture is a matter of one's own interpretation, for no prophecy was ever made by an act of human will, but men moved by the Holy Spirit spoke from God" (2 Peter 1:20–21 NASB).

In this context, *prophecy of Scripture* refers to the speaking and creating of the Bible. The Scriptures were given to us through human instruments by the means of the Holy Spirit, as Jesus promised. A word picture to describe the Greek word for *moved* is that of a sailboat sitting quietly on a placid lake, unmoved. Suddenly the wind picks up, the boat's sails fill out, and passengers grab the side rails as the vessel begins bouncing across the frothy waves.

The same Spirit that moved to create the world created God's Word. He is available also to teach the Bible to us and to make it real for our lives (John 14:26). I recall the day I received Jesus Christ as my Savior at age seven. Finding the tattered

> **Ministry Essential #10:**
> With God, nothing is impossible and no one is unreachable.

paperback Bible that I had hidden under my mattress, I opened it up to read, and it was as though, for the first time, someone had turned on a light. The words jumped out at me. They were personal. I wept as God spoke to me by the Holy Spirit. No longer was this just another book. It was my meeting place with God, a channel through which the Lord spoke to me directly.

Before attending Princeton Seminary, I visited my pastor, the late Dr. Richard Halverson, for advice. I was concerned about protecting my relationship with God in this new environment, in which the Bible was treated more like a textbook to be analyzed than a revelation to be obeyed. He described to me the day early in his seminary journey when he knelt before the open Bible and said, "Holy Spirit, be my teacher and guide." His relationship with God and his trust in the authority of God's Word thus remained intact. The same has been the case for me, and I hope for you as well.

When Love and Truth Unite

Meleah Allard

Meleah Allard is a personal friend whose life was changed when the Spirit of God moved powerfully in her life, calling her to put aside lesbianism and to live for God's glory. Her story is a testimony to the difference between knowing the truth and being moved by the Holy Spirit to obey the truth.

I'm a pastor's daughter, and I asked Jesus to be my Savior when I was nine years old. As a child I loved attending church, singing in the choir, and being part of my youth group. I even went on a mission trip at age fourteen. Daddy joined the Navy at seventeen and served our country before his call into ministry. Throughout childhood, I learned valuable things from my parents. Daddy's generosity is legendary. He often picked up hitchhikers, and they'd leave his car with the gospel and my daddy's coat. He's a prayer warrior. I saw him on his knees countless times throughout childhood. I know his faithful prayers for ten years are what brought the deliverance given to me by God.

My mother taught me perseverance—to hang in and not give up. I watched her do it for years—especially related to her husband. Mother said Daddy was either the best husband and father in the world or the worst nightmare. He was a rage-aholic, totally controlled by his inability to manage his anger. When he would lose his temper, he'd become verbally and physically abusive to my mother, my sisters, and me. One name I remember being called

---

* Meleah is the founder and director of Truth WNC (www.truthministry.org). She and her husband, Mark, and two of their four children reside in Hendersonville, North Carolina. She can be reached at mallard@truthministry.org.

often was "the devil's prostitute." *Words have power!* Mother was usually discouraged and depressed. There wasn't much physical affection, either between my parents or toward us girls. I remember hearing the words "I love you" only a few times in my life. One of those is a vivid memory of lying in a hospital bed at the age of fifteen after I'd attempted suicide with two bottles of pills. Thankfully God had other plans for me.

Compounding these serious family problems was the abuse I suffered at school. I was a gangly girl, extremely tall for my age and terribly thin, with a long, crooked nose. Through most of my formative years, I was berated with names like Beanpole, Telephone Pole, Ski Slope, and Witch's Nose. I became interested in boys at a young age. Mother called me a "boy chaser." In reality I was a love chaser. I was desperately seeking love and affection. Boys took advantage of that weakness. I became pregnant at fifteen after having sex for the first time and was abandoned by the father of my baby. My parents supported me and helped to raise my daughter so I could graduate, but I made a serious turn at that point. I had begged God for years to change my messed-up family. I knew he could. I knew he was all-powerful, but he wasn't changing anything. There was also my church family. They weren't blatantly ugly, but I remember the looks of disdain and whispers as I walked by. The message came through loud and clear: I was the scarlet-letter girl and had been demoted from the preacher's kid on the front row to the prodigal on the back pew. I was mad, and I blamed God. My understanding of God was immature. I hadn't studied the Word or lived enough to really know him. I'd heard all about his wrath, justice, and holiness but little of his love, grace, and mercy. I only saw God as I saw people, hard to please and angry with me. I remember saying, "OK, God, if this is what you have to offer, I don't need you." At that point I chose the path of a rebel, a prodigal.

The Wrong Pathway

When I was eighteen, my daughter and I moved to Florida, where some of my friends lived. They invited me to a gay bar for the first time. Although apprehensive, I was curious, so I went. The experience was surreal and unlike anything I had ever experienced.

One of the things that drew me in was how totally accepted I felt. I didn't feel judged for my past, and people were interested in *me*. In a short time, they began to feel like my family. It also wasn't long before I was pursued by a woman. I'd never had that kind of attention before. I don't know how else to explain it other than that I just fell. That's how sin is, a deep, dark pit that we fall into when we walk too close to the edge of it. It wasn't about sex. I was desperately seeking love, affection, and acceptance, and I was buying Satan's lie about how to attain it.

After moving home to Hendersonville, I found in Asheville a large gay community. I became entrenched in it quickly, and before long they felt like family. Soon after, I met and began a relationship with a woman. She and I lived and raised my daughter together for eight years. I felt what I thought was love. It sure was powerful. It had such a grip on me, but during the last few years my discontent grew. I was like a drug addict, but the drug wasn't effective. I'd tried everything (drugs, alcohol, people, places, and things), but I was still in pain. I remember lying on my couch late one night. I was crying and staring at the ceiling. I said out loud, "I know this is wrong, but I love her and I can't leave. Please, God," I begged, "change my feelings so I can leave." I can hear his response as plainly today as I did that night. He said, "Leave, and I'll change your feelings." That was not the answer I was seeking.

The Spirit Uses the Church

It was another two years before I left. During this time I lost my job and was sacked out on the couch eating chocolate and Cheetos and watching Oprah. She interviewed an author. (I later discovered the author was a leader in the New Age movement.) Shortly thereafter, I read her book. I kept reading the name Jesus in it. They do talk about Jesus but not truthfully. It didn't matter because every time I read his name, it pricked my heart. Our great God can even use Oprah Winfrey and a New Age author to reach his wayward child. Not much later, I gave my daughter a birthday party for her tenth birthday. Some of the girls had made fun of her for having two moms. Believe it or not, it was the first time I realized how my choices were hurting my child. It was as if the blinders had come off and I could finally see. It also occurred to me she might not be a Christian. I hadn't taken her to church or taught her the truth. I made plans to visit a church. My girlfriend stayed home cooking dinner while we attended services. Interestingly, just a few weeks earlier, someone had invited me to church. I remembered they had told me it was a great place for kids. Never underestimate the power of inviting someone to church.

And never underestimate the power of the Holy Spirit to move in a church service. We went to a large Baptist church that Sunday, and it was the warmest, friendliest place I'd ever been to. They didn't have fake smiles. They exuded the joy of the Lord. Within a few minutes of arriving, people were hugging us. We were strangers, but they treated us like long-lost relatives returning home. The music was vibrant and moving. They were singing praise and worship songs I had never heard before. These folks were worshiping, uninhibited and unashamed. The presence of God was so real in that place. The well within me began to be filled. As I sang those worship songs, tears streamed down my face. I knew what I would do. Then through the pastor, the God of the universe spoke directly to me that day. It was a message about God's love, mercy, and grace.

At the end of the service, I ran down the aisle and asked Jesus to be the Lord of my life. It wasn't surreal — it was *so real*. I knew what other decision I was making. There was no way I could stay in the sinful relationship; God's Spirit was pushing me out of my old way of life and onto a new path. In that moment, the love I experienced from *him* overshadowed all other love, even my love for her. After that church service, my girlfriend and I spent the next three days crying together. She tried to talk me out of leaving. I tried to witness to her, but she couldn't hear me through her own pain. She eventually gave up and left. It was very hard. She'd been my best friend for eight years.

The Spirit Uses Words

That was in 1992, after having lived as a gay woman for almost ten years. Since then, God's Spirit and God's people in the church have helped me to grow in my faith and in obedience to his will. In 2003, we began a support ministry for families dealing with gay-identified loved ones, and then a group for men and women wanting to overcome same-sex attractions. Today it is a full-time job. God allows me the awesome blessing of sharing how he redeemed my life to individuals as I counsel them, to families as I help them learn to love their broken family member, and to the church in equipping them to minister grace and truth. God has blessed me with a husband, and with him I have experienced true covenant love. God has blessed me with three wonderful sons and two beautiful granddaughters, from my lovely "born again" daughter.

If you think my story is unique, you would be incorrect. I meet hundreds of people just like me at the Exodus conference every year. Many of them are preachers' kids and deacons' kids with testimonies very similar to mine. God is doing a work in this area. People are being set free. The church is being equipped. If God will do it for us, he will do it for others because he is no respecter of persons. They just have to be willing. Yes, people struggling with homosexuality need the truth, but they don't care how much you know until they *know* how much you *care*. The Christian counselor at my church has no idea how much her words of encouragement conveyed her care when one day she called me a prodigy. Words have power. *The Spirit is powerful.* I don't feel like a prodigy, but I *know* I'm not the devil's prostitute or a prodigal anymore either! I'm a better *P* word today — my heavenly Father calls me *his* princess. I'm starting to believe it!

Part 3

ACTION: BUILDING MINISTRY

Foundation: What Every Church Needs

Structure: Your Unique Ministry

Chapter 10

BLUEPRINT
Six Ministry Spheres

> I told them how the hand of my God had been favorable to me and also about the king's words which he had spoken to me. Then they said, "Let us arise and build." So they put their hands to the good work.
> — *Nehemiah 2:18 NASB*

I recently listened to the testimony of a man from New York City who had invested his life in gay culture for sixteen years until he ran into an emotional dead end. The social scene had lost its glamour, and the excitement had waned. He told me, "I didn't come close to finding the stable gay relationship I had wanted." Frustrated, he sought help and support through a local church and began living faithfully for the Lord. He has since found a new, deeper, settled joy through Christian fellowship and service. As he described the experiences he has had with churches through the years, I was struck by his words. "Even today," he said, "when I walk into a church, I can discern right away whether or not it's a safe place."

How do we make our congregations "safe" places for people who have experienced sexual and relational brokenness? Like Nehemiah, the Old Testament governor of Israel, we need to build walls.

The Construction Crew

It was several hundred years before the birth of Jesus. Jerusalem, the capital of the once-powerful Jewish empire, had been destroyed in 586 BC by the Babylonians. Thanks to the leadership of Judah's governor, Zerubbabel, and later a scribe named Ezra, a rebuilt temple stood proudly in the center of the ruined city. But the city had no walls, and God's house of worship was unprotected. Yet, by the grace of God, the temple was still standing, shivering under its exposure to the elements for ninety years.

Nehemiah arrived on the scene with a vision and a plan and, with the help of God, rallied the people. For more than 150 years the walls had been down. Many people had talked about constructing them, but it was Nehemiah who turned the people's dreams into reality. Together they created a protective hedge around Jerusalem in just fifty-two days.

The Walls We Need Today

Walls provide security. In the day of Nehemiah, a city without walls was susceptible to attack. In our day, a church without walls is not a safe place either. A church leadership team may have a hundred wonderful program ideas and a fat bankroll to finance them, but if there are breaches in their protective walls, ministry for those struggling with unwanted same-sex attractions will not grow. Walls, in this context, represent the commitment of a congregation to protect those who come into their midst. A church with protective walls is one that receives each visitor with the embrace of God's love and seeks to help him or her know Christ and grow strong in faith and faithfulness. Such a church protects those laden with guilt and shame by showing love and proclaiming grace. It also corrects the confused and ill informed by proclaiming truth.

Such walls are not constructed simply by stacking stones and slopping on mortar. Nehemiah involved all of the people in a carefully laid-out process. Each family worked on the wall in front of their own house. If we hope to engage our churches in a mission that will change lives and make a positive impact on our communities, we can learn a lot from this great leader.

Six Ministry Areas

Over a year ago, as I was preaching a sermon series from the book of Nehemiah, I was also researching ministries for the sexually broken. I was struck by the parallels between Nehemiah's success and churches that have been effective in building ministries. Six themes in Nehemiah's strategy were part of the unfolding work of God in each of these churches. Focusing on these six areas will enable you, not only to better support and help people who struggle with sexual brokenness, but to improve ministry and outreach in nearly every sector of your congregation's life.

The six areas, summarized by people's inner drives and their corresponding external focus are:

Inner Reality	**Outer Focus**
1. Motivation	Prayer
2. Vision	Leadership
3. Healing	Family values
4. Growth	Mentors and counselors
5. Support	Small group ministry
6. Celebration	Outreach

Jerusalem's walls were not meant to isolate its residents but to give them unity and strength that they might bless the nations around them (Isaiah 62:6–7). In the same way, the above sectors should enlarge our ministries rather than contain them. It can be helpful to visualize these areas of ministry as *spheres*. With prayer at the center of all that we do, the spheres are like walls being built out, one layer at a time—old walls giving way to new as the ministry expands.

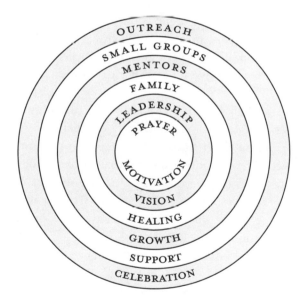

It is important to notice that these spheres are:

- *organic*, describing vital sectors of ministry that should already be part of every healthy church; the goal is to strengthen and sharpen each ministry sphere.

- *interdependent*, building on each other while also working together; to improve ministry in any one area will benefit the rest.
- *broad in scope*, overlaying in general terms unique and specific God-given opportunities in your congregation; the details are up to you and the Lord.

Most churches are stronger in one or two of the ministry spheres than they are in the others. A church leadership team will be wise to recognize and celebrate their strengths while seeking ways to shore up their weaknesses. Interestingly, ministry for sexual brokenness often begins in congregations through their areas of natural strength. Some churches birth their outreach through prayer, others through the vision of the leaders, and still others through their counseling or mentoring ministries, and so forth. As you follow Nehemiah's story and read the brief summaries that follow, consider which spheres represent strengths in your congregation and which need further development.

Sphere 1: Motivation/Prayer

Nehemiah was a man of prayer. As recorded in Nehemiah 1, he bathed his concerns in prayer, fasting, and mourning before the Lord. He meant business with God. He focused his requests on the King of the universe before approaching Artaxerxes, the great monarch over Persia. He recognized that his access to the God of heaven was a greater privilege than his direct access, as cupbearer, to the most powerful earthly ruler of his day. God honors such faith.

We see in Nehemiah 4 and 6 that Nehemiah's campaign to rebuild Jerusalem's walls was fraught with resistance and conflict, and we see how that opposition pushed him closer to God. Any significant ministry for the Lord will likely be met with opposition from spiritual powers in the heavenly places (Ephesians 6:11–12). This is not a reason to give up, but rather to follow Nehemiah's example, to look up and cry out to God for wisdom, strength, and victory. Nine different times we see this bold servant of the Lord bending his heart in supplication (1:4–11; 2:4; 4:4; 5:19; 6:9, 14; 13:14, 22, 29). Even the final sentence of the book of Nehemiah is a prayer: "Remember me with favor, O my God" (13:31). Let this serve as a reminder to us that when we establish ministry for the sexually conflicted, addicted, and dejected, we must bathe our work in prayer from beginning to end.

Nothing can be more important to the ministry of your church family than prayer. Through conversation with God, you will receive guidance about the right thing to do and the right way to do it. Even when you don't know God's will, if you have bathed your hopes in prayer, you can trust in

God to guide you and to accomplish his purpose. Prayer not only lays the foundation of ministry; it creates a roof of protection as ministry grows.

How serious is your church about the ministry of prayer? Do you have a prayer ministry or group that includes ministry to the sexually broken in its prayer focus?

Sphere 2: Vision/Leadership

Nehemiah brought his vision directly to the leaders who could do something about it—first the king, then the nobles in Jerusalem. He also prayerfully explored his options and waited for the right time to move into action. He spent three days in Jerusalem surveying the city and contemplating his approach. Then, under the cover of night, he examined the broken-down walls more carefully to discern the extent of the need. Still he "said nothing to the Jews or the priests or nobles or officials or any others who would be doing the work" (2:16).

If you have received a burden from God to help your church develop ministry for those who struggle with sexual brokenness, first survey your situation. Where are the walls of God's protection breached in your congregation? What are the barriers to developing and sustaining ministry in your context? What are your church's natural points of connection with those who are sexually broken? If you were asked to suggest an initial plan that could stir the leaders of your church and engage your whole congregation over time, what might it look like?

Ministry is motivated by a compelling vision based on true need. Nehemiah got right to the point. He told his leadership team, "You see the trouble we are in: Jerusalem lies in ruins, and its gates have been burned with fire. Come, let us rebuild the wall of Jerusalem, and we will no longer be in disgrace" (2:17). They replied, "Let us start rebuilding," and they got to work (2:18).

Ministry will only go as far as the leaders of your church are willing to take it. Be wise, patient, and persistent as you educate your leaders about this ministry. Nehemiah went back to the nobles again and again to muster their support with each new phase of the construction project.

Are your leaders united and captivated by a godly vision for your church? Does that vision incorporate ministry for people who struggle with sexual and relational brokenness?

Sphere 3: Healing/Family Values

Families are the backbone of the church, and they must be protected. It would not be an exaggeration to say that most of the spiritual drift in Western society during this past generation could have been abated if families had maintained true Christian values such as honesty, transparency, unity, and love. Conversely, when local congregations function as healthy families, they are able to aid the restoration process for our marriages, our children, and our extended family relationships.

Nehemiah called his people to work as a united team by engaging family units for specific tasks. Families often took portions of the walls that were "in front of" or "beside" their own homes (3:23). Similarly today, ministries related to sexual brokenness involve reuniting family units and helping our churches reflect more fully the love and unity and mutual support one would expect from Christian communities. Together we are the family of God. We must help our local congregations reclaim this spirit, that they might become havens of healing.

Do the people of your church love each other like a true family? Is your church a place of healing for its own families and visitors?

Sphere 4: Growth/Mentors and Counselors

Mentors and counselors are the coaches and specialists in ministries of discipleship for recovering homosexuals. In Nehemiah's time, the expertise of the masons and construction workers was essential to the functioning of each team at points along the wall's assembly line. And after the walls were complete, ongoing guidance was needed to strengthen the souls of the people. In Nehemiah 8, for example, we find Ezra the scribe reading God's Word to the masses with a team of priests serving as interpreters and counselors to help the people understand and apply the message (8:1 – 8). So today we should avail ourselves of resource people both inside and outside our congregations to facilitate spiritual growth and faithfulness in people seeking recovery from addictions, sexual brokenness, and same-sex attractions.

One does not need extensive training or expertise to fill an informal mentoring role. Most people who come to a church looking for help regarding same-sex attractions do not want to be singled out as different, but rather to develop healthy friendships with those of the same sex. Anyone with a heart of love has the potential to meet this need.

Solid biblically based counseling is also important. Most Christians who are seeking help in overcoming unwanted same-sex attractions or sexual addictions would be wise to engage in Christian counseling to speed the healing process.

Does your church offer mentoring for people with same-sex attractions and related issues? Does your congregation have a counselor or options for counselor referrals?

Sphere 5: Support/Small Group Ministry

Nehemiah recognized the wisdom of establishing small group ministry teams to rebuild Jerusalem's walls (chapter 3). One of the most consistent strategies employed by churches that engage in ministry to the sexually broken is that of support and therapy groups. Some congregations have developed numerous focus groups designed to concentrate on addictions, divorce recovery, unwanted attractions, sexual brokenness, and other life-dominating issues.

Such groups may be defined by age and gender, as well as by area of concern. All kinds of people need all kinds of support groups.

Never before in history has such a vast supply of books and discipleship materials been available to help Christians glean wisdom for ministry in recovery groups. Through the use of literature and audiovisual resources, any small group can invite the nation's experts into their shared conversation. In addition, the list of available speakers and mentors who specialize in this arena is expanding each year. Many of these specialists are willing to help churches develop their own support groups and mentoring ministries.

Traditional small groups for fellowship, Bible study, and prayer can also be channels of God's purpose for this ministry. If these groups are guided to use materials that build family values, they will more readily come together with a common vision. Nehemiah successfully involved nearly everyone in the rebuilding process. He assigned forty-one parties to rebuild forty-two sections of the wall and the ten city gates. From nobles to common laborers, everyone was expected to participate. Teams formed around areas of giftedness. The high priest himself and his "fellow priests" were the first to put their hands to the work as positive role models, reminding the people that everyone was expected to participate (3:1). The leadership didn't settle for a small group gathering here and there for the few in Jerusalem who showed the first spark of interest. Instead, they expected everyone to build the walls through the venue of small groups. Chapter 15 in this book offers a proven strategy to help our congregations do the same.

Does your congregation have one or more support groups for the sexually confused, addicted, or abused?

Sphere 6: Celebration/Outreach

Once the Jews had their walls erected and understood God's purpose for their lives, their joy could not be contained inside the walls of the city. Gathering in their handmade booths to celebrate the Feast of Tabernacles, "their joy was very great" (8:17). Following the seven-day feast, they had an assembly during which they freely confessed their sins to the Lord and to each other (chapters 9–10), and they brought new residents into the now-fortified city (chapter 11). The community of faith was experiencing a spiritual renewal that overflowed into spiritual and practical blessings to the world around them.

When churches become healthy enough to minister to the sexually conflicted and broken, their ministries rarely remain within the four walls of their buildings. Chapter 16 provides ministry samples to demonstrate that outreach is the natural outflow of a church brimming with the living water of our Lord. Christlike outreach to your community may attract visitors and potential new members and will bring glory to God.

Has your congregation taken such ownership of ministry for people with unwanted same-sex attraction that its ministry naturally spills out into the community?

Ministry Samples

The following chapters include experiences from churches around the country and world that are growing in these six ministry spheres. When I first began calling these congregations to interview their pastors and ministry leaders, I informed them that I was looking for "ministry models." The nearly universal response was "I don't see our church as a model." Each one explained that ministry is messy and that their ministries were by no means ideal. Contemplating my own weaknesses and challenges in ministry, I understood immediately. Each person and each church I contacted were real-to-life, just like those in the Bible. If the protagonists in the Bible were demigod-like archetypes of strength, their examples would diminish our hope of joining their ranks. Instead, evidences of their humanity show through their cloaks of salvation as doubts, temptations, and weaknesses. This is what makes them useful to us. They were not perfect. They stumbled and fell, got hurt and bled. If God was able to use them, he can use us.

These ministry samples encompass a wide variety of churches as evidence that ministry for people struggling with their sexuality can be established or improved in your congregation as well. These examples include not only the best, the biggest, and the most spectacular church programs; they also include the smaller congregations that illumine our land like the vast array of stars glimmering through the canopy of a night sky. The combined brilliance of these small churches brightens the landscape of our sin-darkened culture. Every congregation matters, regardless of size, location, or denominational affiliation. Together our churches can shape the future of our society.

> Ministry Tips: Look for ministry tips at the end of each of the following seven chapters, and discern which are most helpful for your church family.

Looking Back, Looking Ahead

The challenge we all face is to allow ministry to unfold in our churches in a manner that is unique to our own contexts. As you analyze the status and potential in your church in the course of the following pages, celebrate your congregation's strengths. If you are in a large church, your people may have the muscle, money, and management expertise to create unique programs that surpass what I describe in the following pages. If your church is small, capitalize on the familial warmth, the simplicity, and the built-in accountability you can create more easily in your church than can people in larger congregations. And regardless of your church's size, don't neglect any of the spheres. Remember also that any church can develop support and outreach to the sexually broken, but those that give special attention to the first three spheres are best able to sustain it.

MOTIVATION
Prayer

> I tell you that if two of you on earth agree about anything you ask for, it will be done for you by my Father in heaven. For where two or three come together in my name, there am I with them.
>
> —*Matthew 18:19–20*

The Village Church is nestled in the Lower West Side of Manhattan's Greenwich Village. This primarily residential area, located below 14th Street and west of Broadway, has been home to the creative, the rebellious, and the bohemian for over a hundred years. "The Village" fostered many famous writers and artists, including Henry James, Edgar Allan Poe, Mark Twain, and Walt Whitman. The Beat Generation began there. Before rent hikes sent many starving artists looking for new digs, the likes of Bob Dylan, Dylan Thomas, and Jack Kerouac once roamed the Village's tree-lined streets.

Greenwich Village is the birthplace of the gay rights movement that began in 1969 on Christopher Street, across Seventh Avenue, in a historic clash in front of the Stonewall Bar. The gay rights parade commemorating that event now shuts down the lower half of the city as an annual reminder that the Village is a capital for gay culture.

In November 2002, Sam Andreades accepted a call to pastor The Village Church, which is affiliated with the Presbyterian Church in America (PCA). If an expert on the development of posthomosexual ministries was told to survey the thousands of Christian congregations in New York City at that time, he might have chosen The Village Church as one of the least likely to establish ministries for those struggling with same-sex attractions. With only a hundred members, this congregation didn't have much interest in influencing the culture around them; they also lacked the financial and staffing resources of many of the larger churches. But they did have a praying pastor.

For more than six years, Sam quietly asked the Lord to enable their congregation to become a place that offers a redemptive response to people who have unwanted same-sex attractions. God led him to preach gently and thoughtfully on the values that would undergird such a vision, and he began training his leadership team. People seeking God's wisdom and help related to their sexual identities began coming to him for counsel and support. God then brought the necessary leadership to facilitate The Village Church's first support group for this ministry.

Before launching this group, Sam got the endorsement of his leadership team and congregation. Without any major disruption to the life of the church, not only was the support group established, but the ministry continued to grow, steadily and solidly. It was birthed in prayer. The Village Church is currently the only congregation in New York City that is affiliated with the Exodus International church network.[1] When brokenhearted parents search for support for their children who have run off to this dense metropolis to experience gay culture, they often search this network on the Exodus website. The Village Church receives approximately two calls a week with such referrals. When pastors and churches in the Big Apple are looking for advice on how to help people with unwanted same-sex attractions, they often call The Village Church.

The Burden of Prayer

Both small and great works of God can nearly always be traced to a burden for prayer. Nehemiah carried a burden in prayer. Before taking action about the needs in Jerusalem, he "sat down and wept." He wrote, "For some days I mourned and fasted and prayed before the God of heaven" (Nehemiah 1:4).

Young Welsh coal miner Evan Roberts wrote in his journal, "For ten or eleven years I have prayed for revival." He carried this burden of prayer until God lifted it in the fall of 1904 and cast it over Wales to sow a spiritual awakening. Thousands of people were converted, and society was changed. Historians tell us that society was so affected by the Welsh Revival that judges soon had no cases to try. The policemen, when asked what they did with their time after the spiritual awakening, said, "We have three men's quartets. If any church wants a quartet, they simply call the police station." The Welch Revival swept through Great Britain and reached into Scandinavia, Germany, Australia, Africa, India, Canada, the United States, and parts of South America. Breakthroughs in ministry often begin with a burden from on high.

I was recently pulled aside at a conference by a woman who carried a burden of prayer for a prominent gay musician and for the church he attended. As she poured out her heart to me, I said, "I don't know how I can help you, but one thing is obvious. God has given you a burden to pray for this individual and the church he attends. Count it a joy and responsibility to pray until the burden is lifted. God is at work."

United Prayer

The Bible emphasizes the importance of united prayer. In the Old Testament, where victory in warfare depended on God's protection and power, one person could put a thousand enemies to flight, but two could "put ten thousand to flight" (Deuteronomy 32:30). We can be sure that Nehemiah wasn't the only one praying for the restoration of Jerusalem. His brother Hanani and other men from Judah brought to him the report and burden of a city without walls (Nehemiah 1:1–3). He and a few key men carried the vision for repairing the walls into the city, and everything changed (2:11–12). Jesus described the great efficacy of united prayer (Matthew 18:19–20). In the New Testament, where victory is in the spiritual realms, the prayers of one can be used greatly, but the prayers of two or three united intercessors can be used mightily. Let us at least begin with two.

Prayer Partners

Throughout my Christian life, I have nearly always had a prayer partner. I remember once when I had been laboring alone in prayer for several weeks but could not overcome nearly a dozen major challenges in my ministry. Finally, my prayer partner and friend joined me for a time of united intercession. I once again lifted my concerns to God, one by one. Within minutes my burdens were lifted, and within days each concern was resolved. That was a dramatic illustration of a general principle that should guide our lives and ministries: *we need each other.* Perhaps Jesus gave us the promise of increased power in prayer when we unite with a few others to encourage us to act according to what we really are—"the body of Christ" (Ephesians 4:12). He calls us to live the Christian faith together. A natural first step in obedience to this principle is to find a prayer partner. A comrade in the ministry of prayer can provide consistency and strength for our daily lives and challenges.

Intercessory Prayer Groups

We sometimes make the mistake of thinking that prayer is always better when our prayer meetings are bigger. But agreement and focus in prayer are more important than size. A laser beam and a lightbulb both emit photons. The laser, however, is focused. A lightbulb can warm your hand, but a laser beam can bore through steel. The focused prayer of a few in the book of Acts lit a fire that spread throughout the Roman Empire and eventually engulfed the world (Acts 1:12–14; 2:1–2).

A few years ago, I was praying over my city with other pastors in our ministerial association. As we lifted up to God our local community, school system, government, churches, and nearly every facet of our society, I became convicted by the Spirit that I had been neglecting prayer with and for my own congregation. God helped me to see my need to gather a small team of intercessors who would stand with me in confidentiality and confidence as we lifted up to God the people, problems, and needs in my own church. I realized that it was hypocritical for me to labor hard in church work without first praying for God to accomplish his will in each aspect of the ministry.

Within several weeks, I found a few people who felt a sense of call to be on such a prayer team. We have been meeting ever since, and this is probably the most important meeting of my week. Like Moses, whose hands were held heavenward with the help of Aaron and Hur as his people engaged in battle with the Amalekites (Exodus 17:8–13), I needed the help of other intercessors if my congregation was to succeed in its frontline battles for the Lord. Someone once described prayer as "our weakness leaning on God's omnipotence." I attribute every ministry success to prayer, including our efforts to help the sexually conflicted. If your church does not have such a group, form one. Remember that ministry to the sexually and relationally broken is a spiritual battle requiring God's protection and power, which are released through united prayer.

Expanding Your Prayer Ministry

God may lead you to create a prayer ministry for your church, which could include:

- a prayer chain for passing on immediate requests through phone or email networks
- prayer gatherings and retreats for your church leadership team
- a sermon series, Sunday school class, or special programs on prayer
- a prayer watch through which people sign up for time slots to pray, enabling intercession to cover a span of time[2]

Prayer Therapy

Prayer not only changes the atmosphere of a church; it also changes individuals. Francis MacNutt, whose ministry emphasizes the healing power of God through prayer, writes:

The most important thing to realize is that God can transform the wounds of our past when we pray for inner healing. This is an extraordinary secret that some Christians have discovered but that most have never even heard about. Sadder yet, the leaders of most churches — bishops, district superintendents, moderators, and the like — have not, for the most part, ever heard about the power of inner-healing prayer to transform our deepest wounds, the pains that shape our lives without our even knowing it.[3]

MacNutt recognizes the complexities that shape a person with same-sex attractions but does not shy away from the solutions that can be found through prayer. Leanne Payne has also had a powerful ministry of healing people's inner brokenness through prayer. She does not look for instant answers but uses both group and private prayer to help people surrender their lives to God in the deepest realms. Prayer is a vital tool in the Christian counselor's toolbox and a basic ingredient in recovery groups for all kinds of human need.

A Dynamic Prayer Ministry

It was the early 1990s. The Reverend John Yates, pastor of The Falls Church, an Anglican congregation in Falls Church, Virginia, was burdened by God for a ministry of healing to be established in his congregation. John describes the Sunday that he preached on the healing power of the Holy Spirit, and then he handed his burden to the congregation, saying, "Friends, the need for God's healing power is absolutely real. But I don't know how to lead you into it. If we're going to become a healing church, it's up to you."

In response to John's challenge, people began writing, calling, and visiting the pastor to ask what they could do. Soon a group began praying and dreaming about the possibilities. The spiritual logjam broke open, and the Spirit of God began to create new possibilities. Ministry teams were trained. Appointments for those needing prayer were scheduled. Now, more than a decade later, John reflects, "It blows my mind that we have these prayer ministry teams scheduling appointments and praying over people for hours. They've done so much more than a busy pastoral staff ever could have accomplished."

> **Ministry Tip #1: Prayer is essential from beginning to end for ministry to people with sexual brokenness.**

Having drawn insights from prayer ministries around the country, The Falls Church currently has about a hundred prayer leaders who engage in teams to meet the needs of their church and of those who visit. The teams are available after each worship service and throughout the week, whether a person wants to receive healing prayer for a half hour a week, an hour a month, or much more. For those who need deep healing, the team offers intensive individual prayer, typically consisting of six two-hour sessions. Ongoing training for new ministry team members is provided through informal mentoring and a twenty-six-week class.

The Reverend Kathleen Christopher, who directs the prayer ministry, was herself touched and healed powerfully through the prayers of others. When I asked her whether people with issues of sexual brokenness have been helped through this ministry, she said, "God does amazing things through these prayer sessions. Often the change is gradual, and people don't experience the change until after the prayer times. First the temptations diminish. Then they have more strength to focus on what is good. Eventually they are attracted to the opposite sex. We may not hear the results from some of them for a year or more. We also refer them to ministries such as Regeneration. We believe counseling is important too, and we encourage people to find counselors who will support the prayer-healing process."

God Answers Prayer

When I began preaching from the book of Nehemiah during the last quarter of 2008, our country was slipping into a deep recession. Challenging our people to pray for the fifty-two days of our sermon series, I reminded them that this was the amount of time it took God's people to erect walls around

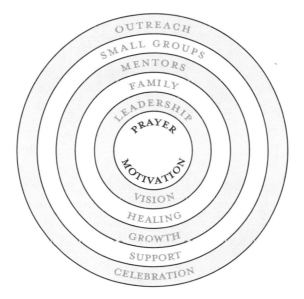

Jerusalem. One of the prayer goals we adopted for this two-month span was financial—we wanted to end the year in the black. When our fifty-two days ended and as the year closed out, I was unnerved to learn that we had a significant shortfall and that the books were closed. That night, however, a large check came in from someone who knew nothing of our need, putting the church in the black by $105. What amazed me most at the time was my lack of faith and my accompanying surprise when God answered the prayers of his people once again.

The same God who enabled God's people to build the walls of Jerusalem in Nehemiah's day is standing by and ready to assist our ministry efforts. *But we must pray.*

Looking Back, Looking Forward

All ministry is difficult, but ministry to people who are conflicted sexually is one of the most difficult. Spiritual resistance, societal confusion, interpersonal conflicts, and personal wounds face the person who seeks to establish ministry in this arena. To engage in such ministry without prayer would be as foolish as visiting the North Pole without protective clothing.

Chapter 12

VISION
Leadership

> When a woman who had lived a sinful life in that town learned that Jesus
> was eating at the Pharisee's house, she brought an alabaster jar of perfume,
> and as she stood behind him at his feet weeping, she began to wet his feet
> with her tears. Then she wiped them with her hair, kissed them and poured
> perfume on them.
>
> When the Pharisee who had invited him saw this, he said to himself, "If
> this man were a prophet, he would know who is touching him and what kind
> of woman she is—that she is a sinner."
>
> *—Luke 7:37–39*

Jesus was reclining at the dinner table with a Pharisee named Simon and his
guests. Consider what it may have been like as a surprise guest wandered in
from the street and hesitated at the edge of the courtyard where the meal
was being served. The text implies that she was a prostitute, leaving our
imaginations to fill in the blanks about her history and character. But for
Simon, no extenuating circumstance could excuse her abrupt and socially
unacceptable interruption of his dinner party. He was a Pharisee, a well-
respected religious leader in the local synagogue, a teacher of the truth, a
man who followed the standards of the Jewish oral and written law with great
care. For him, to look at any woman in public could be construed as sinful.
But to have this notorious sinner *in his house* was downright offensive. Jesus,
however, had a point to make. And he would teach by his own example.

Preaching Isn't Enough

When we talk about Christian leadership, Jesus Christ, whose name we carry,
sets all the standards. Going against the norms of his day and aware of the
talk that would follow, Jesus invited a social outcast, who likely had fallen
into sexual sin, into his life and ministry. That was not a coincidence, an

afterthought, or a regrettable blunder. Jesus broke with social convention to advance his kingdom. Through his example, the Lord calls us to allow social outcasts to join us in our work and worship.

Let us look at the world around us and ponder. If Jesus behaved in this radical manner in his day, how would he direct ministry in our day and in our culture? Would he make a special effort to involve those the church tends most quickly to reject? If so, which classes or groups of people would he engage?

One Sunday morning, a homeless person came through our sanctuary doors and meandered down the center of the aisle in the middle of our worship service. He approached the chancel steps as everyone looked on in shock. He stood at the base of the pulpit and waited for the hymn to end. It was awkward, and nobody approached him. I moved from the chair behind the pulpit, came down the steps, and whispered in his ear, asking him what he wanted. He explained with alcohol-laden breath that he would like to sing a solo.

Stunned, I recalled the text in James that I would be preaching on the following Sunday:

> My brothers, as believers in our glorious Lord Jesus Christ, don't show favoritism. Suppose a man comes into your meeting wearing a gold ring and fine clothes, and a poor man in shabby clothes also comes in. If you show special attention to the man wearing fine clothes and say, "Here's a good seat for you," but say to the poor man, "You stand there" or "Sit on the floor by my feet," have you not discriminated among yourselves and become judges with evil thoughts?
>
> —*James 2:1–4*

I led him to the worship leader's chair, and the two of us sat next to the pulpit in sight of the congregation. If any seat was considered "honorable" in the church, he was now in it. I didn't need to say a word to remind him to remain seated. His sense of privilege held him high and straight in his chair, and the perplexed eyes of the congregation buckled him down.

After the benediction, I invited him to follow me down the aisle. At the back of the church, he complained, in slurred speech, that he hadn't yet sung his solo. I explained that he would need to come back sober and then we'd talk about it further. Besides, he had done more than sing; he had already preached next Sunday's message.

To this day, church members still talk about the incident with the unexpected guest, but probably not one of them recalls the following week's sermon about homelessness. Honestly, they probably don't remember many of my sermons. But they will always remember my stumbling effort to show hospitality to a street person. Nor do they remember my sermons about ministering to the sick, but they will not forget when I visited them in the hospital—or when I neglected them in their time of need. My words are forgotten, week after week, but my actions make an impact that lasts—for good or for bad.

Actions Speak

Jesus' words carried authority because of his integrity. He lived what he taught, and his actions gave weight to his voice. He fulfilled a principle that applies to each of us: people are influenced by the way we live.

In a *Harvard Business Review* article titled "Personal Histories: Leaders Remember the Moments and People That Shaped Them," prominent leaders in business, education, and the arts were asked to describe the person, experience, or writing that taught them most about effective leadership. The conclusion of those interviewed, from Disney's Michael Eisner to General Electric's Jack Welch, was clear and direct: leadership is about showing, not telling; about setting a right example, not describing it.[1] This holds true for all kinds of leaders.

If leaders in your church show love and compassion to all kinds of people with all kinds of needs, their gracious spirit will permeate the whole church. Christlike convictions lead to biblical actions. By living in Christ's way, leaders open the way for the Lord to revolutionize their congregations. Our ministries need not be showpieces for the world to see, but if we are really "Christian" churches, people should see Jesus in us.

When I first began building ministry in my church for the sexually broken, word leaked out to the community. I live in a small town in a county with about a hundred thousand people. We offered training for our church leaders, hosted a community support group for parents of children with same-sex attractions, and confirmed that we had good counseling available. I preached sermons, hosted a conference for our area on the topic, and was interviewed by our local paper. Soon the letters to the editor began flying, and I began emotionally dodging verbal swings of public opinion from the right and the left. One person's editorial comment knocked me right back to center with a humorous mention of all the letters to the editor and fuss over such a ministry, since "we don't have enough homosexuals in town to float a raft."

Because of demographics, many congregations around the country, such as mine, may never develop booming ministries to homosexuals like the ones I have been studying in certain larger metropolitan congregations. But I can tell you from experience that lives of local pastors, parents, and children in the community and in my own congregation have already been touched, and this makes it abundantly worthwhile. I believe every congregation can be guided to live out the implications of the gospel toward the sexually and relationally broken. Once churches begin doing so, other ministries and outreaches in their congregations may be enhanced as well.

How Leaders Are Motivated

In his book *The 21 Irrefutable Laws of Leadership*, John Maxwell describes the "Law of the Lid." The concept is that a leader's effectiveness can only rise as high as his or her vision and ability. If a leader's vision and skill level don't grow, neither will his or her influence. Leaders will either lead the way or get in the way of progress.

How does a church leadership team move from inaction to action? They must be motivated. Motivation comes through vision built on godly values. The values a church leadership team owns today will shape their ministry for tomorrow. Values are the foundation for every vision and ministry of your church. Transparency, grace, truth, humility, and the like are the basis for developing healthy and vital congregations. If it takes months or even years for your leaders to embrace these values, it will be time well spent. When a ministry fails, people are reluctant to try it again. If a leadership team will build its vision and action steps on the sure footing of clear biblical values, however, the team will be motivated to keep the ministry going and improving over the long haul.

GOALS AND ACTION STEPS

VISION

VALUES

If all of this sounds like work, it is. Do not attempt to build a ministry for
people with unwanted same-sex attractions without obtaining the blessing
of church leaders. You must build such ministry *through* your leaders rather
than *around* them. If the leadership team is united, your congregation can be
as well.

Sizing Up Your Congregation

If you are a pastor, you have probably attended enough seminars related
to church ministry, growth, and health to make your head spin. You have
undoubtedly returned to your church over and over, conference notebook
in hand, and found that while ideas are a dime a dozen, insights for effective
implementation are invaluable. What is often lacking in such seminars is a
plan for making the concepts work in your situation.

Each church is unique, and yours is no exception. If the last sentence made
you think twice, so should any book or seminar that offers a one-size-fits-all
approach to ministry. Your church has an exclusive *history* that will influence its future, distinctive *demographics* that factor into its growth, a unique
theological bent that plays into its ministry focus, a one-of-a-kind *community*
that shapes its outreach, and a specific *denominational affiliation* that guides its
worship and government.

An often-overlooked factor that makes ministry unique in your congregation is the *size* of your church. Fifty-nine percent of congregations in the
United States have fewer than 100 members, 94 percent have fewer than 500
members, and less than 3 percent have over 1,000 attending their churches.
Most pastors are in small congregations; however, most *people* are impacted
by larger churches. Fifty percent of churchgoers attend the largest 10 percent
of congregations, those with attendance of 350 or more.[2] In other words, pastors of larger churches are caring for approximately half of the regular church
attendees in our country.

In the booklet *Sizing Up a Congregation for New Member Ministry*, Arlin
Rothauge discusses how the size of a church influences the pastor's approach
to ministry.[3] Her insights have provoked articles and books on the subject
that are worth considering for the development of ministries to the sexually
broken. She recognizes four general types of churches, based on active membership. As you study the four church-size models below, consider where your
church fits in. Does your leadership style fit with the size of your church? If
your church is growing or downsizing, are you prepared to adjust with the
trend? And, most specific to this book, notice how your approach to the
spheres of ministry may vary based on your congregation's average worship
attendance.

The Family Church — Fewer Than 50 Active Members

In congregations of this size, authority and decision-making power often rest in key patriarchs or matriarchs more than in the pastor. Like a family, this church has parental figures who call the shots when the pressure is on. Because smaller churches typically cannot afford a full-time pastor, many fresh seminary graduates use these congregations as stepping-stones to larger churches. As a result, key lay leaders find themselves holding the family together during times of transition until the next inexperienced pastor comes along with a new set of ideas and a new bag of tricks. The longer a pastor remains in a family-size congregation, the more authority will potentially shift to that pastor.

I once preached a sermon about sexual brokenness while I was a temporary pastor for a church of this size, and I soon met with "the powers that be." If there was any question about who considered himself a patriarch in the church family, all it took was one edgy sermon to find him visiting my home. He let me know, without mincing words, that I needed to stick with the straight and narrow or look elsewhere for my employment. He didn't wait to call a meeting of the elders, nor did he dig through a notebook of church policies on hiring and firing. He saw himself as the head of the family, period.

Pastoral leadership and the ministry spheres. Authority in a church family of any size is not always neatly contained in the persons who are given titles such as pastor, elder, or deacon. Authority may be informally granted by the congregation based on a person's history of service, faithfulness of character, connections and relationships, strength of personality, wisdom and insight, and (I hate to mention these last two) family name and financial clout. The smaller a congregation, the more these untitled authority figures become a reality. They exist in every size congregation, however, and if you are new to a congregation, you are wise to discern who carries authority in your church and how best to work with them to help them grow spiritually and become a part of your leadership team if needed.

If you are ministering in a family-size church, you will likely find that the six spheres of ministry will not develop much further than the powerbrokers in your church. You will also find the lines between the spheres to be blurred. All will tend to grow together or not at all. Still, give primary focus to the first three spheres. If your church has natural propensities and strengths related to one or more of the outer spheres, make that your next area of focus.

The Pastoral Church — 50 to 150 Active Members

The pastoral-size congregation depends heavily on the pastor for visitation, teaching, counsel, leadership, and everything everywhere always. The church is still small enough for everyone to know each other, but it is too large for a

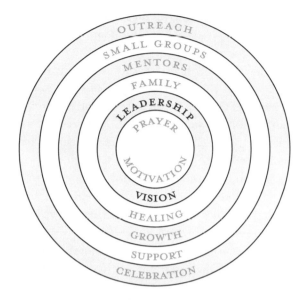

matriarch or patriarch to lead it. A small leadership team typically guides this size church with the pastor and under the pastor's authority. Pastors with strong interpersonal skills may do well in a congregation of this size. If the church continues to grow, however, the pastor may burn out physically, emotionally, and spiritually if he or she doesn't learn to build programs and to delegate responsibility.

Pastoral leadership and the ministry spheres. Leadership in a church of this size requires a balance between caring for God's people and building programs for the people — although caring for the people must win out. When the church experiences significant growth or shrinkage, the role of the pastor may shift toward spending more time with the people (as it shrinks) or toward building more excellent programs (as it grows).

If your congregation is of the pastoral size and ethos, the demarcation between the spheres will be more pronounced than in the family-size church, and your focus will tend toward the first three. You may find it natural to develop a prayer ministry, leadership vision, and family care system for those with unwanted same-sex attractions. Mentoring and counseling, support groups, and outreach, however, may be more seasonal and difficult to maintain unless your congregation matures significantly in a unified vision and commitment to ministry for this unique audience. Partner with other churches and interdenominational postgay ministries in your community as needed.

The Program Church — 150 to 350 Active Members

Once a church reaches 150 active members, it is generally necessary for the pastor to give more emphasis to programs than to the people. A church of this size functions best with a pastor who thrives on group goal setting, congregational consensus building, and lay leadership training and delegation. The parishioners can expect the pastor to make hospital calls but may not see him or her in their kitchens around a pot of coffee. The success and growth of a church this size depends largely on the effective building of all kinds of programs.

I pastored a church of this size for seven years and remember once looking at all the programs of our church and thinking, I feel like a plate-spinning performer on the stage of the church, receiving alternating cheers and frowns depending on whether all of the plates are safely spinning on their narrow bases of support. At times, I wanted to cancel every one of the programs. Then I would look around and recognize how essential each program was to the health of the church. Once again I would begin the cycle of training more leaders and delegating more responsibilities.

Pastoral leadership and the ministry spheres. We must not measure the success of our church ministry by the programs we have but by the health of our people. Programs must be flexible, expendable, and focused on the spiritual growth of our members and on reaching others for the Lord. If you are in a program-size church, you will most likely find the lines between the ministry spheres to be well differentiated as they work themselves out in the life of your congregation. You may find each sphere to be important, and each dependent on the others. Unless your circumstances dictate otherwise, consider following the spheres sequentially to develop a holistic ministry for the sexually conflicted.

The Corporate Church — 350 or More Active Members

In a church of this size, the pastor puts most of his or her energy into creating an experience of excellence in the worship service and into managing a large church staff. He cannot be expected to do all of the visitation or to know each member by name. The abundant resources that come with a church of this size create expectations for excellence in programming and ministry options for the church members. The senior pastor, therefore, must be a keen administrator, a gifted preacher, a skilled manager, an encourager of people, and, above all, a leader with a passion and vision that is captivating.

The strength of the corporate-size church is that a host of excellent resources make possible a plethora of quality programs for the congregation and community. The weakness is that people can easily become anonymous and hide in the system for years with little accountability toward spiritual growth.

The pastor and leadership team in a corporate-size church should recognize their opportunity and responsibility to guard the life of the other churches in their community. Larger churches can unintentionally suck the life and existence out of smaller congregations, much like a new Lowe's may put the mom-and-pop hardware stores out of business. Alternately, they can bless smaller congregations by assisting and supporting them in ministry.

When I was in a program-size church, one of the corporate-size congregations in the area was drawing away my members. To keep me from having an attitude of resentment toward the pastor of that congregation, I took him out to lunch, and we became good friends. Now in a larger congregation, I'm involved in bringing pastors together in the community to build mutual support and foster strength in each church. Rather than hosting our own community outreach programs, for example, we often work with the other churches in town to cohost seminars. When we find new programs that work in our church, we seek to help smaller congregations implement them in their churches as well. This approach is especially needed in ministries related to homosexuality, because resources and knowledge in this area of specialty tend to be scarce.

Pastoral leadership and the ministry spheres. If you are in a corporate church, the lines of demarcation between the spheres are very clear, and you can easily build programs for any of the spheres. It is all too easy in a large congregation to become satisfied with programs that are not actually changing the lives of people. Do not neglect the first three spheres, for they are the foundation of the rest. Without prayer, strong leadership training, and the promotion of family values in your church, the other programs may become empty shells, devoid of life-giving power. I advise large congregations to discern their natural areas of strength and excel in them, while ensuring that the other spheres are not neglected.

Size and Success Are Not Synonymous

I intentionally address all sizes of congregations in this book. The corporate church can develop what might be classified as "flagship ministries" in the sight of church growth gurus. But in the sight of God, the *outworking of each church's natural strength* is what matters. When a teenager with a frame and aptitude for cross-country running feels he is less of a man if he doesn't play linebacker on the high school football team, his problem isn't his size. He needs to find a new scale on which to weigh success.

God provides all types and sizes of churches to meet the needs of all kinds of people. Each church model is important, and God gifts pastors to serve in the congregations to which they are called, whether for a season or for decades. The American corporate measurement of bigger programs and budgets as a measurement of accomplishment has captivated the hearts of too many pastors, and it can lead to idolatry. The Lord is more concerned about quality in our ministries than quantity, about fruitfulness in our outreach than showiness, and about bringing honor to his Son than about bringing honor to any particular church.

Training Your Leadership Team

If you are the pastor, or if you are working with the pastor, how can you strengthen vision for this ministry focus in your church leadership team? Let me suggest four possibilities. I encourage you to begin with one and eventually incorporate all four, not necessarily in this order:

- Bring in a guest speaker. Please see *www.exodusinternational.org* for possibilities.
- Bring your leaders to an Exodus-affiliated conference or a similar event.
- Have your leaders read this book and guide them through the discussion questions in the back, either during your regular meetings or at a weekend retreat.
- Use the leadership training resources referenced in the back of the book. See also *www.ChurchReflections.com* for a complete leadership training packet.

A Word to the Pastor

When I took my first long-term pastoral position, I nearly split my congregation more than once as I pushed programs and policies too firmly or rigidly. Now, years down the road, I lead my local ministerial association and observe younger pastors making the same mistakes. Several times I have watched pastors divide their churches and deeply damage their ministries because they weren't willing to keep the health of the church a priority above innovative concepts, their people above programs, and individuals above the latest new ideas. Nothing should be more important in your first few years at a church than loving your people and building trust with them. Beyond those early years, your responsibility to nurture and shepherd them should remain a top priority. If you are too far ahead of the flock, you may lose their trust. You are no longer a leader if you have lost your followers.

A Positive Example

Bob Stith had been the pastor of Carroll Baptist Church in Southlake, Texas, for twenty-five years and knew very little about homosexuality. As Bob spent time in prayer, God gave him compassion for the broken and marginalized people in his community—the homeless, drug addicts, mothers with unwanted pregnancies, and alcoholics. He preached, prayed, and worked with his congregation over many years until they, too, were moved with the compassion of Christ, and new ministries began to develop.

One day someone asked Bob, "If someone heard you preach about homo-sexuality, would they come to you for help?" He pondered the question and realized that anything he said publicly about homosexuality would probably cause gays and lesbians to keep a wide distance from the church. This led him to question how he managed to show such compassion for nearly every other human condition, but not for homosexuality. Wanting to learn more, he attended an Exodus conference in 1995. Within months, he was invited to serve on the board of Living Hope Ministries in Arlington, Texas, whose mission is "to proclaim God's truth as we journey with those seeking sexual and relational wholeness through a more intimate relationship with Jesus Christ." Bob resisted, explaining that he knew very little about homosexual-ity. He was told, "Bob, you don't know how much it will mean to the men if you will just come alongside them and be their friends."

Bob decided to try out the board position as he continued to pastor his congregation. The members of Carroll Baptist were already committed to the values that make a church welcoming and caring and full of grace and truth. It was not a great leap to learn with Bob about homosexuality and to embrace this new ministry concern. Bob continued to pastor and to serve Living Hope Ministries for another twelve years. He is one of the many examples of pastors who have guided their congregations gracefully and wisely to live out the grace and truth of Jesus Christ in all aspects of church ministry.

In 2007, Bob completed his thirty-second year at Car-roll Baptist Church and was called to serve as the national

> **Ministry Tip #2:**
> **Change occurs through church leaders who demonstrate and teach godly values in a congregation.**

strategist for gender issues with the Southern Baptist Convention. He has a special interest in equipping pastors, church leaders, and entire congregations to develop biblical understanding and compassion for people with unwanted same-sex attractions. Bob seeks to teach other pastors to emulate Jesus, who stepped into Simon the Pharisee's house and demonstrated compassion to an unwanted visitor.

Looking Back, Looking Forward

Your congregation can rise no higher in its expression of compassion and ministry to the sexually broken than does your church's leadership team.

Every ministry of your church should be initiated through appointed leader-ship—how much more is this true for ministry to the sexually and relation-ally broken, one of the most difficult of all ministries. Better to move slowly together than to move too quickly and fall apart. It has taken decades for our churches and our country to become so confused and conflicted about homosexuality; we cannot correct the problem in a day. We must be patient and gentle as we instill godly values and vision in the hearts and minds of our people.

Chapter 13

HEALING

Family Values

For this reason I kneel before the Father, from whom his whole family in heaven and on earth derives its name.

—Ephesians 3:14–15

"Pastor, my daughter is gay, and she's planning to marry her partner. She's asked me to go to the wedding. What should I do?"

"There are some deeper issues than whether or not you attend the wedding," I replied. "Tell me more about her."

This dear woman described her heartbreaking struggle with her lesbian daughter, which had continued for nearly twenty years. She had tried preaching to her daughter, praying for her, cajoling her, yelling at her, listening to her, and being patient with her. One thing she never did was give up on her. How could she? This was her own daughter. Now the mother was facing a tough decision. How could she continue to show her daughter that she loved her without affirming a leap in the wrong direction? And how does a church support members who desperately need support as they strive to show grace and speak truth to their loved ones? Solutions are found in churches that learn to function as families.

The Church as Family

Jesus told his followers they were part of a family that knit them together with ties stronger than blood (Matthew 5:23–24; 12:48–50; 19:29). His disciples in turn described the church as a family (1 Timothy 5:1–2; 2 Timothy 1:2–5; Hebrews 12:7–10; 1 Peter 4:17; 1 John 3:1; Jude 1). We must remember that Jesus and his disciples were referring to the ancient Middle Eastern model of family, not to family in the modern Western context.

One of my brothers married into a Greek family. Even though his wife's parents and siblings do not all live in the same town, they constantly talk to each other on the phone or through their computers and support each other through thick and thin. If they were in the same town, they would validate the experiences in the humorous movie *My Big Fat Greek Wedding.* In biblical times, families were not only confined to the same town but typically lived under one small roof with the chickens and goats. When the Bible describes the church as a family, it means we are close to each other — *really close.*

When I have Sundays off, I enjoy visiting other churches with my wife and children. Even as a pastor, it feels awkward to walk into a house of worship for the first time. I look around as I slip into the sanctuary, hoping the people will receive us well. I don't want to be ignored, but I also don't want to become a public spectacle. I want to be included as part of the family. Technically, every brother and sister, parent or child, grandparent or grandchild in the faith is already part of my family. We are kin under the fatherhood of God (Matthew 12:46 – 50).

Churches that understand they are true family in Christ become homes where people with same-sex attractions feel welcomed and loved. Perfection is not required for acceptance in such congregations. The light of God's love and holiness is brought forth in such a manner that people find hope, healing, and accountability to grow. Heterosexual sin as well as homosexual sin is confronted with humility and grace, and even visitors know they are accepted with all of their weaknesses as part of this caring family.

Kristin Tremba is the director of OneByOne, a ministry designed to help churches in the Reformed tradition become places of healing for the sexually broken. Her commitment to building family values in Christian congregations has been an inspiration to me. I recently joined the OneByOne advisory board and immediately realized I had joined a new family. She and her ministry team are transparent with one another, dependent on one another, laugh with and at one another, and support one another through the challenges of life and ministry. They have given their lives to each other. They are family. That, too, is her vision for the church. In the book *Sexual Wholeness in a Broken World*, she challenges churches:

> It is not by coincidence that the gay community is often called "the family." The need for family is acute among gays and lesbians because many of them have experienced some degree of dysfunction in their own biological families. It is important to understand that same-sex attraction in and of itself is not a sin. At the root of same-sex attraction is a longing to be loved by people of the same sex, and that longing is a God-given need that should be met. For many gays and lesbians, the need for intimacy and identification with the same sex was — to some degree — not met in childhood in the

arms of a loving mother and father and in a family system of caring sisters and brothers.

The same can be said for those who struggle with sexual addiction, drug addiction, and those who have experienced the effects of verbal, physical, emotional and/or sexual abuse. I have heard many testimonies of people being healed of life-debilitating addictions and wounds via the local church. However, the healing always occurs within the context of caring relationships. Sermons, Bible studies, retreats, and conferences play their part to heal and restore, but true and lasting healing always comes through personal relationships.[1]

How can a church develop intimacy, transparency, and support between its members and toward its visitors? The development of mentoring pairs, support groups, and other programs described in this book can help. But the most critical factor is the standard set by a church's pastor and leaders. If the pastor is transparent about his weaknesses and failures, the congregation will follow her or his example. If visitors are warmly welcomed from the pulpit, they will soon experience the same loving reception from the pews.

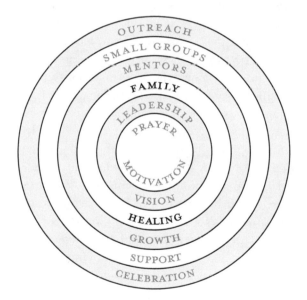

The Father of the Family

Dale and Joan Evrist moved from California to Tennessee in 1993 to plant a Foursquare church in the Nashville area. That church, New Song Christian Fellowship, has grown significantly in size and outreach and now meets in four different locations. It has also grown in its understanding of what it means to be the family of God. Programs for all ages emphasize discipleship, community building, and strengthening marriages and families based on biblical truth. The most significant ministry, Dale says, often happens during church fellowship functions and around the kitchen table in members' homes. Relationship building with one another and with the Lord is the heart of New Song's ministry.

From the church's inception, Dale has emphasized the fatherhood of God and the truth that every member of the church is part of a spiritual family. Pastor Jack Hayford, Dale's spiritual father, had a significant impact on Dale early in his ministry. "Jack loved fatherless men. He never got caught up in a person's outer shell," Dale says. "He looked right past the jar of clay with all of its marks and marring and considered the potential glory within each person. If a man appeared more feminine than most men, it didn't matter. And if a woman came into worship manifesting rough masculine characteristics, that didn't move him." Following Jack Hayford's example, Dale tells such individuals, "There's none among you who have brokenness that is any different from anyone else's brokenness in terms of the big redemptive picture. We believe there are a million and one ways to get broken in life, but only one way to be made whole—through the cross of Christ. Welcome. You're safe here."

Word soon got out that New Song was a church that helped people with sexual brokenness, and they came out of the woodwork. Dale asked the Lord what he could do to help these men and women. The Lord told him, "Become a strong spiritual father who loves these sons and daughters equally and unconditionally. They need a father's touch, acceptance, and love."

Jeff Buchanan, for example, was living homosexually before moving to Nashville, where he joined New Song church in 1996. He found the family he needed for support as he matured in the faith. When Dale asked Jeff what the church has done for him, he replied, "You accepted me and modeled healthy manhood and brought me into family structures and taught me the Scriptures." Jeff became one of Dale's associate pastors, and Jeff's wife, Angela, became Dale's assistant. As Jeff guided people who are sexually broken on a journey of healing in Christ, he developed a curriculum called "Journey Ministry." He and Angela are now moving to Florida to serve with Exodus International. The leader of the church ministry network for Exodus International, Jeff has a vision that all local congregations will function like the New Song family that nurtured and supported him in his own journey. His testimony blends with that of many other persons who have been touched and changed through the New Song family.

When Families Face Homosexuality

If you are a pastor, you have probably had church members visit your office to ask your advice about family members who have homosexual attractions.

Pastors and congregations that offer ministry to the sexually broken, addicted, or abused are often recipients of the news that a child, sibling, or parent has suddenly announced he or she is gay. When homosexuality shows up at home, where can family members turn for healing, advice, and support? The right answer should be, "the church." This can be the case for every church that chooses to function like the family of God. But the pastor must lead the way.

When my friends Bob and Susie Michaels learned that their son Shane was hiding homosexual feelings, they were devastated. Bob, the pastor of a Baptist church in North Carolina, had introduced the topic of homosexuality to his congregation several months before the concern became so much a part of his life. When Bob and Susie informed the church staff about their crisis, the staff team encouraged them to take a sabbatical. Bob agreed, thinking the break would be an opportunity to remind his son Shane of his clear obligation before God to repent and to give up homosexuality. Shane had been a faithful and committed member of the church for his entire life. Surely a month would be enough time to get things back in order.

Bob and Susie soon discovered that Shane, who was due to begin his first year in college, had decided that his faith experience must have been more emotional than real and that his same-sex attractions would not just "go away." He was intent on living his life as a homosexual. The family began weekly counseling at a local Exodus-affiliated ministry and began to learn how much more complicated homosexuality is than they had always supposed. The parents reaffirmed their commitment to biblical values and at the same time told Shane that they would love him unconditionally. Shocked by his parents' selfless love, Shane told them he nevertheless would live according to his inner inclinations.

In the meantime, the congregation questioned why their pastor was away, and rumors began to spread. Some suggested that perhaps the pastor's marriage was unraveling. Others feared Bob and Susie were leaving the church or that their son Shane had run away from home. After being informed about these rumors, Bob and Susie realized they had to return and set the record straight. Susie considered simply telling the church generically, "Shane is dealing with some issues." But she felt the Holy Spirit tell her, "If you don't tell the truth and name it, you won't be able to help someone else with it." Shane agreed to join them and to publicly announce his decision and his new identity. They sent a message to the church that they would be at the upcoming Wednesday evening service to make an announcement.

When the family arrived at church, the parking lot, normally half full for the Wednesday evening service, was packed. So was the church. As the three came to the front of the sanctuary, tension filled the air. Bob put his arm around Shane, who explained that he had chosen to live a homosexual lifestyle. Bob and Susie affirmed their commitment to following the scriptural call to holiness but said that they would love their son without reservation as they walked with him through this journey. The response of the church was overwhelming. The people stood and began shouting, "We love you Bob, Susie, and Shane. We are here for you." For nearly an hour, the members came up, one by one, to embrace the family and to express their love.

Bob's church is now more of a true Christian family than before because of the open hearts of their pastor and his family. The pastor they once put on a pedestal is now seen as more approachable. In fact, several families came to Bob in private and thanked him for being so honest. They sought his help, confessing that they, too, were facing the challenge of homosexuality in their families.

Some members, however, asked Bob not to talk about homosexuality anymore because they didn't want their children to start asking about it. Yet, in spite of the understandable angst some feel as this issue has been introduced to the congregation with unusual force and rapidity, the church is staying together and growing together. Shane has every opportunity to worship with his church family as he comes to understand the source of his same-sex attractions. Had he been rejected by his family and church, he would have felt great pressure to dive into the gay community for support.

I asked Bob and Susie what advice they can give to other pastors as a result of their experience. They said, "We've got to teach the churches that we are never more Christlike than when we love the prodigals." They told me with deep conviction, "We have to let this issue be talked about and understood in our churches. Otherwise, when families face the challenge of homosexuality, their only place to go for help will be the gay-affirming churches."

Bob and Susie are a key part of the support group for families struggling with homosexuality that meets in my church—a group that is touching others in our community with compassion and understanding. The woman I mentioned at the beginning of this chapter joined this group and has found something much better than private counsel in a pastor's office; she has found friends who care for her and support her on the path of loving her daughter without compromise while upholding God's standards for sexuality. This woman is part of a family that seeks to help families. Neither Bob's congregation nor mine has "arrived" and become a model church family. We are flawed pastors who encourage our congregations to embrace flawed people. With churches around the country, we are just beginning to understand what it means to be the family of God.

Building Family Values

Most pastors won't experience the same trauma Bob Michaels experienced with his son. Every pastor, however, has a trail of flaws and failures that can become points of connection with their congregation. When a pastor shows vulnerability with the congregation, church members will be motivated to do the same with each other.

When I took my first long-term pastorate, congregants approached me with humorous stories about the mistakes of their former pastor. I listened and shook with fear. Within weeks I made my first major blunder in worship. I was so emotionally engaged in my preaching that immediately after the sermon I moved right into the benediction, not noticing that the service had not yet ended. As I marched down the aisle, the ushers marched me right back to the front, offering plates in hand. We all had a great laugh. It was at that moment I realized the congregation had laughed at and with the former pastor because they had loved him so much. We were becoming family. When I humbly and appropriately share my hurts, pains, and failures with my church members, they reciprocate.

It Can Start with Church Members

Eddie Hammett, a church consultant, former pastor, and author of several books related to church life and health, shared this story with me about how one woman in his congregation, Ellen, helped his church become a more loving family:*

Ellen was a member of my inner-city congregation in Durham, North Carolina, where we were trying to get a handle on how best to represent Christ to a growing AIDS and gay population in our community. Our church was close to Duke Hospital's AIDS clinic. We were hosting a series of seminars on topics relevant to inner-city churches, and after the session on AIDS, Ellen pushed an anonymous note under my office door. She thanked me for the seminar and shared that her grandson had AIDS and had come to her house to die. She had not shared this with anyone in our close-knit church family due to her embarrassment and fear.

After a while, Ellen came forward and shared her story from the perspective of a church member who was faced with the issue of AIDS through her grandson, who had contracted the virus. She was seeking to understand what redemption, reconciliation, and restoration looked like in this situation. Her testimony motivated us to serve her family from that time until her grandson's death. During the funeral, in a spontaneous and personal address, Ellen talked openly and passionately about her grandson Tim. Her grandmotherly

---

* A founding partner of The Columbia Partnership (*www.thecolumbiapartnership.org*), Eddie is the author of several books, including *Reaching People under 40 while Keeping People over 60*, *Spiritual Leadership in a Secular Age*, and *Making Shifts without Making Waves*.

compassion and heartache touched our congregation deeply; her heart affected our hearts. As a result, our church moved out to create partnerships with community agencies, with other families, and with an AIDS clinic. Who knew that an awareness seminar and one elderly church member could so transform lives and a congregation's ministry!

Looking Back, Looking Forward

As we venture into the next three ministry spheres, we will be talking about focused discipleship and ministry programs. These ministries and programs can change lives, strengthen families, and reshape our churches. But programs are only as good as the people who guide them. If your congregation is living out the biblical mandate to be God's family, programs will enhance and accelerate the

> Ministry Tip #3:
> Families can be healed
> in churches that are
> true families.

success you already enjoy. If, however, you aren't cultivating a loving and transparent family spirit throughout your congregation, any programs you build will surely sink into the sands of indifference and irrelevance. Programs must be constructed on the rock-solid foundation of a loving and transparent church family.

GROWTH
Mentors and Counselors

The things you have heard me say in the presence of many witnesses entrust to reliable men who will also be qualified to teach others.

— 2 Timothy 2:2

The words in 2 Timothy 2:2 were written near the end of Paul's life. The great apostle was challenging Timothy to use their relationship as a pattern for other mentoring relationships, which would in turn foster yet more such discipleship pairs. Paul and Timothy had developed a spiritual "father-son" bond (Philippians 2:22). Beginning with Paul's second missionary journey, they were often travel companions (Acts 16:1–3). From local pastor to personal emissary to steadfast supporter, Timothy stuck by Paul's side all the way to Paul's imprisonment. They forged a relationship of trust and mutual benefit that supported their spiritual growth and the expansion of the early church.

Second Timothy 2:2 is easy to remember, as is the above-mentioned Philippians 2:22, because both biblical references have three "twos." It takes two to establish a mentoring relationship—two men or two women paired for a purpose. We each need those who will take us under their wings, as Paul did for Timothy. And we in turn are called to provide spiritual covering, insight, support, and guidance for others. Giving and receiving. Entrusting one life to another, who reaches out to another, who will touch yet another.

Another Example of Two

One of the most graphic and powerful statements on mentoring is found in the relationship that developed between Jeff Konrad and Mike Haley,

187

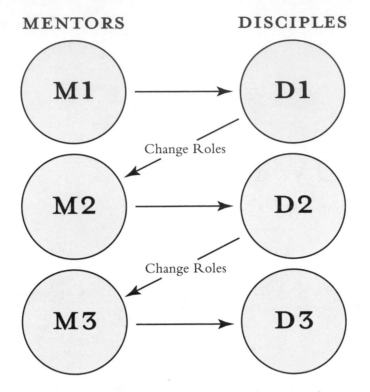

described in part in the letters Jeff wrote to Mike over a four-year period (published in the book *You Don't Have to Be Gay*). Once a self-identified homosexual, Jeff had himself come out of the lifestyle and was studying the root causes of homosexuality when he met Mike. The very idea that a person could walk out of homosexuality was new to Mike, and he wasn't interested. The two of them engaged in correspondence, and it would take several years for Mike to realize that he wasn't satisfied with what the gay community had to offer.

Mike's happiness had depended on being an "attractive commodity." To find worth and value in the eyes of other men, he worked out at the gym for two to three hours a day, injected steroids, and struggled with bulimia. The price of looking and playing the part was too much to pay. In December 1989, he picked up the phone and asked Jeff for help.

Mike's life changed through his relationship with Jeff and through relationships with other caring male mentors. In his words to me, it was "men willing to walk beside me, willing to know me as an individual, who made the difference. It was mentors in churches I could watch and from whom I learned about dating, marriage, and parenting. It was being with men who admitted to having many of the same struggles and insecurities I had. Mentors like Jeff made all the difference." Through Love in Action's residential program, through the support of understanding churches, and especially through Jeff Konrad's steadfast friendship, Mike put behind him twelve years of life in gay culture to begin a journey of growth toward wholeness in Christ. He eventually stepped into leadership positions related to postgay ministry and authored the book *101 Frequently Asked Questions about Homosexuality.* Jeff mentored Mike, whose life has touched countless others, who in turn are mentoring others.

Mike and Jeff's story has been replayed thousands of times in our generation. I have several close friends who have come out of homosexuality and who now experience wholeness and joy in righteous living, and I have interviewed dozens of others. But I have yet to find one who has experienced such victory without the support of mentors. I use this term loosely. A "mentor" might be a church member who is simply available as a friend to a recovering homosexual, or it might be a person who pours his or her life into another through many years of training and life instruction, as Paul did for Timothy and as Jeff Konrad did for Mike Haley.

Why Mentoring Relationships Are Important

In the book of Ecclesiastes, we read, "Though one may be overpowered, two can defend themselves. A cord of three strands is not quickly broken" (Ecclesiastes 4:12). The silk that shimmers in a spiderweb, if woven into thick strands, creates a cord that is stronger than steel. Alone, however, spider's silk cannot bear the elements of nature. Like the single thin strand of a spiderweb, many Christians are not woven into the fabric of church life. They feel alone and isolated. We are not meant to face the elements of the world alone. You can attend a church of twelve thousand and still be lonely. You can join a dozen social clubs and still be without a close friend. You may have a hundred relatives but not have a single person who really knows you. If there is no one in your life with whom you can share your dreams and doubts, secrets and struggles, you are alone.

Jesus modeled mentoring. He worked one-on-one with each of his twelve disciples, and especially with his inner circle — Peter, James, and John. Jesus showed patience toward impetuous Peter until the rugged fisherman was shaped into a solid pillar for God's church. He led James, who sought a place of honor in the kingdom, down the road of humility that he might become a servant of the Most High God. Our Lord poured out love on John until the apostle would become "the beloved disciple" who wrote a gospel and several letters about true agape. Even Jesus himself, the perfect one, had a mentor. Joseph, his godly father, shepherded him and helped him along on the pathway to maturity.

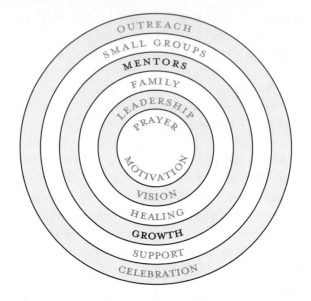

Mentoring relationships are necessary for the accomplishment of God's purpose in our lives. This principle holds true for every Christian, and those struggling with unwanted same-sex attractions are no exception. Through my years of pastoring, I have often had men slip quietly into my office and confess their struggles with sexuality. Some of them have returned again and again, over months and years, to be held accountable for their spiritual walks, to receive grace for the times they stumble, to find relief through talking it out. Their success, however, depends on having other mentors and friends around. I can only be close to a few people. As a pastor, I have been grateful for other people in churches I have served who have stepped into mentoring roles for those in need.

One man whom I love deeply in the Lord benefited from such informal mentoring relationships with me and with other church members for years. He and I didn't talk much about homosexuality even though we both understood our friendship to be a source of his stability. Around the time I accepted a call to a church in another state, several other friends of this man, who also had been part of his support system, moved away. He slipped back into his old lifestyle. It breaks my heart. Mentoring matters.

Leaders in posthomosexual ministries around the country give their lives to mentoring relationships — men to men and women to women. Behind all of the public speaking and ministry, they devote countless hours to phone calls, meetings, counseling appointments, and emotional moments. They come out of these experiences drained and yet energized. They are pouring their energies into those who seek to overcome their same-sex attractions. And they need help.

Great things can happen once churches around the world recognize that they are filled with potential mentors. And people who are called to be mentors must honor their unique opportunities with focused learning about homosexuality through every possible resource and by listening to and learning from the people they mentor.

Mentoring should not be left to professionals and paid ministry workers. God calls each of us to mentor our children and later, to some extent, our grandchildren. God may also give you a mentoring relationship at the work-place, at school, at a place of volunteer service, or in your neighborhood or church. The place isn't what matters, but the person. Whom has God called you to disciple? And who is mentoring you? Do you understand the critical importance of such relationships for spiritual development and growth?

Mentoring is the workout room of the Christian life. It is difficult work. But it is also rewarding. Jesus mentored twelve men, who in turn mentored others, and you and I have come into the blessing somewhere down the line. If you are not motivated and committed to mentoring another person, per-haps you need to be mentored yourself. One sign of spiritual maturity is the natural longing to mentor others in the faith. Just as it is second nature for biological fathers and mothers to provide nurture and safety for their children, so spiritual fathers and mothers step into the mentoring role with a sense of joy and obligation. Most Christians today, including pastors, have not real-ized their own spiritual potential and can benefit greatly from mentoring relationships.

Mentoring and Temptation

In Romans 15:1–2, Paul exhorts us, "We who are strong ought to bear with the failings of the weak and not to please ourselves. Each of us should please his neighbor for his good, to build him up." How do we apply this verse to ministry for the sexually broken? Let me suggest several important consid-erations.

First, recognize that there are different levels of mentoring. You may not be called to invest years into a person's life, but perhaps weeks or months. Let God guide you as you become a role model or encourager for someone of your same gender who is struggling with same-sex attractions. A relation-ship is a dance; it takes two. The very person who needs to spend time with you as part of the healing process may become overly attached, requiring you to pull back. If you enter into such a mentoring relationship, protect your heart. Allow yourself space and time to recover. Be a stable factor in the other person's life. Read books about mentoring and about recovery from homosexuality. Attend conferences about the same. Learn from many who once identified themselves by their sexuality but now identify themselves as sons and daughters of God. Be part of a support group, as described in the next chapter. As you do these things, not only will you help others; you will become a better person and a stronger Christian.

If you have a personal history of sexual sin or abuse, guard yourself. Paul, who exhorts us to "carry each other's burdens," also warns us, "If someone is caught in a sin, you who are spiritual should restore him gently. But watch yourself, or you also may be tempted" (Galatians 6:1–2). If you are helping one or more people with issues of accountability, find someone to hold you accountable as well. As you encourage the weak to become strong, learn to read indicators about your own weaknesses.

Even though homosexuality is not caused by sexual addiction, the addictive nature of sex must be dealt with in the recovery process. If you have issues with addiction of any kind, you must guard your weak side as you minister to others. An addiction can be any habitual, short-lived pleasure or inappropriate activity that you use to medicate your inner pain. People who mentor and counsel those recovering from addictions sometimes use the acronym HALT as a reminder of how to protect themselves and those they are helping from tumbling again into addictive behavior. When you or others are:

•   •   •

Hungry, get food.
Angry, get away and deal with it.
Lonely, recognize and meet your need through appropriate friendship and support.
Tired, get rest.

•   •   •

Hunger and tiredness relate to physical needs. Anger and loneliness reflect needs of heart and emotion. Ron Smith, the director of New Hope Ministries, described to me how useful this simple acronym has been for him. In his counseling, he has often encountered both homosexuals and heterosexuals who had been walking in victory over their past addictions and sins for many years. Then suddenly, out of the blue, they were hit between the eyes with temptations they thought had been laid to rest. People have told him, "It's like I'm back at ground zero," or "I feel like I'm starting all over again." That is the reality of being human. And this is why we need safeguards and accountability partners.

God can use temptations and trials to make us stronger. Jesus himself was tempted by the devil when he began and ended his ministry. Peter learned to stand against temptation by first being knocked down (1 Peter 4:12). Paul warns us, "So, if you think you are standing firm, be careful that you don't fall!" He then adds these words of promise: "No temptation has seized you except what is common to man. And God is faithful; he will not let you be tempted beyond what you can bear. But when you are tempted, he will also provide a way out so that you can stand up under it" (1 Corinthians 10:12–13).

Counselors

Professional counseling has the potential to accelerate the healing and recovery process for persons struggling with same-sex attractions. Yet, many psychiatrists, clinical psychologists, and professional counselors assume that a person should be affirmed in his or her "homosexual orientation," and that any form of "change therapy" is intrinsically harmful. The American Psychiatric Association's governing council, for example, recently encouraged their therapists to respect the religious convictions of their clients as their own code of ethics requires but to refrain from encouraging them to believe that change is possible.[1]

Christian therapists who put God into the equation potentially have more to offer their clients, assuming other factors, such as the counselor's training and natural gifting, are comparable. Compare the secular and Christian approaches:

APA approach: The focus of therapy should not be on changing homosexuals to heterosexuals. If persons with unwanted same-sex attractions are seeking to change their orientation because of religious convictions, they should be helped to realize they might need to change their convictions or at best remain celibate. If their church is exacerbating their inner tension, they might need to look for a different church.

Christian approach: Christian therapists generally agree that the focus of counseling should not be on converting homosexuals to heterosexuals but on helping homosexuals find health and wholeness as they live in a manner that honors God and fulfills their lives. The term *holiness* simply suggests that a person has set his or her life apart to honor God. That person's identity is no longer rooted in sexual preferences or attractions but in the glorious freedom and joy found in Jesus Christ. Once a person begins living for God, his or her life becomes reshaped by the power of God. Every aspect of a person's life is touched, and over time, even one's sexual attractions may change.

It is agreed that a person with unwanted same-sex attractions should not focus on "trying to become heterosexual." One's so-called "orientation" may change, however, as a person draws near to God and finds healing and strength in other areas of life. *Celibacy* and *celebrate* come from the same root word. Both heterosexuals and homosexuals whose lives are no longer identified by sexual issues have reason to celebrate! If a person does decide to change churches based on issues of sexuality, he or she should avoid both gay-affirming and gay-bashing churches and find a congregation that unites truth and grace.

A completely secular approach to counseling cannot adequately understand our human orientation. Everyone is affected by the fall of humankind into sin. Even our genes and environment are tainted by sin and can provoke rebellion against God. When a Christian counselor helps counselees surrender their lives to Christ, reorientation can begin on the deepest level, influencing one's past, present, and future. A person who is oriented toward God can turn from self-centeredness to generosity, from being sexually driven to being spiritually driven, from self-medication through improper channels to fulfillment, growth, and service.

> **Ministry Tip #4:**
> **Mentoring and counseling relationships cultivate personal growth.**

There are excellent Christian counselors and therapists around the country who understand same-sex attraction and who have experience in this arena. Still, we wish there were far more. For a partial list of such counselors, visit *www.exodusinternational.org*. If you are unsure about a counselor or therapy program in your area, contact them and ask the following questions. (If they are not willing to discuss their approach, you should ask yourself why you would want to subject yourself or others to their counsel.)

- Do you take a Christian approach to counseling? If so, what do you mean by that? Do you respect a client's religious convictions?
- What is your training? Are you licensed? (Is licensure required by your state's laws?) Accredited? Certified?
- Are you affiliated with a particular network, church, or agency? If so, please tell me about it.
- Have you counseled people with unwanted same-sex attraction before? What do you believe is the cause of homosexuality? What approach do you take in treating it? What challenges might you face in treating it?

- What is your fee structure? Do you work on a sliding scale, based on a client's income? Can you do third-party (insurance) billing?
- What results can I expect from your approach to therapy? To what extent is the client involved in determining the course of treatment? How will you decide when to end therapy? What follow-up care do you provide?

Looking Back, Looking Forward

People who struggle with their sexual identities can accelerate healing through mentoring and Christian counseling. Jesus set the standard by mentoring others, as did Paul. The Bible encourages every Christian to engage in mentoring relationships. We are not meant to be alone. We should help each other carry the burdens of life. The help of a close and trustworthy friend can make all the difference.

Chapter 15

SUPPORT
Small Group Ministry

> Jesus went up on a mountainside and called to him those he wanted, and they
> came to him. He appointed twelve — designating them apostles — that they
> might be with him and that he might send them out to preach and to have
> authority to drive out demons.
>
> — *Mark 3:13 – 15*

Two church members joined Pastor Mark Batterson for the first worship service of National Community Church in Washington, D.C. — his wife, Lora, and his son, Parker. Within months, a core group of twenty-five people met in a school. When the leadership team received notice that the school was closing, they found a home in a movie theatre at Union Station. National Community Church's spiritual DNA was being established. They would be a church in the middle of the marketplace. Orthodox in belief but unorthodox in practice, they would bring the church to the people.

The interdenominational National Community Church (NCC) now meets in five locations — four theatres and one coffeehouse. Small group ministry is central to their inreach and outreach. Their website states, "Even though you are never required to join a small group, we believe it's the best thing going at NCC." Dozens of intentional gatherings for outreach and discipleship meet weekly throughout the Washington, D.C., metro area in workplaces, homes, and coffeehouses. The focus of these groups ranges from Bible study and core discipleship to special interest and ministry. They have groups for men, women, and couples. They also have groups for special needs, such as sexual and emotional brokenness.

Heather Zempel, the discipleship pastor for National Community Church, described to me the significant growth in ministry they experienced as a result of their support and recovery groups for sexual brokenness. "It was a shock," she said, "to have people just walk into my office and talk about their struggles with sexuality. Yet they come in so often now that it's no longer shocking. There's so much experimentation, especially with twentysome-things." Small group ministry for all kinds of people and all kinds of needs is changing lives at National Community Church.

Small Groups throughout History

Small group discipleship was central to Jesus' ministry on earth. He began his outreach by pulling together twelve men. Living and working with them, he trained his disciples to become leaders in the church he would leave behind. They followed his pattern and developed small groups as the heart and soul of their disciple-making mission.

Throughout history, great movements of renewal and church growth have been fostered through small groups. From the time of the early church, Christians supplemented large worship gatherings with house meetings for intimate fellowship and growth. Small groups have played a critical role in the drama of the Christian story (Acts 2:46–47). They enhance every denomina-tion and can cultivate spiritual and numerical growth in any congregation. John Calvin, the father of Reformed theology, encouraged people to recog-nize their families as churches within the church. John Wesley established small groups that taught "methods" of spiritual accountability, out of which arose the name "Methodists." Regardless of the label—Protestant, Catholic, Episcopalian, Eastern Orthodox—when small groups are an ingredient in any church ministry, Christians can benefit.

Interdenominational and nonsectarian organizations have long recog-nized small group ministry as critical for people's recovery, growth, and sup-port. From more than five decades ago, when the first Alcoholics Anonymous group was launched, to fifteen years ago, when Celebrate Recovery began, regular gatherings in clusters of about a dozen people have found the ben-efits that Jesus once shared with his disciples. In a small group, secrets can be shared, struggles understood, truth imparted, accountability fostered, stability developed, relationships forged, spiritual growth realized, and disciples made. Small group ministry is important for every Christian. It is the heart and soul of ministry for those recovering from sexual brokenness.

Why Small Groups in Your Church?

If your leaders are committed to offering ministry for people with unwanted same-sex attractions, it will be strategic to provide one or more groups for sup-port and recovery. Recalling the six spheres of ministry, *prayer* should under-gird such groups from the start, *leadership* must endorse their formation and

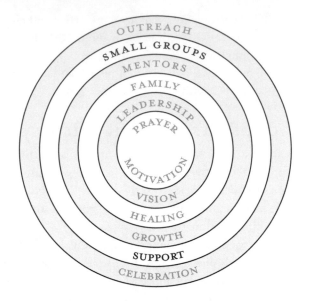

provide an umbrella of protection over them, *families* will need them for support, *mentors and counselors* may be involved in their composition, the *congregation* should be aware of their existence, and they can become natural vehicles for *outreach*.

Support groups provide a component of recovery that one-to-one mentoring and counseling cannot. Individuals who have unwanted same-sex attraction are prone to isolation. A small group gathering can promote social development—a vital part of the restorative process for many. Regular gatherings with fellow believers also create accountability; group members report to each other at each meeting. And relationships of trust that develop within the groups become a network of strength for meeting the challenges of life.

Small Group Resources

Tens of thousands of congregations around the world wisely incorporate small group ministry to build their membership, promote spiritual growth, and encourage outreach. It is hoped that many more will take the next logical step of adding support groups for recovery from addiction and abuse, gender identity issues, and other areas of human need. One key consideration is the selection of good curriculum.

Living Waters

Living Waters is one of several excellent courses offered by Desert Stream Ministries (*www.desertstream.org*). This twenty-lesson teaching and discipleship series is a Christ-centered program for people seeking healing in areas of sexual and relational brokenness. Ann Cohrs, ministry associate for Regeneration Ministries, says, "I don't know of any Christian who would not benefit from using Living Waters, regardless of issues you may have or may not even know you have." Desert Stream Ministries' offerings are currently being used in churches around the world more than any other curriculum on sexual and relational brokenness. Andy Comiskey, the founder and director of Desert Stream Ministries, told me, "Because the course is done in a local church, the church that hosts it becomes much loved by the course participants. It actually transforms an aspect of the life of the church in that it creates an approach to body life that is profound."

The small group format is the heart and soul of the ministry. Andy explained, "In a good small group setting, you're immediately beginning to connect with others in areas of need and vulnerability. You are given the opportunity to engage with other men or women in a way that breaks down the sense that 'I'm so different, so alone.' Typically no more than 30 percent of the participants in a Living Waters group are dealing with same-sex attractions. Others in the group are struggling with more general problems of besetting sexual sin like Internet pornography and marital strife. This mix helps break down the false idea that there's an otherness to homosexuality, as though it's a group of people all its own—an idea that fuels distorted thinking and activism, which is truly unnecessary in the kingdom of God."

Celebrate Recovery

Celebrate Recovery (*www.celebraterecovery.com*) was created by Saddleback Church to help people overcome life's hurts, habits, and hang-ups by providing a biblical and balanced program to help them deal with issues such as abuse, addiction, and anger. Broader in scope than Living Waters, the Celebrate Recovery program guides its participants through eight principles based on the Beatitudes of the New Testament and twelve biblical steps to recovery. Through a DVD-guided twenty-five-lesson course, participants are encouraged to discover a new level of care, acceptance, trust, and grace. Celebrate Recovery works well in churches as a general outreach tool because it encourages the formation of support groups to meet all kinds of needs ranging from financial instability to issues faced by adults of dysfunctional families. Congregations may also form separate groups to help people struggling with same-sex attractions. Where such specialized groups are not formed, people wishing to overcome homosexual attractions will probably not open up about their unique temptations and may not experience the healing they seek.

Homosexuals Anonymous

One of the most widespread small group recovery programs for homosexuality is also one of the least known due to anonymity. Inspired in part by Alcoholics Anonymous (AA), Homosexuals Anonymous (HA) operates with a fourteen-step small group process (*www.ha-fs.org*). These steps focus on same-sex attraction issues and therefore are not actually an adaptation of AA's well-known twelve steps. Doug McIntyre, a cofounder of this ministry almost thirty years ago, has come back into the leadership of HA and is passionate about the potential for change for people with unwanted same-sex attraction. Once engaged in a homosexual lifestyle, Doug has been living faithfully for Jesus Christ for more than twenty-five years and estimates that thousands of people have come out of homosexuality around the world, many of them through Homosexuals Anonymous. They offer free information and resources to help pastors and churches establish groups.

Other Options

Smaller congregations may not be able to afford the leadership training and resource expenses associated with courses like Living Waters, or even Celebrate Recovery. Working together, though, several churches can jointly host such programs for their community.

Alternately, there are many good books and workbooks that can supplement and guide the support group process. The American Association for Christian Counselors offers a number of helpful training and group tools (*www.aacc.net*), and Exodus International's online bookstore is comprehensive (*www.exodusinternational.org/books/*). For groups that are focused specifically on same-sex attraction issues, Frank Worthen's books are excellent.[1] See the resources section in the back of this book for further suggestions.

Types of Groups

The type of group or groups you form will depend primarily on the needs of the people you are called to help. It is best to launch a variety of groups to meet a variety of needs. If your church is only capable of establishing one group, consider partnering with churches in your community to establish multiple groups for the needs in your area.

Meetings designed for Bible study, fellowship, and discipleship can include participants with same-sex attractions and related issues without singling them out. Specialty groups dealing with addictions, sexual abuse, homosexuality, or any other special focus, however, can help people get to the root of their issues more freely. When dealing with sexuality, it is generally best to have separate support groups for men and women, enabling participants to talk openly about their personal concerns. Support groups for married couples in which one spouse has a history of same-sex attractions may be formed in larger congregations.

Support groups for parents whose children struggle with their sexuality are also needed. This is often the most logical place to begin small group ministry for sexual brokenness in a church. You *may* have people who are impacted personally by unwanted same-sex attractions in your church, but you almost certainly *do* have family members and friends of those who experience homosexual attractions. If we do not provide biblical answers and emotional support to parents who are asking for help, they may look elsewhere. Many, for example, have been pulled into support groups sponsored by Parents, Families & Friends of Lesbians & Gays (PFLAG), which functions under the rubric of the gay rights agenda. A more balanced and biblical alternative is offered by Parents and Friends of Ex-Gays and Gays (PFOX). Avoiding both the gay-affirming and gay-bashing extremes, PFOX helps parents love their homosexual children unconditionally without approving potentially harmful behavior. PFOX can help you locate or establish a support group for your church or local community (*www.pfox.org*).

Other Important Details

There are several additional considerations for those who wish to establish small group ministry: group openings, group leadership, group beginnings, and proper group facilitation.

Group Openings

Consider whether your groups will be open or closed to visitors and new group members. There are benefits either way, and often groups can be closed for a season and then opened up. Groups that are constantly closed to new people may become cloistered and inward looking. Regular visitors, on the other hand, can diminish the sense of intimacy and continuity that develops within a group over time. It is generally best for a church to have one or more groups that are open to visitors, either part or all of the time, and to have one or more groups that remain intentionally closed for at least a few months to facilitate bonding and intimacy. If your congregation has only one support group, you may wish to cycle between open and closed meetings through a mutually agreed-on pattern that fits well with the group.

Group Leadership

Select leaders for each group based on the group's composition and goals. A group of males overcoming same-sex attractions, for example, should be led by a male. A support group for the sexually abused may require a mature Christian leader or a trained counselor. Ideally, each leader should have a partner who has a passion for this ministry and who can be a support and accountability factor in the group.

It is important that each leader and group function under the authority of a local church. People who come to such groups need the stability of a support structure that will not crumble under the kinds of challenges that often arise with recovery ministries. Under the church's umbrella, the group may also enjoy a covering of prayer, financial support, authoritative guidance when needed, and help in integrating interested group members into the church family.

How Should a Group Begin?

During the first meeting, group leaders should establish goals and standards, including the members' input, where possible, to encourage members' ownership of the group dynamic. Questions to answer include:

- What will be the composition of the group?
- What is the group's focus?
- Where will it meet and when?
- Will it be open to others? If so, how often?
- Will members maintain confidentiality about what is said in the group?
- How will group members show honor to each other in their interactions verbally, emotionally, and relationally?
- If a person violates the group covenant, how will discipline be enacted?

Many times these and other policies are written out in a simple covenant that group members endorse as a commitment to their common values. When people later join the group, they can be asked to agree to the same terms, thus resetting expectations to a common starting point.

Facilitating the Group

A good length for a support group meeting is between two and three hours, depending on the group's objectives and the curriculum. Allow some time for mixing and interaction before and after people gather. Snacks or a shared meal before or after the meeting are good options. Food promotes fellowship. A typical meeting should include time for worship, learning, sharing, and closing prayer.

Groups that focus solely on listening to each other's problems rather than on listening to the Lord can become depressing and even debilitating to their members. Sharing time can become healing time, however, when the group is centered on Scripture and excellent teachings about God and his power to assist us in recovery. A skilled leader knows how to use Scripture or available resources to guide a discussion that will pull everyone into the conversation and make each person feel important. Please visit *www.ChurchReflections.com* for more tips on leading a group and for the typical life cycle of a group.

Unique Characteristics of Recovery Groups

Recovery groups require more energy to facilitate than small groups that meet simply for fellowship, Bible study, prayer, and spiritual growth. Group members seeking to overcome the pain of abuse, the pull of addiction, and the palpitations of heart and soul as they struggle with issues of identity and self-worth naturally require more attention in the group mentoring and discipleship process. Therefore, it is important to keep a good balance in your group between those whose needs are great and those who are able to bring stability and support to the ministry. Likewise, group members may find a need to shift from one group to another as they seek the environment best suited to their growth.

Frank Worthen, a patriarch in the posthomosexual movement, describes three levels of growth in recovering homosexuals that he has observed through small group ministries he has established.[2] A *level one* group is comprised completely of people who struggle with unwanted same-sex attractions. When a person has become comfortable sharing at this level, he or she may be ready for *level two*, which includes people of the same gender who have not experienced same-sex attractions. Having previously been rejected by people with "straight" backgrounds, it takes courage and trust to open up in this context. *Level three* involves opening up with members of the opposite sex about one's struggles.

Each of these levels represents a stage of growth and maturation. If a person with homosexual attractions jumps to level three by dating and marrying someone of the opposite sex in an effort to "fix" himself or herself before true healing and recovery have occurred, that person may experience significant setbacks. It should be remembered that the desire for intimacy with people of the same sex reflects a deep personal need that often goes back to childhood. A person in recovery should go through levels one and two, whether formally or informally, until healing has taken them far enough to justify closer relationships at level three.

Access to these levels of growth may be created in a church by developing several types of groups to meet the stages of recovery for many different people. They may also be fostered within one group by allowing the composition of the group to change as it progresses through the three levels. Theory rarely squares with reality, however, and there is no way around the fact that recovery groups can be a trying and messy business. But they are worth it. They are the muscle of ministry for people recovering from issues of sexual and relational brokenness.

Engaging Your Whole Church through Small Groups

A careful study of the life of Jesus shows that he engaged his disciples in three primary ways: He taught them publicly, he ministered to them as a group, and he supported them one-on-one. These three modes of mentoring—from the crowd to a small group to private teaching—were not neatly separated in his ministry but flowed together day to day and week to week. Jesus often spoke to a large gathering and then stepped aside to converse with his disciples. At other times, he worked with one or more of his followers and then sent them into the crowd to multiply loaves or to fetch a coin from a fish's mouth. Each circumstance was a setup for teaching, and every challenge was an opportunity for growth. They shared their lives together.

The Western model of "doing church" is less relational than that given to us by Jesus. We strive to build our worship services and touch all kinds of people with all kinds of programs. But how deeply are our church members growing, really? In 2007, the Willow Creek Association published the shocking results of a ministry effectiveness survey taken by people in the twenty-thousand-member Willow Creek Church and in several other congregations. They found that ministries that measure success by numbers and program participation have the potential to produce spiritual stagnation in many people's lives.[3] Approximately 26 percent of church members, primarily the believers who wanted to move beyond the basics, were either "stalled" or "dissatisfied" with their spiritual growth. This study demonstrates the overwhelming need for ministries that move congregations beyond programs designed to attract a crowd to personal mentoring, small group ministries, and the spiritual development of church members.

I have seen a possible solution to the spiritual stagnation that so easily permeates our congregations through my experience with the ministry of Community Bible Study. Started by my parents in 1975, Community Bible Study has blossomed into an international ministry with more than six hundred classes around the country and growing movements in other nations. Their method of discipleship is very effective. Through an integrated process of teaching, small group interaction, and personal study, CBS classes walk through books of the Bible. In the nine years I served as one of the teaching directors, I often wondered why a similar method of united learning and discipleship wasn't being used more often in the average church.

I focused my doctoral study on the implementation of this concept in the church, and over nearly two decades, I've developed materials and a ministry called Connections. Through this new ministry, interested congregations are provided with materials that can link a pastor's sermon to small group discussion and personal devotion. One of the outgrowths of this ministry is the production of materials that supplement this book to help you educate, inspire, and engage your whole congregation in Christlike outreach to the sexually and relationally broken. Specifically, a prayer guide, leadership training resources, sermon ideas, small group study materials, and a church leadership packet have been designed to assist you in your ministry (visit *www.ChurchReflections.com*).

Small Groups in Manila

Located on the eastern shore of Manila Bay, the city of Manila is one of the most densely populated urban centers in the world. This capital of the Philippines sits as a central hub for a metropolitan area with 19 million people, an area that has no lack of opportunity for the gay community. Manila has also become a setting for Christians to provide help for those who want to come out of homosexuality.

Rollie delos Reyes II found freedom to turn from his homosexual lifestyle and live for Christ in 2001. When he began his graduate studies in counseling, he wrote a thesis titled "Counseling the Filipino Homosexual." He was surprised to find a dearth of understanding about homosexuality in the Filipino academic community. It was the same in most churches, which were either supportive of homosexuality or against both the practice and persons who had same-sex attractions. Not so, however, among some in the Roman Catholic Church. In 2002, Rollie joined Courage Philippines, an Apostolate of the Roman Catholic Church, which encourages a life of chastity. Within about four years, he became one of their leaders. Rollie told me that the Catholic catechism teaches that homosexual acts are morally sinful and that the homosexual condition is an objective disorder, but it also teaches to have respect and compassion for persons experiencing such attractions. Sadly, in Rollie's opinion, Filipino clergy remain unaware about these official teachings of the church, and they sway on either extreme — either they strongly condemn the homosexual person (together with the homosexual sin), or they are becoming too compassionate to the point of accepting the homosexual lifestyle. He believes that Filipino clergymen should still be properly educated to respond with truth and love. He tells me, "I would personally be happy if the Catholic Bishops' Conference of the Philippines would issue an official stand of the Philippine Catholic Church on the issue of homosexuality — much like what the U.S. Conference of Catholic Bishops has done."

Rollie also became involved as a helper for one of the local Living Waters programs and is grateful for three other ministries for people with unwanted same-sex attractions sponsored by his church. Small group ministry has made all the difference for Rollie, and he is watching these ministries change many lives.

On the eastern side of the Manila metropolitan area, Christ Commission Fellowship also has a significant ministry for people seeking to come out of the homosexual lifestyle. This church of about twenty-five thousand members is serious about small groups. Their ministry for posthomosexuals, Living Free Ministry, uses the small group format as an essential part of the recovery process.

> Ministry Tip #5: Small groups are the muscle for ministries of recovery.

Its leader, Alberto Rodriguez, is enthusiastic about the people who have been helped to live in holiness and to find healing in Christ. The initial leadership team for Living Free was mentored by Frank Worthen, former chairman of Exodus International, and the ministry team has incorporated Frank's discipleship materials. For Alberto, small group ministry is an essential component in the change and growth process for all people, including those with unwanted homosexual attractions.

These are just two of the churches in one city, Manila, that recognize the power of small group ministry. This same story can be told over and over in many parts of the world.

Looking Back, Looking Forward

We have discussed support groups for people recovering from sexual and relational brokenness and have considered how small groups can be used by God for congregation-wide renewal. Jesus used small group ministry to shape the lives of his disciples, who followed this pattern and changed their world. Have you adequately utilized small group ministry in your congregation?

Chapter 16

CELEBRATION
Outreach

Philip went down to a city in Samaria and proclaimed the Christ there. When the crowds heard Philip and saw the miraculous signs he did, they all paid close attention to what he said. With shrieks, evil spirits came out of many, and many paralytics and cripples were healed. So there was great joy in that city.
—*Acts 8:5–8*

The joy in the city of Samaria was great because of the good news that had come from Jerusalem through God's servant Philip. That's how it is when the walls of ministry are established—the gospel spills over, and whole communities are touched outside the confines of the church.

So it was in Nehemiah's day. After he and the people had completed the walls, "the sound of rejoicing in Jerusalem could be heard far away" (Nehemiah 12:43). While choirs marched in opposite directions along the top of the walls, cymbals, harps, and lyres accompanied their unbridled voices in an unparalleled celebration.

But one thing was missing.

The Samaritans.

Why Include the Samaritans?

Let your mind drift back four and a half centuries, and imagine yourself in Nehemiah's sandals. The Samaritans were not part of the celebration. But why should they have been? Wouldn't their inclusion have been politically incorrect? Weren't the Samaritans an amalgamation of Jewish and Assyrian blood, a painful reminder of the invasion of the northern kingdom of Israel two centuries prior to Ezra and Nehemiah's reconstruction work? And hadn't Ezra the scribe set a precedent when he refused the Samaritans' request to help build the temple two decades before Nehemiah arrived on the scene to work on the walls (Ezra 4:1–3)? Perhaps the Samaritans were angry that the Jews wouldn't let them back into their lives. Add to this the Samaritans' opposition to Nehemiah's rebuilding process, and one can understand why Nehemiah refused to invite them to the celebration once the walls were complete.

Back to Philip

By the time of Jesus, the hostility between God's people and the Samaritans had escalated, and the divide between them was cavernous. The temple that the Samaritans had built at the base of Mount Gerizim, near Shechem, had been destroyed in 128 BC by the Judean king John Hyrcanus. The Samaritans were not permitted to offer sacrifices in Jerusalem or to intermarry with the Jews. They were shunned, avoided, and despised by the Jews, and the feeling was mutual.

In this climate of conflict, the Samaritans felt the need to develop a religion of their own. Still claiming the God of the Jews, they carved out a place for themselves on the religious landscape by rejecting key parts of the Jewish Bible. The Samaritan version of the Holy Writ retained the first five books, the Pentateuch, but made alterations to substantiate their claim that Mount Gerizim was the rightful site for the temple, not Jerusalem, where Jews gathered to worship. Samaritan scholars taught that Ezra had corrupted the original texts of Scripture, making the Jewish version of the Bible less accurate than the Samaritans' Bible.

Our Samaritans

Most churches today avoid talking about homosexuality—and not without reason. In the minds of many evangelical Christians, a long history of political strife between gay rights advocates and the church justifies the shunning of homosexuals from our places of worship and from our lives. After all, aren't homosexuals living reminders of the erosion of Christian values and the invasion of secularism in our land? And haven't gays and lesbians sought leadership posts in some of our churches? They wanted to have a hand in building our temple, and naturally we have refused to let them in. Perhaps we shouldn't have been surprised when they erected a temple of their own. Entry gates into gay-affirming worship can be found just outside the true Jerusalem. Identifying signs above the portals usually carry words like "Metropolitan Community Church" or "An Affirming and Welcoming Congregation." It is just as well that they keep their distance. After all, the Bible does not support their beliefs. Seeking to justify their existence, their progay scholars actually claim to offer a more accurate reading of Scripture based on the reinterpretation of a few key texts. New light today has made it all clear, they claim.

In the meantime, we build our ministries and travel to the ends of the earth to make new converts. We seek to reach people of all races and languages with the gospel. Our missionaries bring back the spoils through story, and we celebrate. Without the Samaritans, of course.

But wait. Jesus is coming soon to inspect our walls.

Inspection Time

When Jesus appears to take us home, will he congratulate us for living according to the principles and promises he left with us? Let's review the main application points of this book by carrying our analogy into each ministry sphere to see what we find.

Prayer. We quote this famous verse on prayer at our missionary conferences: "The harvest is plentiful but the workers are few. Ask the Lord of the harvest, therefore, to send out workers into his harvest field" (Matthew 9:37–38). What about the parallel verse: "Do you not say, 'Four months more and then the harvest'? I tell you, open your eyes and look at the fields! They are ripe for harvest" (John 4:35). Jesus spoke these words as he pointed to the Samaritans, bounding over the hillside in their white garments like wheat waving in the breeze and ready to be reaped. They were coming to the Savior.

Do your church members pray for God to help them bring in the sheaves in Samaria?

Leadership. Jesus gave leaders to the church. He also gave vision to its leaders: "You will receive power when the Holy Spirit comes on you; and you will be

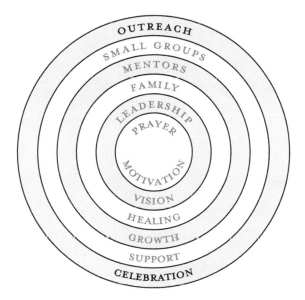

my witnesses in Jerusalem, and in all Judea and Samaria, and to the ends of the earth" (Acts 1:8). Missiologists tell us that *Jerusalem* represents people in our immediate vicinity: our families, relatives, and neighbors—those who are most like us. *Judea* represents our own community, our near neighbors. And the *ends of the earth* refer to people from every tribe, language, people, and nation, for heaven will not be complete without them all (Matthew 28:18–20; Revelation 5:9; 7:9; 14:6). One problem though. What about Samaria? Why did he have to include that one? For most of us, it's been taken off the map.

Do your leaders have a vision to reach Samaria for Jesus Christ—or at least the Samaritans who come to visit?

Family. Jesus rebuked the priests and religious leaders of his day for emphasizing dress codes and religious rules more than justice and kindness. He instilled in his followers family values such as love, truth, transparency, and mercy. Jesus reinforced his teaching when he mingled with tax gatherers, forgave prostitutes, and included women in his inner circle. But perhaps nothing was as shocking to the disciples as his talking kindly to a Samaritan woman. Worse than that, he humbled himself before her and asked her to give him a drink (John 4:7). The Pharisees would not talk with women in the streets or even look at them. As a result, some of them were constantly bumping into pillars and walls and became known as the "bleeding and bruised Pharisees."[1] Here was Jesus, not only talking to a woman in public, but to a *Samaritan* woman. Worse yet, she was a *sinner,* living with a man who was not her husband. This would be comparable to a theologically conservative pastor today sitting down in public view with gays and lesbians to listen to their stories and let them know that they are important to God.

Does your church embrace truly Christlike family values?

Mentors and counselors. When asked how to apply the Great Commandment to their lives, Jesus told the religious crowd in his day the story of the good Samaritan (Luke 10:30–35). This classic parable demonstrates an outreach of personal love and compassion. The Samaritan applied medicine, bandaged wounds, put the needy man on his own donkey, brought him to an inn, took care of him, and paid the bill for his complete healing. Consider how upsetting this story must have been to the Pharisees. The Samaritan was a hero of outreach and personal care. Jesus told his listeners, "Go and do the same."

Are you and members of your church offering one-on-one mentoring and pastoral care or counseling for modern-day Samaritans?

Small group ministry. We read in John 4:4 that Jesus "had to go through Samaria." Normally when Jews took a trip north or south across Palestine, they would avoid the middle section, the land of Samaria. They took the long way around by crossing the Jordan, turning a three-day journey into a trip of twice the length. It was safer and more socially acceptable to avoid the political enemies of the Jews. Why, then, did Jesus lead his disciples right into the heart of Samaria? Was he taking a shortcut to his next appointment? No. Samaria *was* his next appointment. His goal was not to *save* time but to *spend* time with the people the Jews had long rejected. He and his disciples remained in Samaria for two days (John 4:43). By his example Jesus not only helped the Samaritans find God's grace; he showed his disciples how to share it. Jesus taught his small group of disciples how to reach out to Samaria.

Have you utilized small group ministry to help your church embrace Christian family values? Do you have small groups designed for people with unwanted same-sex attractions or related issues like addictions and abuse? Have you considered creating a support group for Christian parents whose children are gay? Your church need not implement all of these ideas today, but why not begin forming ideas for tomorrow?

Outreach. This final stage of the ministry would be launched after Jesus' ascension. When the disciples followed him into Samaria, seeds of truth were sown in their hearts that would later result in a spiritual harvest. But it would take the sovereign hand of God to scatter the early Christians and get them back to Samaria with the gospel of God's grace. We read in Acts 8:1 that "a great persecution broke out against the church at Jerusalem, and all except the apostles were scattered throughout Judea and Samaria." Three verses later, we learn that "those who had been scattered preached the word wherever they went. Philip went down to a city in Samaria and proclaimed the Christ there" (8:4–5).

God used governmental pressure to accomplish his purpose. He can do it again today. Gay marriage, hate-crime legislation, and the like may be his means of scattering the seed of the gospel into Samaria and of bringing Samaritans into churches and into the kingdom of light.

Outreach Examples

When Philip preached the redemptive grace of the gospel in Samaria, "there was great joy in that city" (Acts 8:8). He was completing spiritually what God started symbolically through Nehemiah. So, too, when we build the walls of protection in our churches, the good news of God's grace will naturally overflow and bless people in our communities and beyond. Outreach is ministry spilled over, the nearly effortless outcome of a deep inner work of God. The overflow tends to occur at a church's point of natural strength. Consider:

Prayer. In chapter 11 we considered the prayer ministry of The Falls Church in northern Virginia. They could not keep the celebration of God's life-changing power within the confines of their house of worship. Now they host regular conferences and seminars for anyone interested in issues of sexual and relational brokenness and healing prayer and have a vision to help other congregations develop prayer ministry as well.

Leadership. Those who persevere in the bold task of leading posthomo-sexual ministries can often trace their success to leaders who have supported and mentored them in the context of the local church. In chapter 1, we noted that Alan Chambers, president of Exodus International, credits most of his early spiritual success to Discovery Church, which brought together grace and truth to foster an environment of acceptance and growth. Now consider the rest of his story.

In 1996, Alan joined Calvary Assembly of God in Winter Park, Florida, where Clark Whitten was senior pastor. Alan and Clark found a connec-tion in Christ, and within a few years Alan was offered a staff position in this several-thousand-member congregation. When Alan accepted the call as president of Exodus International, Calvary Assembly fully backed his deci-sion. In support of Alan, Clark accepted an offer to serve on the board of directors of Exodus International.

In 2005, Clark Whitten began a new church in Longwood, Florida, called Grace Church. Alan made Grace his home church. These two men continue to model what needs to happen in churches around the country. If the head of Exodus International is serving in a local church, it is hoped that the leaders of Exodus-supported ministries around the country will follow in his steps. For this to happen, however, pastors and church leaders must, like Clark Whitten, receive them and support them as they use their gifts to make disciples—even in the local church context.

Alan and Clark demonstrate a truth that has been illustrated in churches around the country: Godly church leaders who develop ministries for homo-sexuals cannot help but influence other leaders.

Family values. In chapter 6, we noted how Mike Goeke was challenged by his wife and his extended family not to give up on his marriage. Chapter 3 ended with the story of Mike's pastor, Patrick Payton, encouraging members of his congregation to embrace the family values of transparency, humility, truth telling, and love. We saw how Mike and Stephanie came forward with the history of Mike's same-sex struggles and how the church was changed. This was the beginning point of a significant outreach. Just as Mike and Stephanie were finding grace for their marriage, they formed a ministry for people with marriages shaken by same-sex attraction. And the ministry could not be contained within the confines of the congregation.

Probably more than half of the people today who struggle with same-sex attractions are married to someone of the opposite sex.[2] Mike partnered with his church, Stonegate Fellowship, to create Cross Power Ministries (*www.crosspowerministries.com*), which offers not only lay counseling to people with unwanted same-sex attractions but also a four-day annual conference for people whose marriages are affected by homosexuality. Their second annual conference, in 2009, drew fifty-three couples, including thirteen mentor couples from fourteen states, Canada, and the Philippines.

Mentors and counselors. When Roy Blankenship began his pastoral counseling ministry at First Baptist Church in Woodstock, Georgia, he had no idea what he was in for. He would experience a phenomenon that has been lived out by several other congregations as well—a counseling or mentoring program that meets all kinds of needs and involves all kinds of people. First Baptist Woodstock has grown to include recovery groups for alcohol and substance abuse, sexual brokenness, same-sex attractions, and a variety of life-dominating issues. In 2004, Roy put several of the ministries under an umbrella organization called The HopeQuest Ministry Group, Inc., while remaining

> **Ministry Tip #6: If we build ministry in each of the first five spheres, outreach will occur naturally.**

on the staff of the church. First Baptist, in conjunction with HopeQuest, leads one of the few church-based residential recovery programs for sexual brokenness and life-dominating concerns in the country. Every six weeks, HopeQuest offers a twelve-week recovery program that ministers to about seventy-five to eighty people per year, and their nonresidential services reach far more.

Small group ministry. When Andy Comiskey formed his first small group for people with sexual and relational brokenness, he had no idea that Desert Stream Ministry would eventually be established and launch groups around the world. Doug McIntyre didn't expect that the initial small group that helped him walk in obedience to Christ would become a prototype for small groups in other countries under the Homosexuals Anonymous umbrella. People involved in Saddleback Church's first Celebrate Recovery group never dreamed their model of ministry would have such impact worldwide.

By following linkages through these and similar ministries around the globe, I've caught a glimpse of how difficult it is for effective small groups to keep the good news to themselves. From Germany to New Zealand, from South America to Egypt, from India to Thailand, the stories of changed lives through small group discipleship has been repeated in country after country, and small group ministry is the unifying factor that makes it possible.

Outreach. Regardless of a congregation's size or strengths, when a church engages in the first five ministry spheres, outreach happens. A church that embraces cutting-edge ministry cannot help but influence its community. The gospel is needed in Samaria, and by his Word and Spirit, Jesus is leading the way.

The Big Picture

Then we will no longer be infants, tossed back and forth by the waves, and blown here and there by every wind of teaching and by the cunning and craftiness of men in their deceitful scheming. Instead, speaking the truth in love, we will in all things grow up into him who is the Head, that is, Christ. From him the whole body, joined and held together by every supporting ligament, grows and builds itself up in love, as each part does its work.

—*Ephesians 4:14–16*

Some years ago I visited the state of my birth, Oregon, to see family and friends. Traveling back roads, we forged southeastward through pristine territory. Deciding to gain perspective on the portion of the state we had yet to explore, we chugged up the twenty-mile ramp along the backbone of Steens Mountain. The vegetation grew shorter and scarcer, and the air thinner, until only grass, rock, and wildflowers painted our landscape. Suddenly we reached the top—or, should I say, the edge. Steens Mountain is the largest geological fault in North America, dropping more than a vertical mile to the expansive Alvord Desert. What I saw gave me a new appreciation for the word *breathtaking*. I peered over a visual plummet into expansive countryside far below, stained red and orange by the setting sun. If you have ever wondered what it would be like to hang outside of an airplane at seven thousand feet, visit Steens Mountain.

Paul's view of the church as described in the book of Ephesians is even more stunning. The apostle takes us up the road of spiritual realities to heavenly heights in the first half of the book. In chapter 4, a sudden drop from lofty teaching shows us the panorama of earthly application. He beckons us to peer over the ragged edge that joins heaven to earth to see the breathtaking view of "how wide and long and high and deep is the love of Christ, and to know this love that surpasses knowledge—that you may be filled to the measure of all the fullness of God" (Ephesians 3:18–19).

215

Paul envisions a church that is

- *committed to truth*, not "blown here and there by every wind of teaching and by the cunning and craftiness of men in their deceitful scheming" (Ephesians 4:14), and that
- *communicates God's grace*, "speaking the truth in love" (v. 15), because it is
- *centered on the Lord*, on "him who is the Head, that is, Christ" (v. 15).

In short, Paul wants us to recognize the potential for spiritual maturation and growth in our congregations.

Christian Maturity

My search for churches that have established ministries for people with unwanted same-sex attractions has brought me to the doorstep of healthy and vital congregations that are keenly focused on Christ. We must measure our success not by the size of our *programs* but by the *person* of Jesus Christ. Christian maturity is the nonnegotiable essential for Christlike ministry.

An immature church may launch into certain ministries and look good on the outside while being spiritually anemic within. No church should attempt ministry to people with sexual brokenness, sexual abuse, and unwanted same-sex attractions without putting the spiritual growth of its membership first on the list of priorities. Love for one another, transparency with each other, truth spoken with clarity, prayer for each ministry, and unity among leaders are essential foundations for this work.

The Open Door

San Rafael, California, is a small town with an urban feel. Named after the archangel Rafael, the apocryphal angel of healing, this town has been marked as a source of healing and help for hundreds of people who have struggled with unwanted same-sex attractions. Michael and Mona Riley began their ministry in San Rafael in August 1972, and as of this writing they are still there. For nearly four decades they have served in what may be considered the first and most enduring proof in the United States that local congregations can indeed create and sustain ministry for people with unwanted same-sex attractions and other forms of sexual brokenness.

Their congregation, the Church of the Open Door, was born in the midst of the Jesus movement, an era of experimentation and reckless abandon, for better or for worse. Michael and Mona were hoping for better when their ministry team established more than a dozen Christian discipleship houses. They took in drug addicts, street people, and others with a variety of needs. The door was indeed wide open at the Church of the Open Door.

In 1973, a man named Frank Worthen came to visit. Frank had been involved in San Francisco's gay subculture for more than twenty years, had become a Christian, and was seeking to help homosexuals find salvation and freedom to walk in holiness. When Frank shared his vision for launching a ministry to homosexuals, Michael and his leadership team didn't spend much time pondering whether to join him or how it could be done. In Michael's words, "To us, it was just another ministry, another interesting outreach." They didn't have a clear model to copy, a proven strategy to embrace, or a time-tested manual to follow. As one of the first churches to venture into this new territory, they stepped out in faith.

A similar bold faith is required today for churches that establish ministries for people with unwanted same-sex attractions and related concerns. When we understand that God wants us to reach people with his love and truth more than we can imagine, we can also trust that he will show us the way.

Help along the Way

As I've stated and illustrated throughout this book, one of the best resources to help a church launch ministry to the sexually broken is someone who has experienced such brokenness and is now walking in holiness before the Lord. In many cases, such an individual will arise from within one's own congregation. Likewise, many churches have created partnerships with leaders of posthomosexual ministries outside their fold. Either way, mature Christian leadership is needed to help our churches become mature in Christ.

"When Frank walked into our office many years ago," Michael Riley explains, "our destinies became entwined forever. Working with young people and working in ex-gay ministry are two of the most exciting things I've ever done in my ministry life. It's been incredibly rewarding."[3]

Now in his early eighties, Frank tells about writing one of the first Christian books about coming out of homosexuality. He also helped launch Exodus in the United States, then Exodus International, and then other posthomosexual ministries overseas. His starting point, however, was the formation of Love in Action.

For more than twenty years, Love in Action and the Church of the Open Door hosted live-in programs that drew up to twenty people a year from around the world. Residents involved themselves in Love in Action's discipleship courses and participated in the life of the Church of the Open Door as part of their recovery process. This shared ministry was for decades the source of media attention as God used it to change lives and to spread the vision. In 1994, Love in Action strategically relocated to Memphis, Tennessee, where it continues to flourish. This, the first of Exodus's 230 affiliated ministries in North America, is also one of the strongest.

Shortly after Love in Action's move, Frank launched New Hope Ministries in 1994, which now offers a biannual seven-day residential program and a variety of services and resources in conjunction with the Church of the Open Door. Michael and Frank give thanks to God for their wives, whose contributions to the ministry through their writings and personal support have been invaluable.

A Word of Advice

I asked Frank for a word of advice for pastors. He expressed to me his understanding that many churches are divided on the topic of homosexuality before it is even introduced, and he advises pastors not to force the issue on their people but to build ministry incrementally: "Tell them that I understand they're facing many issues we never had to face before. The typical response to homosexuality for churches today is either to reject gay people or to accept homosexuality without questioning whether or not that's where it's at. Too many pastors are avoiding the issue. It is time for pastors to get some knowledge on this subject and to build churches that can tell gay people, 'We love you, and if you want to know Christ better, we're here to help you.'"

This book has offered rationale, testimonies, models, and guidelines for ministry. Now it is up to you. If you doubt the great purpose God has for your church, please reread the first half of Ephesians, pause at the end of chapter 3, take a deep breath, and look at the end of chapter 4 once again. The love of God is wide enough to reach all kinds of people, long enough to keep your church on track through time, high enough to change any life, and deep enough to heal every wounded heart.

> For this reason I kneel before the Father, from whom his whole family in heaven and on earth derives its name. I pray that out of his glorious riches he may strengthen you with power through his Spirit in your inner being, so that Christ may dwell in your hearts through faith. And I pray that you, being rooted and established in love, may have power, together with all the saints, to grasp how wide and long and high and deep is the love of Christ, and to know this love that surpasses knowledge—that you may be filled to the measure of all the fullness of God.
>
> Now to him who is able to do immeasurably more than all we ask or imagine, according to his power that is at work within us, to him be glory in the church and in Christ Jesus throughout all generations, for ever and ever! Amen.
>
> —*Ephesians 3:14–21*

Questions for Personal or Group Reflection

Introduction: Putting Christ Back into "Christian"

1. In what ways has the issue of homosexuality been controversial in the church at large? In your congregation?
2. List several topics other than homosexuality in which truth and grace must be embraced if Christians are to avoid harmful extremes.
3. What are the greatest barriers in your church to finding peace and unity about the topic of homosexuality?

Chapter 1: The Feet

1. Do you tend to lean more toward grace or truth? Do you find it difficult to bring them both together without compromising either? Answer with specific examples.
2. Where would you place your church on the triangular preparedness paradigm (p. 29)? Why?
3. Think of three practical steps your church members might take to blend grace and truth as they engage in Christlike ministry.

Chapter 2: The Heart

1. Complete this sentence as you think of needs in the world and of people in pain all around you: "I am greatly moved to compassion by _____."
2. Do you feel any compassion for gays and lesbians and for those who do not identify themselves as homosexual but who quietly suffer with unwanted same-sex attractions? Why or why not?
3. How would our society change if we had absolutely no compassion for homosexuals? And, on the other extreme, describe how things would change if marriage were allowed in our country in any shape or form imaginable.

Chapter 3: The Head

1. List five reasons why godly leadership is needed in the church today.
2. Do the leaders in your church (or denomination) tend more toward the extreme of the Pharisees or the Sadducees? Explain.
3. Does your church allow people who have been divorced but are now repentant to serve in leadership capacities? Does it allow people who were once practicing gays or lesbians but who now love and obey the Lord to serve in leadership? If not, should it? What about those who have overcome alcoholism or drug addiction? What about someone who has overcome sexual addictions?

Chapter 4: The Landscape

1. Respond to this statement: "There are only a few texts about homosexuality in the Bible—fewer than there are about how an Old Testament priest should dress for service. We don't talk about priests' garments much anymore, so let's stop making such a big deal about homosexuality."
2. Chapter 4 talks about the great emphasis in the Bible on marriage as God designed it. What do you think about the legalization of homosexual marriage? Why?
3. What most impressed you about the testimony of Tim Wilkins?

Chapter 5: The Source

1. If scientists were to discover a "gay gene," would it make any difference in how you view homosexuality? Explain.
2. Can you think of ways our society tends to use genetics as an excuse for behavior? Do you ever do so yourself? If so, how?
3. What insight did you gain from Bill Henson's testimony? Be specific.

Chapter 6: The Law

1. Have you heard people say that the Old Testament laws against homosexuality are outdated? How do you respond to such claims?
2. Give three examples of Old Testament ceremonial laws that are not relevant for today. Give three examples of moral laws from the Old Testament that are timeless.
3. Do you agree with the approach taken by Mike Goeke's family to get him back, as explained in his testimony? Why or why not?

Chapter 7: The Wisdom

1. Do you agree with the American Psychological Association's declarations that homosexuality cannot be changed and that attempts to do so may harm the one being treated? Why or why not?

2. Do you personally know any gays or lesbians who have come out of a homosexual lifestyle and who now live in holiness? If so, how do they impress you?

3. What are your reactions to the Mel White story? How might the world and our churches be different today if we had been more engaged in ministry to homosexuals a few decades ago?

Chapter 8: The Grace

1. Comment on this statement: "Sodom and Gomorrah is the clearest statement in the Bible of the coming judgment on the sodomites in our land."

2. What is the danger of elevating one sin above all others? What is the danger of redefining sin?

3. What most impressed you about Terrence Toon's testimony? Why?

Chapter 9: The Potential

1. Have you ever experienced such a powerful move of God's Spirit or such deep conviction from God's Word that it changed the direction of your life? Briefly describe what happened.

2. Do you believe God's Word is trustworthy through and through? Why or why not?

3. Regarding Meleah's testimony, do you think her early years of growing up in the church helped her to come back to the Lord when she was older? Read Proverbs 22:6 and discuss ways in which we can help children in our homes and in the church become grounded in Scripture.

Chapter 10: Blueprint

1. Do you believe your church should create (or improve) ministry for people who struggle with unwanted same-sex attractions? Why or why not?

2. Which of the ministry spheres do you think is most important? Why?

3. Which ministry sphere represents the area of greatest need for your church's growth? Why?

Chapter 11: Motivation

1. Have you ever experienced a powerful answer to prayer? If so, explain.

2. On a scale of one to ten (ten being best), how would you rank the level of prayer in your church?

3. Give three steps you will take to improve your personal prayer life, and suggest three ways your church might strengthen its prayer ministry.

Chapter 12: Vision

1. Have you witnessed a homeless person or someone with a special need interrupting a worship service, a church potluck, or a similar religious function? If so, how did people respond? How do you think Jesus would have responded?
2. Which of the different size models described in chapter 12 does your church fit into? What did you learn from the discussion about different-size congregations?
3. What damage could be caused in your church if your leadership attempted to build any ministry in the church too quickly, especially ministry for homosexuals?

Chapter 13: Healing

1. Describe a time you visited a church and did not feel welcome. Describe also a time you visited a church and felt part of the family almost immediately.
2. Describe the Christian family values that would make any church more Christlike for visitors. Which of these values would be most important for people who are struggling with sexual brokenness?
3. Name three things you and others in your church might do to incorporate these values into the life of your church.

Chapter 14: Growth

1. Have you been mentored by someone, whether formally or informally, who has helped shape and change your life? Explain.
2. Have you to some extent mentored any person, whether a child, a person in church, or a person on the job? What worked well? What do you wish you would have done differently?
3. Do you have a positive or negative opinion of the counseling profession? Do you believe some counselors can be of great help to people? Explain. (Please do not violate anyone's confidence.)

Chapter 15: Support

1. Have you ever been in a small group for spiritual growth, fellowship, support, or therapy? As you are comfortable (and without breaching anyone's confidence), share what you liked and didn't like about your experience.
2. Considering Jesus and his disciples and other examples in the Bible, what might be the benefits of being part of a regular small group gathering for accountability and spiritual growth?

3. Does your church have support or therapy groups for special needs? What needs are you aware of that could possibly be better met if your congregation offered a specialized group for that need?

Chapter 16: Celebration

1. Do you like or dislike the comparison in this chapter between Samaritans and homosexuals? Explain your answer.
2. Which of the ministry spheres do you believe reflects your congregation's greatest natural strength? Why? Be specific.
3. Describe what the ideal ministry to people with unwanted same-sex attractions might look like in the context of your church, given enough time and leadership.

Conclusion: The Big Picture

1. Why is spiritual maturity in your church of first importance for developing ministry in the context of sexual and relational brokenness? What kinds of problems might develop if people are not focused on the Lord above all else?
2. Looking back on your study in this book, what was the most important insight or challenge you would like to implement in your life and in your congregation?
3. Which resources or books (as listed in the next section) will you utilize for your next stage of growth and understanding?

Additional Ministry Resources

Recommended Reading

The Church

Chambers, Alan. *God's Grace and the Homosexual Next Door*. Eugene, Ore.: Harvest House, 2006.

Dallas, Joe. *A Strong Delusion*. Eugene, Ore.: Harvest House, 1996.

Theology

Gagnon, Robert. *The Bible and Homosexual Practice*. Nashville: Abingdon, 2001.

Grenz, Stanley. *Welcoming but Not Affirming*. Louisville: Westminster, 1998.

Apologetics

Haley, Mike. *101 Frequently Asked Questions about Homosexuality*. Eugene, Ore.: Harvest House, 2004.

Satinover, Jeffrey. *Homosexuality and the Politics of Truth*. Grand Rapids: Baker, 1996.

For Men

Dallas, Joe. *Desires in Conflict*. Eugene, Ore.: Harvest House, 1991.

Konrad, Jeff. *You Don't Have to Be Gay*. Newport Beach, Calif.: Pacific Publishing House, 1987.

For Women

Howard, Jeannette. *Out of Egypt*. Baltimore, Md.: Regeneration Books, 1991.

Paulk, Anne. *Restoring Sexual Identity*. Eugene, Ore.: Harvest House, 2003.

For Parents and Family

Dallas, Joe. *When Homosexuality Hits Home*. Eugene, Ore.: Harvest House, 2004.

Nicolosi, Joseph. *A Parent's Guide to Preventing Homosexuality*. Downers Grove, Ill.: InterVarsity, 2002.

Worthen, Anita, and Bob Davies. *Someone I Love Is Gay*. Downers Grove, Ill.: InterVarsity, 1996.

Resource Ministries

Association of Christian Counselors (*www.aacc.net*). An association that equips clinical, pastoral, and lay caregivers with biblical truth and psychosocial insights to minister to hurting persons and to help them move to personal wholeness, interpersonal competence, mental stability, and spiritual maturity.

Celebrate Recovery (*www.celebraterecovery.com*). A ministry that helps people resolve their pain in a fellowship-based environment while implementing a Christ-centered recovery that helps people discover dignity, strength, joy, and growth.

Courage (*www.couragerc.net*). Provides spiritual support for men and women striving to live chaste lives in accordance with the Roman Catholic Church's pastoral teaching on homosexuality.

Desert Stream Ministries (*www.desertstream.org*). Equips churches to establish healing ministries to the sexually and relationally broken.

Exodus International (*www.exodusinternational.org*). The largest referral and resource network that proclaims freedom from homosexuality through repentance and faith in Jesus Christ. Exodus also helps church leaders deal pastorally with issues related to homosexuality. The Exodus International network includes more than 230 affiliated ministries in the United States and Canada and is linked to regions outside the United States through the Exodus Global Alliance.

Homosexuals Anonymous (*www.ha-fs.org*). A nondenominational Christian Fellowship of men and women seeking to live free from homosexuality through support groups that follow a fourteen-step process based on biblical values.

National Association for the Research and Therapy of Homosexuality — NARTH (*www.narth.com*). An organization that seeks to make effective psychological therapy available to homosexual men and women who seek change. NARTH offers research information and an international referral service of licensed therapists.

OneByOne (*www.oneby1.org*). A Presbyterian Church USA (PCUSA) renewal organization that seeks to educate and equip the church to minister the transforming grace and power of Jesus Christ to those in conflict with their sexuality. OBO offers educational resources, church presentations and seminars, as well as limited phone and counseling referrals.

Parents and Friends of Ex-Gays — PFOX (*www.pfox.org*). A Christ centered network of parents, friends, and family of loved ones struggling with homosexuality.

The Way Out (*www.sbcthewayout.com*). The ministry of the Southern Baptist Convention's Gender Issues Office that provides resources and guidance for congregations and individuals struggling with same-sex attraction.

Transforming Congregations (*www.transcong.org*). A ministry that provides information, resources, and training to churches related to the transformation of homosexuals with a special focus on the United Methodist Church.

For additional resources, visit *www.ChurchReflection.com*

Notes

Introduction: Putting Christ Back into "Christian"

1. Dietrich Bonhoeffer, *Life Together* (New York: Harper, 1954), 54–55.

Chapter 1: The Feet

1. Michael Todd Wilson and Brad Hoffmann, *Preventing Ministry Failure* (Downers Grove, Ill.: InterVarsity, 2007), 15–16.
2. J. C. Abma et al., "Teenagers in the United States: Sexual Activity, Contraceptive Use, and Childbearing, 2002," National Center for Health Statistics, *Vital and Health Statistics*, ser. 23, no. 24 (December 2004).
3. U.S. Census Bureau, "America's Families and Living Arrangements: 2000" (June 2001), 12.
4. Centers for Disease Control and Prevention, "Adverse Childhood Experiences Study: Prevalence of Individual Adverse Childhood Experiences," *www.cdc.gov/nccdphp/ace/prevalence.htm* (December 12, 2005).
5. Fred Phelps, the founder of Westboro Baptist Church in Topeka, Kansas, is notorious for his extreme antigay and anti-American positions. Convinced that God will judge America and the world for homosexuality, he has developed slogans such as "God Hates Fags" (the header on his website: www.godhatesfags.com), "America Is Doomed," "Thank God for Dead Soldiers," and "God Hates the USA."
6. The popularization of streaking in 1974, naturalist groups, and those making political statements have promoted the riding of bikes nude for some time, and the world's first international bike ride was in 2004. While such events have received national and international publicity for some time, traditional Christian churches have not endorsed them because of the Bible's call for purity in thought and the avoidance of temptation (Philippians 4:8–9; Colossians 3:5; 2 Timothy 2:22; 1 John 2:16). To this end, this author does not recommend searching the Internet for more information on this topic.
7. Mark Chaves, "National Congregations Study," *www.soc.duke.edu/natcong/Docs/NCSII_report_final.pdf* (June 2009).
8. SBC Gender Issues Office, "Lifeway Research Issues Survey Results," *www.sbcthewayout.com/survey.html* (April 10–12, 2008).
9. From a telephone interview, October 12, 2009.

10. Alan Chambers, *God's Grace and the Homosexual Next Door* (Eugene, Ore.: Harvest House, 2006), 80–81.

11. From a telephone interview, October 12, 2009.

12. Ibid.

13. Chambers, *God's Grace and the Homosexual Next Door*, 83–84.

14. Alan Chambers, *Leaving Homosexuality: A Practical Guide for Men and Women Looking for a Way Out* (Eugene, Ore.: Harvest House, 2009), 63–64.

15. Chambers, *God's Grace and the Homosexual Next Door*, 84–85.

Chapter 2: The Heart

1. Articles suggest the rate of homosexuality in the Deaf world is about 15 percent higher than in the general population (see, e.g., Tina Gianoulis, "Deaf Culture," *www.glbtq.com/social-sciences/deaf_culture.html*).

2. See Mark R. Laaser, *Healing the Wounds of Sexual Addiction* (Grand Rapids: Zondervan, 2004), 10, 15.

3. Alan Chambers, *God's Grace and the Homosexual Next Door* (Eugene, Ore.: Harvest House, 2006), 134–36.

Chapter 3: The Head

1. J. Oswald Sanders, *Spiritual Leadership* (Chicago: Moody, 1967), 35.

2. Leroy Eims, *Be the Leader You Were Meant to Be* (Wheaton, Ill.: Victor, 1975), 7.

3. Jack Rogers, *Jesus, the Bible and Homosexuality: Explode the Myths, Heal the Church* (Louisville: Westminster, 2006), 18.

4. Derrick S. Bailey, *Homosexuality and the Western Christian Tradition* (London: Longman, 1955).

5. See, e.g., Acts 1:12–14; 2:17–18; 16:13; 17:12; 18:26; 21:9; Romans 16:1–7, 12; 1 Corinthians 11:5; Philippians 4:3; 1 Timothy 3:11.

6. Rogers, *Jesus, the Bible and Homosexuality*, 44.

7. Kenneth S. Wuest, *The New Testament: An Expanded Translation* (Grand Rapids: Eerdmans, 1961), 15.

8. Scriptural texts related to the topic of homosexuality include Genesis 2:21–25; 9:20–27; 19:1–29; Leviticus 18:22; 20:13; Deuteronomy 23:17–18; Judges 19:22–25; 1 Kings 14:24; 15:12; 22:46; 2 Kings 23:7; Ezekiel 16:50; Romans 1:18–32; 1 Corinthians 6:9–11; 1 Timothy 1:8–11; 2 Peter 2:6–10; Jude 7; Revelation 21:8; 22:15.

9. Max De Pree, *Leadership Is an Art* (New York: Doubleday, 1989), 11.

Chapter 4: The Landscape

1. Troy Perry, *Don't Be Afraid Anymore* (New York: St. Martin's, 1990), 40.

2. See Reuven P. Bulka, *One Man, One Woman, One Lifetime: An Argument for Moral Tradition* (Lafayette, La.: Huntington House, 1995), 9; Neil Whitehead and Briar Whitehead, *My Genes Made Me Do It!* (Lafayette, La.: Huntington House, 1999), 106. Whitehead explains that homosexuality was so rare among Orthodox Jews

that learned rabbis "usually allowed men to sleep in the same bed, because the likelihood of sexual contact was considered negligible" (chapter 6).

3. See Matthew 19:3−9. Such questions were asked because adultery was an issue in the Jewish community, even if it was not widespread. Among the Jews in Jesus' day there were two schools of thought about adultery and divorce. Shammai held that the "something indecent" for which a man was allowed to divorce his wife (Deuteronomy 24:1−4) meant "marital unfaithfulness." The school of Hillel, however, taught that a man could divorce his wife if she did anything he disliked (based on the phrase in Deuteronomy 24:1, "becomes displeasing to him"); not cleaning house well or burning the husband's food could be grounds for divorce. Interestingly, the continued practice of levirate marriage (Deuteronomy 25:5−10) among the Jews led to polygamy in Jesus' day, which was countenanced by the school of Shammai but not Hillel. See W. Günther, "Marriage, Adultery, Bride, Bridegroom," in *New International Dictionary of New Testament Theology* (ed. Colin Brown; Grand Rapids: Zondervan, 1976), 2:578−79.

4. C. S. Lewis, *Mere Christianity* (New York: Touchstone, 1980), 104−5.

5. See, e.g., Alix Kirsta, "Genetic Sexual Attraction," *The Guardian, www.guardian. co.uk/weekend/story/0,3605,956454,00.html* (May 17, 2003); Arthur P. Wolf and William H. Durham, eds., *Inbreeding, Incest, and the Incest Taboo* (Palo Alto, Calif.: Stanford University Press, 2004).

6. Jessica Bennett, "Only You. And You. And You," *http://www.newsweek.com/ id/209164* (July 29, 2009).

7. Beyond Marriage, "Beyond Same-Sex Marriage," *http://www.beyondmarriage.org/ full_statement.html* (April 2006).

8. Quoted in Walter A. Elwell and Philip W. Comfort, eds., *Tyndale Bible Dictionary* (Wheaton Ill.: Tyndale, 2001), 169.

9. See, e.g., Robin Scroggs, *The New Testament and Homosexuality* (Philadelphia: Westminster, 1980).

10. See David E. Malick, "The Condemnation of Homosexuality in Romans 1:26−27," *Bibliotheca Sacra* 150, no. 599 (1993): 327−40.

11. Whitehead and Whitehead (*My Genes Made Me Do It!* 100) comment on extensive research by D. F. Greenberg, a progay advocate, on the practice of homosexuality in different cultures and times (see Greenberg, *The Construction of Homosexuality* [Chicago: University of Chicago Press, 1988]; Robert A. J. Gagnon, *The Bible and Homosexual Practice* [Nashville: Abingdon, 2001], 350).

12. Joe Dallas (*A Strong Delusion* [Eugene, Ore.: Harvest House, 1996], 195) points out that the words selected for men and women are rarely used in the New Testament and emphasize *gender*. Paul was clearly stating that the activities committed in this context were unnatural to humans as *males* and *females*. The idea of specific sexual orientation does not enter into the logic of the text.

13. See Perry, *Don't Be Afraid Anymore*, 342, who states, "The homosexual practices cited in Romans 1:24−27 were believed to result from idolatry ... in this larger context, it should be obvious that such acts are significantly different than loving, responsible lesbian and gay relationships seen today."

14. For a good summary of various efforts to cloud the rather plain meaning of this Romans 1 text, see Gagnon, *The Bible and Homosexual Practice*, 229–329.

15. Quoted in Roy B. Zuck, *Basic Bible Interpretation: A Practical Guide to Discovering Biblical Truth* (Wheaton, Ill.: Victor, 1991), 45.

16. Lewis, *Mere Christianity*, 95.

Chapter 5: The Source

1. John J. McNeil, "Homosexuality: Challenging the Church to Grow," in *Homosexuality in the Church* (ed. Jeffrey S. Siker; Louisville: Westminster, 1994), 53.

2. Quoted in Larry Thompson, "Search for a Gay Gene," *Time*, http://www.time.com/time/magazine/article/0,9171,983027,00.html (June 12, 1995).

3. See Stephen Bennett, "Dr. Albert Mohler, A 'Gay' Gene and The 'Cure' for Homosexuality," *Christian News Wire*, http://www.christiannewswire.com/news/609722522.html (March 19, 2009).

4. Quoted in R. McKie, "The Myth of the Gay Gene," *The Press* (New Zealand) (July 30, 1993), 9.

5. Neil Whitehead, "The Importance of Twin Studies," NARTH *Bulletin* 26, http://www.narth.com/docs/whitehead2.html (April 2001).

6. D. H. Hamer et al., "A Linkage between DNA Markers on the X Chromosome and the Male Sexual Orientation," *Science* 261, no. 5119 (1993): 321–27.

7. Anastasia Toufexis, "New Evidence of a 'Gay Gene,'" *Time* 146, no. 20 (November 13, 1995): 95.

8. Neil Whitehead and Briar Whitehead, *My Genes Made Me Do It!* (Lafayette, La.: Huntington House, 1999), 145.

9. Ibid., 27.

10. Ibid., 26.

11. See A. C. Kinsey, W. B. Pomeroy, C. E. Martin, *Sexual Behavior in the Human Male* (Philadelphia: W. B. Saunders, 1948); A. C. Kinsey et al., *Sexual Behavior in the Human Female* (Philadelphia: Saunders, 1953). Whitehead (*My Genes Made Me Do It!*) points to more than thirty surveys of homosexual incidence by the mid-1990s based on genuinely representative samples.

12. See, e.g., E. O. Laumann et al., *The Social Organization of Sexuality* (Chicago: University of Chicago Press, 1994). This 1992 National Health and Social Life Survey is the most extensive survey to date of the sexual practices of Americans. See also Robert A. J. Gagnon, *The Bible and Homosexual Practice* (Nashville: Abingdon, 2001), 416–29.

13. C. S. Ford and F. A. Beach, *Patterns of Sexual Behavior* (London: Eyre and Spottiswoode, 1952), quoted in Whitehead and Whitehead, *My Genes Made Me Do It!* 98.

14. D. F. Greenberg, *The Construction of Homosexuality* (Chicago: University of Chicago Press, 1988), 74–77.

15. Stephen Goldberg, *When Wish Replaces Thought: Why So Much of What You Believe Is False* (New York: Prometheus, 1992), 53, 63.

16. Simon LeVay, *Queer Science* (Cambridge, Mass.: MIT Press, 1996), 273.

17. American Psychological Association, "Answers to your questions: For a better understanding of sexual orientation and homosexuality" (2008), *www.apa.org/topics/sexuality/sorientation.pdf.* Copyright © 2008 American Psychological Association.

18. U.S. Census Bureau, "Educational Attainment, 2006–2008 American Community Survey 3-Year Estimates," *http://factfinder.census.gov/servlet/STTable?_bm=y&-geo_id=01000US&-qr_name=ACS_2008_3YR_G00_S1501&-ds_name=ACS_2008_3YR_G00_.*

19. Cited in Jeffrey Satinover, *Homosexuality and the Politics of Truth* (Grand Rapids: Baker, 1996), 96.

20. Martin Luther, *Luther's Works* (Philadelphia: Muhlenberg, 1960), 3:80–81.

21. The New Catechism reads, "Homosexual persons are called to chastity. By virtues of self-mastery that teach them inner freedom, at times by the support of disinterested friendship, by prayer and sacramental grace, they can and should gradually and resolutely approach Christian perfection" (*Catechism of the Catholic Church* [New York: Doubleday, 1995], 625–26). This is the general approach adopted by Courage, the primary Catholic ministry reaching out to help people with unwanted same-sex attractions.

22. Elizabeth Moberly, *Homosexuality: A New Christian Ethic* (Greenwood, S.C.: Attic, 1983), 18.

Chapter 6: The Law

1. John Boswell promoted it in his *Christianity, Social Tolerance and Homosexuality* (Chicago: University of Chicago Press, 1980), 100, as did Troy Perry in his *Don't Be Afraid Anymore* (New York: St. Martin's, 1990), 341. The argument is still used widely today.

2. For example, in Leviticus 18 the term is linked to all forms of incest (vv. 6–18), adultery (v. 20), child sacrifice (v. 21), homosexuality (v. 22), and bestiality (v. 23); and in one verse out of thirty, we find it refers to approaching a woman during her period (v. 19). Twenty-six of the twenty-seven verses in the chapter connect the word *detestable* to gross violations of the Ten Commandments and God's timeless moral law. One verse (v. 19) was likely slipped in because of the focus on so many proscriptions and prohibitions related to sexual behavior.

3. Arthur Goldberg, *Light in the Closet: Torah, Homosexuality and the Power to Change* (Beverly Hills, Calif.: Red Heifer, 2008), 301–75.

4. See, e.g., John R. Diggs Jr., "The Health Risks of Gay Sex," Catholic Education Resource Center (2002), *http://www.catholiceducation.org/articles/homosexuality/ho0075.html*; Alysse ElHage, *Family North Carolina Magazine* (July/August 2007), "The Physical Health Risks of Homosexuality," North Carolina Family Policy Council, *http://www.ncfamily.org/FNC/0707S3.html*.

5. Chad Thompson, *Loving Homosexuals as Jesus Would: A Fresh Christian Approach* (Grand Rapids: Brazos, 2004), 57–58.

6. Ibid., 35.

7. Jeff Konrad, *You Don't Have to Be Gay* (Newport Beach, Calif.: Pacific, 1987).

Chapter 7: The Wisdom

1. Quoted in Jeffrey Satinover, *Homosexuality and the Politics of Truth* (Grand Rapids: Baker, 1996), 32.

2. Ronald Bayer, *Homosexuality and American Psychiatry: The Politics of Diagnosis* (New York: Basic, 1981), 102.

3. Ibid., 3.

4. Cited in Merton P. Strommen, *The Church and Homosexuality: Searching for a Middle Ground* (Minneapolis: Kirk House: 2001), 40.

5. Harold I. Lief, "Sexual Survey Number 4: Current Thinking on Homosexuality," *Medical Aspects of Human Sexuality* 11 (1977): 110–11.

6. See Satinover, *Homosexuality and the Politics of Truth*, 169.

7. Neil Whitehead and Briar Whitehead, *My Genes Made Me Do It!* (Lafayette, La.: Huntington House, 1999), 67.

8. Strommen, *Church and Homosexuality*, 42.

9. Bruce Rind, Philip Tromovitch, and Robert Bauserman, "A Meta-analytic Examination of Assumed Properties of Child Sexual Abuse Using College Samples," *Psychological Bulletin* 124 (July 1998): 22–53.

10. Louise Silverstein and Carl Auerbach, "Deconstructing the Essential Father," *American Psychologist* 54 (June 1999), 397–407.

11. Strommen, *Church and Homosexuality*, 42.

12. Joseph Nicolosi, *A Parent's Guide to Preventing Homosexuality* (Downer Grove, Ill.: InterVarsity, 2002), 60–61.

13. Rogers Wright and Nicholas Cummings, eds., *Destructive Trends in Mental Health: The Well-Intentioned Path to Harm* (New York: Routledge, 2005), xxx.

14. Ibid., 22.

15. Quoted in Warren Throckmorton, "Is Psychology Losing Its Way?" *http://www.drthrockmorton.com/article.asp?id=176* (December 21, 2005).

16. See Warren Throckmorton, "My Interview with Dr. Robert Spitzer, *www.drthrockmorton.com/interviewdrspitzer.pdf* (March 2004).

17. See Stanton L. Jones and Mark A. Yarhouse, *Homosexuality: The Use of Scientific Research in the Church's Moral Debate* (Downers Grove, Ill.: InterVarsity, 2000), 54.

18. S. Fisher and R. Greenberg, *Freud Scientifically Reappraised: Testing the Theories and Therapy* (New York: Wiley, 1996), 135.

19. Satinover, *Homosexuality and the Politics of Truth*, 104.

20. Cited in Strommen, *Church and Homosexuality*, 32.

21. See, e.g., NARTH Scientific Advisory Committee, "What Research Shows: NARTH's Response to the American Psychological Association's Claims on Homosexuality," *Journal of Human Sexuality* 1 (2009), 9–37.

22. J. C. Abma et al., "Teenagers in the United States: Sexual Activity, Contraceptive Use, and Childbearing, 2002," National Center for Health Statistics, *Vital and Health Statistics*, ser. 23, no. 24 (December 2004).

23. Mark R. Laaser, *Healing the Wounds of Sexual Addiction* (Grand Rapids: Zondervan: 2004), 15.

24. Satinover, *Homosexuality and the Politics of Truth*, 141–42.

25. See William Consiglio, *Homosexual No More: Practical Strategies for Christians Overcoming Homosexuality* (Wheaton, Ill.: Victor, 1991).

26. See Anne Paulk, *Restoring Sexual Identity: Hope for Women Who Struggle with Same-Sex Attraction* (Eugene, Ore.: Harvest House, 2003), 237–47.

27. Cited in Strommen, *Church and Homosexuality*, 34.

28. See Nicolosi, *Parent's Guide to Preventing Homosexuality*, 75.

29. Jones and Yarhouse, *Homosexuality*, 98.

30. American Psychiatric Association, "Psychiatrists' Views on Homosexuality," *Psychiatric News* (September 1993), a survey conducted by the Office of International Affairs.

31. Satinover, *Homosexuality and the Politics of Truth*, 185–87.

32. William H. Masters and Virginia E. Johnson, *Homosexuality in Perspective* (New York: Bantam, 1979), 400.

33. Warren Throckmorton, "Attempts to Modify Sexual Orientation: A Review of Outcome Literature and Ethical Issues," *Journal of Mental Health Counseling* 20 (October 1998): 283–304.

34. Warren Throckmorton, "I Am Not a Reparative Therapist," *http://www.drthrockmorton.com/article.asp?id=183*.

35. APA Task Force on Appropriate Therapeutic Responses to Sexual Orientation, "Report of the Task Force on Appropriate Therapeutic Responses to Sexual Orientation" Washington, D.C.: American Psychological Association, 2009), 5, *http://www.apa.org/pi/lgbt/resources/therapeutic-response.pdf*.

36. Psychotherapist Joseph Nicolosi, for example, is a leading proponent of reparative therapy, which seeks to help homosexuals become reoriented toward heterosexuality. He has counseled more than 1,000 homosexuals. When asked about the percentage of those who have been helped, Nicolosi replied, "The success rate is the same as for any kind of psychotherapy: one-third success, one-third improved, and one-third unsuccessful" (cited in Strommen, *Church and Homosexuality*, 67). When I interviewed Dr. Nicolosi, however, he explained that their counseling practice has since become so efficient that "almost all of our clients experience significant diminishment of same-sex attractions." But even this is not a claim to 100 percent success.

37. The 38 percent claiming success included 15 percent who reported change that led to successful heterosexual dating or marriage, and 23 percent who remained chaste. The first group experienced "a complete or nearly complete resolution of homosexual orientation issues," and the second group experienced "a very substantial resolution of homosexual orientation issues" (Jones and Yarhouse, *Homosexuality*, 279–86).

38. Jones and Yarhouse, *Homosexuality*, 387.

39. Alan Chambers, *God's Grace and the Homosexual Next Door* (Eugene, Ore.: Harvest House, 2006), 122.

40. Mel White, *Stranger at the Gate: To Be Gay and Christian in America* (New York: Plume, 1995), 13–14.

Chapter 8: The Grace

1. For a comprehensive treatment of both biblical and extrabiblical references to the Sodom account, see Robert Gagnon, *The Bible and Homosexual Practice* (Nashville: Abingdon, 2001), 79–100. A long-trusted tool in the scriptural interpretation toolbox is the comparison of theologians' perspectives through the broad sweep of history, all the way back to the church fathers. In this case, the overwhelming majority have understood the Sodom account to be a judgment on homosexual activity, along with other sins. For example, Thomas Schmidt (*Straight and Narrow?* [Downers Grove, Ill.: InterVarsity, 1995], 41) writes, "The second-century BC *Testament of the Twelve Patriarchs* labels the Sodomites 'sexually promiscuous' (*Testimony of Benjamin* 9:1) and refers to 'sodom, which departed from the order of nature' (*Testament of Nephtali* 3:4). From the same time period, *Jubilees* specifies that the Sodomites were 'polluting themselves and fornicating in their flesh' (16:5, compare 20:5–6). Both Philo and Josephus plainly name same-sex relations as the characteristic view of Sodom."

2. Several prominent authors use this argument, such as John Boswell (*Christianity, Social Tolerance and Homosexuality*] Chicago: University of Chicago Press, 1980], 93–94), Derrick S. Bailey (*Homosexuality and the Western Christian Tradition* [London: Longman's, 1955], 3–4), and John McNeill, (*The Church and the Homosexual* [Boston: Beacon, 1993], 54–55).

3. Occurrences of the word *yādaʿ* that mean sexual intercourse in Genesis include 4:1, 17, 25; 19:8; 24:16; 38:26. The other uses in the Hebrew Bible include Numbers 31:17, 18, 35; Judges 11:39; 19:22, 25; 21:11; 1 Samuel 1:19; 1 Kings 1:4.

4. James De Young ("The Contributions of the Septuagint to Biblical Sanctions against Homosexuality," *JETS* 34 [1991]: 158–65) points to Scroggs, Greenberg, Edwards, Nissinen, Springett, Grenz, and Wold as examples of progay authors who disagree with the conclusions of Bailey and Boswell.

5. Robin Scroggs, *The New Testament and Homosexuality* (Philadelphia: Westminster, 1980), 108.

6. David F. Wright, "Homosexuals or Prostitutes? The Meaning of *arsenokoitai* (1 Cor. 6:9; 1 Tim. 1:10)," *Vigiliae Christianae* 38 (June 1984), 125–53.

7. Gagnon, *The Bible and Homosexual Practice*, 312–36.

8. David Kinnaman and Gabe Lyons, *unChristian: What a New Generation Really Thinks about Christianity . . . and Why It Matters* (Grand Rapids: Baker, 2007), 27.

9. Quoted in Adelle M. Banks, "Youth see Christians as judgmental, anti-gay," Religion News Service, October 11, 2007.

10. See The Henry J. Kaiser Family Foundation, "HIV/AIDS Policy Fact Sheet: The HIV/AIDS Epidemic in the United States" (September 2009).

11. Centers for Disease Control and Prevention, "Fact Sheet: HIV and AIDS among Gay and Bisexual Men" (August 2009), *http://www.cdc.gov/NCHHSTP/ newsroom/docs/FastFacts-MSM-FINAL508COMP.pdf*; see also CDC, "HIV and AIDS in America: A Snapshot" (April 2009), *http://www.cdc.gov/nchhstp/docs/ AAA-HIVFastFacts-42309-508comp.pdf*.

12. Cited in Jeffrey Satinover, *Homosexuality and the Politics of Truth* (Grand Rapids: Baker, 1996), 57. Satinover describes the incidence as "roughly 430 times greater than among the heterosexual population at large." See also R. S. Hogg, S. A. Strathdee, et al., "Modeling the Impact of HIV Disease on Mortality in Gay and Bisexual Men," *International Journal of Epidemiology* 26, no. 3 (1997): 659.

13. Kay Warren, *Dangerous Surrender: What Happens When You Say Yes to God* (Grand Rapids: Zondervan, 2007), 232–33.

14. The idea that being gay or bisexual is an "in thing" encouraged experimentation among teenagers as early as 1993 (see David Gelman, "Tune In, Come Out," *Newsweek* [November 8, 1993], 70).

15. See Joel 2:32; Acts 2:21; Romans 10:13; James 5:16, 19–20.

Chapter 9: The Potential

1. Quoted in Mel Tari, *Like a Mighty Wind* (Carol Stream, Ill.: Creation House, 1971), 9.

2. Quoted in Robert E. Coleman, ed., *One Divine Moment: The Asbury Revival* (Old Tappan, N.J.: Revell, 1970), 9.

3. See Henry Blackaby and Claude King, *Fresh Encounter: God's Pattern for Spiritual Awakening* (Nashville: Broadman and Holman, 2009), 123–37.

4. In his book *An Endless Line of Splendor: Revivals and Their Leaders from the Great Awakening to the Present* (Wheaton, Ill.: Tyndale, 1986), Earle Cairns tells the unfolding story of revivals through modern history. Even exceptions like the New York prayer revival of 1857 were based on the unchanging nature of God as revealed in Scripture.

5. Quoted in Paul Lee Tan, *Encyclopedia of 7700 Illustrations* (Rockville, Md.: Assurance, 1979), 1152.

6. Charles C. Ryrie, *A Survey of Bible Doctrine* (11th ed.; Chicago: Moody, 1989), 40.

7. See, for example, Darrell L. Bock, *Can I Trust the Bible?* (Downers Grove, Ill.: InterVarsity, 2007); N. T. Wright, *The Last Word: Beyond the Bible Wars to a New Understanding of the Authority of Scripture* (New York: HarperCollins, 2005); Erwin W. Lutzer, *Seven Reasons Why You Can Trust the Bible* (Chicago: Moody, 1998).

Chapter 11: Motivation

1. To see the church network of Exodus International—the largest umbrella worldwide for posthomosexual ministries—go to *www.exodusinternational.org/church*.

2. For a description of the prayer watch and an example of how it has been powerfully used by God, visit *www.ChurchReflections.com*.

3. Francis MacNutt, *Can Homosexuality Be Healed?* (2001; repr., Grand Rapids: Baker, 2006), 67.

Chapter 12: Vision

1. "Personal Histories: Leaders Remember the Moments and People That Shaped Them," *Harvard Business Review* (December 2001), *http://hbr.harvardbusiness .org/2001/12/leaders-remember-the-moments-and-people-that-shaped-them/ar/1.*
2. See Hartford Institute for Religion Research, "Fast Facts," *http://hirr.hartsem. edu/research/fastfacts/fast_facts.html#mega*; the National Congregations Study, *http://www.soc.duke.edu/natcong/*; U.S. Congregational Life Survey, *http://www .uscongregations.org/charact-cong.htm.*
3. Arlin Rothauge, *Sizing Up a Congregation for New Member Ministry* (New York: Episcopal Church Center, 1983).

Chapter 13: Healing

1. Kristin Johnson, ed., *Sexual Wholeness in a Broken World* (Orlando, Fla.: OneByOne, 2008), 111–12.

Chapter 14: Growth

1. Christopher Munsey, "Insufficient Evidence to Support Sexual Orientation Change Efforts," *Monitor on Psychology* 40 (October, 2009): 29.

Chapter 15: Support

1. Worthen's workbook *Helping People Step Out of Homosexuality* (San Rafael, Calif.: New Hope Ministries, 2002) and the book *Establishing Group Meetings* (San Rafael, Calif.: New Hope Ministries, 2001) can be purchased at *www .newhope123.org.*
2. Worthen, *Establishing Group Meetings.*
3. Greg Hawkins and Cally Parkinson, *Reveal: Where Are You?* (Barrington, Ill.: Willow Creek Resources, 2007).

Chapter 16: Celebration

1. William Barclay, *The Gospel of John* (Daily Study Bible; Philadelphia: Westminster, 1959), 1:143.
2. See Neil Whitehead and Briar Whitehead, *My Genes Made Me Do It!* (Lafayette, La.: Huntington House, 1999), 39, where they take an average of surveys. They report that "in most cases, wives are ignorant of their husband's homosexual behavior."
3. Michael Riley, *A Pastor's Guide to Ex-Gay Ministry* (Orlando, Fla.: Exodus, 1997), 5.

Share Your Thoughts

With the Author: Your comments will be forwarded to
the author when you send them to *zauthor@zondervan.com*.

With Zondervan: Submit your review of this book
by writing to *zreview@zondervan.com*.

Free Online Resources at

www.zondervan.com

Zondervan AuthorTracker: Be notified whenever your favorite
authors publish new books, go on tour, or post an update
about what's happening in their lives at www.zondervan.com/
authortracker.

Daily Bible Verses and Devotions: Enrich your life with daily
Bible verses or devotions that help you start every morning
focused on God. Visit www.zondervan.com/newsletters.

Free Email Publications: Sign up for newsletters on Christian
living, academic resources, church ministry, fiction, children's
resources, and more. Visit www.zondervan.com/newsletters.

Zondervan Bible Search: Find and compare Bible passages in
a variety of translations at www.zondervanbiblesearch.com.

Other Benefits: Register yourself to receive online benefits
like coupons and special offers, or to participate in research.

◤ZONDERVAN®

ZONDERVAN.com/
AUTHORTRACKER
follow your favorite authors